EDUCATION IN A COMPETITIVE AND GLOBALIZING WORLD

OPEN DISTANCE LEARNING (ODL) IN SOUTH AFRICA

EDUCATION IN A COMPETITIVE AND GLOBALIZING WORLD

Additional books in this series can be found on Nova's website under the Series tab.

Additional e-books in this series can be found on Nova's website under the e-book tab.

EDUCATION IN A COMPETITIVE AND GLOBALIZING WORLD

OPEN DISTANCE LEARNING (ODL) IN SOUTH AFRICA

MOEKETSI LETSEKA
EDITOR

nova publishers
New York

Library of Congress Cataloging-in-Publication Data

ISBN: 978-1-63463-890-6

Published by Nova Science Publishers, Inc. † New York

CONTENTS

Preface		**vii**
Chapter 1	Introduction: Open Distance Learning (ODL) in South Africa *Moeketsi Letseka*	**1**
Chapter 2	A Fit for Purpose Mission for Widening Access through Open Distance Learning *Mpine Makoe*	**7**
Chapter 3	Participation in Open Distance Learning *Paul Prinsloo*	**21**
Chapter 4	Assessment in Open and Distance Learning *Motlalepule Ruth Mampane*	**39**
Chapter 5	Best Practices in Open Distance Learning Assessment *Victor Pitsoe and Matsephe M. Letseka*	**51**
Chapter 6	Pass Rates in Open Distance Learning (ODL) *Moeketsi Letseka and Keleco Karel*	**65**
Chapter 7	Throughput Rates in Open Distance Learning: Towards Understanding and Managing the 'Revolving Door' Syndrome *Folake Ruth Aluko*	**77**
Chapter 8	Conceptions of Success in Open Distance Learning *Victor Pitsoe and Gezani Baloyi*	**91**
Chapter 9	Student Support for Open Distance Learning (ODL) *Shakila Dhunpath and Rubby Dhunpath*	**105**
Chapter 10	The Nexus between Open Distance Learning and the Labor Market *Maximus Monaheng Sefotho*	**117**
Chapter 11	Shift from Open Distance Learning to Open Distance e-Learning *Sindile Ngubane-Mokiwa and Moeketsi Letseka*	**129**
Conclusion: After Thought	*Moeketsi Letseka*	**143**
Index		**147**

PREFACE

Access to higher education and the prospect of obtaining a higher education qualification through full-time contact institutions seems a remote reality for the majority of black South Africans who were denied opportunities for higher education during apartheid. The majority of this group is either in full-time employment, part-time employment, temporary posts, unemployed and at most unemployable. This book opens up the debate on the open distance learning (ODL) mode of teaching and learning. The book is written in user-friendly English accessible to professionals in higher education and ODL as well as the non-professional layman.

The book debates among others, the critical issues of access to higher education in South Africa. It offers ODL as a viable alternative to millions of South Africans who were denied opportunities to study in higher education by past policies of apartheid. The book puts across ODL as a viable mode of access to higher education qualifications that are accredited by South Africa's Qualifications Authority (SAQA) and are recognized by the country's labor market. The book tackles the sensitive but necessary issue of assessment in ODL. It discusses best practices in ODL and offers justifications for ODL practitioners to align their practice with internationally recognized benchmarks and examples of best practice. The book explores the sensitive issues of pass rates and throughput rates in ODL. Given their very nature as higher education institutions whose student clientele is mature working adults, ODL institutions' qualifications completion targets tend to be more relaxed and extended than their full-time contact higher education institutions counterparts. Invariably throughput rates in ODL institutions are perceived to be very poor. The book opens up debates on the dynamics of ODL pass rates and throughput rates. It explores the notions of throughput rate and pass rate and interrogates the nuances of perceived ODL poor rates. A question the book seeks to address is whether ODL throughput rates and pass rates are indeed poor or seem poor relative to performances of full-time contact institutions?

Chapter 1 – The timing of putting together a book on open distance learning (ODL) in South Africa in 2014 is significant. The year marks twenty years since the advent of democracy in 1994. A lot is currently taking place at this time in South Africa by way of reflection. The big question on everyone's lips is: "How does South Africa measure up in terms of the ideals mapped out when the new democratic dispensation was ushered in twenty years ago?" This is a heavily loaded question that calls for robust and yet candid self-evaluation of how well or worse South Africa has done in the twenty years that have flown past as far as improvement of the quality of the lives of the ordinary people is concern, and concomitantly, as far as a sense of belonging to this 'new' nation is concerned. We might want to stretch the envelope even further and reflect on South Africa's competitiveness in the global community. Is the country doing well or worse than it did during the dark days of apartheid when it was a global pariah with a system of rule that was declared "a crime against humanity" by the international community? Former leader and founder of Agang South Africa [a then budding political party] Mamphela Ramphele (2013) publicly declared that South Africa's education system "was better before the advent of democracy". Ramphele lamented that "the irony is that the people who ignited the struggle for freedom in 1976 were protesting against poor education. If they were to come back today they wouldn't believe it – that what they had and what they were protesting [against] is much better than what our children in 80% of the schools get".

Chapter 2 – The aim of the chapter is to examine the concept of access to higher education in relation to quality as espoused in the mission statement of the university. In an ODL context, what the institution does and how it does it is critical to understanding the university's purpose. The idea is to provide a critique of the University of South Africa (UNISA's) mission statement as a quality indicator. Given the importance of the mission statement in defining and describing the purpose of the institution, this chapter analyzes UNISA's mission statement in relation to the quality indicators as outlined in the Quality Assurance Criteria that were developed specifically for distance education institutions. To find out whether the UNISA is doing what it claims to do as an ODL institution mandated to widening access to higher education, three distance education Quality Assurance Toolkits developed by the Commonwealth of Learning (CoL), the African Council for Distance Education (ACDE) and the National Association of Distance Education Organisation of South Africa (NADEOSA) were analysed. Although mission statements are ubiquitous in higher education, very little attention is given to what the content of the statement means in relation to university's goals and objectives. This chapter analyzed the Quality Assurance criterion that purports to measure the mission of the university, that is, the general philosophy that guides the values, culture and ethos of an institution. The meaning found in the mission statement suggests that UNISA as an ODL institution should provide higher education guided by the open learning principles of access, flexibility and student centeredness.

Chapter 3 – Increasing or widening participation has been a trend in international higher education since the 1990s. Not only was this in response to increased demand for access to higher education, but also due to a proliferation of different forms of delivery, open education becoming mainstream and, of course, the impact of technology. Distance education and open distance learning (ODL) in particular has been an integral part of the South African higher education landscape since 1873 when the University of South Africa (UNISA) was established. Until recently, UNISA was not only the only dedicated distance education provider in South Africa, but also the only ODL comprehensive institution, the biggest on the African continent and one of the mega universities in the world. To a large extent, participation in ODL is synonymous with UNISA. This chapter provides a socio-critical interrogation of the notion of participation in ODL in the specific context of South Africa. Participation in ODL with special reference to South Africa is, however, influenced by international trends in higher education, and the increasing blurring of the boundaries between traditional residential face-to-face education and traditional distance education modes. This chapter focuses on participation in ODL as a distinct notion different from *access*, and entails a multi-dimensional and complex rite of passage consisting of mostly non-linear, multidimensional, interdependent interactions at different phases in the nexus between student, institution and broader societal factors. I will firstly problematize participation in ODL and clarify a number of terms germane to the discourse. The next section in this chapter will then briefly discuss international trends in participation in higher education and ODL before addressing selected issues in the South African context with specific reference to "White paper for post-school education and training. Building an expanded, effective and integrated post-school system" (DHET, 2013) and the "Policy for the provision of distance education in South African universities in the context of an integrated post-school system" (DHET, 2014). Against this background I will then discuss a number of theoretical constructs informing a socio-critical model of student participation in ODL.

Chapter 4 – This chapter argues that assessment is core to teaching and learning and is used to measure student's knowledge, abilities, skills and attitudes. Assessment results give a measure of success or failure in subsequent work (a probability of subsequent performance). The purpose of assessment in open and distance learning (ODL) is multifaceted and educational. Feedback received through assessment activities enables students to evaluate their learning and for lecturers to measure their teaching. The chapter will demonstrate that as teaching and learning help to introduce, communicate, and expose students to skills, attitudes and new knowledge (local and global knowledge), and enables them to reflect and critically engage with module learning outcomes; assessment is used to evaluate, control and apply knowledge, skills and attitudes learned. Assessment helps to reaffirm the learning outcomes (as meaningful problem) and monitors the effect of teaching and learning (measures if learning outcomes have been achieved). Ultimately, assessment offers the student the opportunity to practically demonstrate their understanding of content learned and learning achieved (learning outcomes), to measure teaching success (determine if teaching was achieved), and to apply and demonstrate knowledge in place (problem solving skills).

Chapter 5 – In this chapter the authors argue that, given the complex and culturally diverse nature of students in ODL, for assessment in ODL to be effective, efficient and have a positive impact in teaching and learning, it should be underpinned by the notions of 'best practice', 'reflective practice' and 'culturally relevant pedagogy'. The authors note that these notions in ODL assessment have gained serious attention from higher education institutions, stakeholders, and scholars. For us, assessment methods should be appropriate to the students, the level and the material to be tested, and embrace the cultures of the students. Notwithstanding the fact that there are pockets of excellence in ODL assessment theory and practice, the authors' take is that with the increase of ICT in higher education there is tangible evidence that assessment of learning in ODL in the 21st century is not free and immune to challenges. They are convinced that the appropriation of 'best practice', 'reflective practice' and 'culturally relevant pedagogy' is critical in the assessment of students' learning in the ODL context. Among others, they consider that best practice account offers unique value, not only by extending the descriptive knowledge base in ODL assessment, but is uncovering significant cognitive and socio-cultural adjustments which are critical to the theory and practice of ODL assessment. This chapter begins with a brief overview of thoughts on the best practice in ODL assessment. The second section explores Reflective Practice and Best Practice in ODL Assessment. In the third section the authors briefly sketch Culturally Relevant Pedagogy as a tool for measurement. The forth section reflects on assessment in ODL through the lens of the emerging paradigms. Finally, they provide some concluding remarks.

Chapter 6 – This chapter interrogates the challenges of poor pass rates at UNISA and the associated trend by which students do not graduate within the specific duration required to complete their designated study program. It briefly describes the ODL framework with a view to providing readers with some understanding of how a distance education institution like UNISA operates. In a country like South Africa, which is marked by high levels of unemployment, adult illiteracy and socio-economic inequalities, an optimally functioning higher education sector that delivers good pass rates and good throughput rates is *sine qua non* to global economic competitiveness and a sense of well-being among its citizenry. Thus the imperative to sufficiently deal with the twin issue of equity and redress in a country that has only just emerged from a system of rule that privileged the white minority while marginalizing, disadvantaging and excluding the vast majority of the Africa peoples from socio-economic opportunities cannot be overemphasized. The chapter briefly describes the open distance learning (ODL) mode that UNISA operates. By its very nature as an ODL institution UNISA targets mature working adults who do not have the time to pursue higher education qualification at full-time contact institutions. At the time of writing UNISA's student headcount enrollments were estimated to be close to 400 000 in a country where national headcount enrollments are close to 1 million. This puts UNISA's share of South Africa's headcount enrollments at just over 40%. The chapter grapples with the challenges of UNISAs pass rates, which have been described as "shocking". A recent authoritative government report on post-school education and training statistics shows that UNISAs percentage of graduation rates in undergraduate, masters and doctoral degrees during 2010 were well below national averages of 16%, 18% and 12%. In fact UNISA's averages in the three categories above were in single digits. The chapter proposes a review of the university's admission policy; a coordinated and sustained student support program, and a tightening of the tracking system of 'at-risk' students.

Chapter 7 – The 'revolving door' syndrome is a term that has been used to describe the low throughput rate in higher education. Even though distance education has been recognized as having the potential to meet the escalating demand for higher education all over the world, the mode is plagued with low throughput rate. This is especially true in South Africa, where almost 50% of newly enrolled students drop out of the higher education system in the first and the second year. In this chapter, the author attempts to provide possible succinct reasons for low throughput rate in distance education in the country; discuss the challenge with calculating throughput rate, and the need to understand the intricacies involved, especially given the historical past and the social context of the country. As well she proffers suggestions on possible ways to stem the tide from the governmental, institutional and student angles. It is hoped that even though scholars have been making attempts to understand the phenomenon and to recommend solutions for it for decades, this chapter would help to move distance education providers closer to answering some of the myriad of questions that confront the phenomenon.

Chapter 8 – Despite the fact Open Distance Learning (ODL) continues to be an alternative or complementary mode of learning, in this chapter, the authors conjure that student support is a fundamental part of the delivery of quality distance education experiences and enhances students' success in a sustainable way. However, this chapter contributes to the debate on student success and academic success in higher education in South Africa, but with a focus on the University of South Africa's (UNISA) ODL. It makes a case for the potential of effective and efficient student success programs/systems to broaden access with success to higher education. For us, supporting students for success in a culturally diverse educational setting remains a complex challenge and calls for a rethinking. While success and the completion of studies are imposed by numerous tenacious factors, the authors argue that lack of appropriate support for ODL students can result in decreased student success and increased withdrawals. Although they acknowledge that the notion of Student Support Services in ODL has always been broadly perceived and a contested terrain, the authors' take is that effective and efficient student support services should draw from theories that are consistent with the culturally diverse needs of the students. Among others, the authors contend that challenges of epistemological access, poor bandwidth and under preparedness (of both students and the institution) have great potential of failing the perceived initiatives of student success. They consider UNISA's *paradigm shift* from correspondence to cyberspace a policy imperative; and that it has far reaching implications for the student success. Central to this chapter is the assumption that with the increase of the barrage of cultural situations facing today's ODL practitioners, there is a need to develop cultural intelligence, as a soft skill, to promote student success systems. The authors' thesis is that cultural intelligence has the potential and prospects to offer practitioners promising realistic, practical skills to meet the demands of a diverse student body, and can be considered to be a tool to improve student success. This chapter begins with conceptualization of "student success" and "student support services." Second, the authors critically reflect on the student success and retention. Third, they look into the designing of student support for success in ODL. Fourthly, they present cultural intelligence as a strategy to promote student success systems in ODL. Lastly, the authors offer the concluding remarks.

Chapter 9 – UNISA's Academic Literacies provisioning over the past 9 years has served a disembodied interventionist role in student support, despite the dire need for substantive support, given the Institution's poor track record of student success. The absence of a clear vision to embed student support in the mainstream curriculum is likely to relegate academic development practitioners to sub-contractors, further marginalizing a vital support function which can be characterized as erratic and incoherent since the existing staff providing this function are on short-term contracts. The chapter argues that not only is this practice pedagogically unsound, but it contradicts UNISA's declared aspiration to be among this country's top universities, focusing more intently on the quality of teaching and learning (Senate Report, 2010:2). It argues that the need for academic development (AD), particularly for Open and Distance Learning (ODL) institutions is now direr than ever before and is central to the university's intention to improve its unsustainable throughput rates. By revisiting some of the theories supporting the need for explicit academic literacies support, the chapter contends that rather than devalue its status, the academic development provisioning at UNISA should be significantly up-scaled and institutionalized for optimal impact.

Chapter 10 – This chapter is about the nexus between Open Distance Learning (ODL) and the labor market. The chapter starts with the review of the philosophy of ODL and links it with andragogy as a philosophical approach and the art and science of adult learning. Central to the discussion is the issue of how ODL provides the much needed qualified human resources to the labor market, found to be complex within the South African context. This is due to many factors paramount to which is labor immigration. Historically, continued labor market discrimination against previously disadvantaged groups, blacks, women and persons with disabilities in senior and executive management positions is a thorn in the South African employment sector. Given the status of South Africa as an emerging market, its labor market is becoming a kaleidoscope with various aspects to be considered. For instance, recruitment and appointments tend to be biased against graduate from historically black universities, many experience extended waiting periods before absorption into the labor market. Their counterparts from historically white universities on the contrary wait less. Sometimes the whites are guaranteed jobs while still studying. The chapter reviews work-based learning as a contributory factor to the development of ODL graduates. The last part links ODL and the labor market with career adaptation of the ODL graduates and how this answers to the needs of the ever changing labor market.

Chapter 11 – This chapter explores the University of South Africa (UNISA)'s immanent shift from open distance learning (ODL) to open distance e-learning (ODeL). It considers UNISA's initial mandate as an ODL institution that provides higher education opportunities to previously disadvantaged, predominantly African students who would otherwise not be able to obtain a higher education qualification were they to be left at the mercy of full-time, campus-based and contact higher education institutions. The move from ODL to ODeL presumes existence of an established culture, use of, and reliance on modern electronic technologies. But while South Africa has pockets of urban cosmopolitan enclaves in the form of major modern cities and sub-urban areas, the larger spatial spread of the country remains rural, communal, invariably poor and excluded from the broader benefits of modern electronic technologies in what is known as the 'digital divide'. UNISA needs to reconcile its commitment to the mandate to provide higher education learning opportunities for the majority poor and previously marginalized Africans with the envisaged shift to ODeL. It needs to vigorously deal with the probable perception that the shift to ODeL might have the unintended consequence of perpetuating inherited socio-economic inequalities; that it might potentially exclude the poor from access to open distance learning opportunities as a result of a policy shift that equates access to higher education opportunities with possession of, and access to modern electronic technologies, which the mass of the poor might not afford. The chapter grapples with the perceived social benefits of the shift to ODeL. It argues that the promise of the global e-learning system can only be realized at UNISA if the university were to strive for a better understanding of the views on teaching and learning that pertain to the specific socio-economic and cultural context of South Africa.

In: Open Distance Learning (ODL) in South Africa
Editor: Moeketsi Letseka
ISBN: 978-1-63463-890-6

Chapter 1

INTRODUCTION: OPEN DISTANCE LEARNING (ODL) IN SOUTH AFRICA

Moeketsi Letseka*
Department of Educational Foundations
College of Education, University of South Africa (UNISA), Pretoria, South Africa

INTRODUCTION AND BRIEF BACKGROUND

The timing of putting together a book on open distance learning (ODL) in South Africa in 2014 is significant. The year marks twenty years since the advent of democracy in 1994. A lot is currently taking place at this time in South Africa by way of reflection. The big question on everyone's lips is: "How does South Africa measure up in terms of the ideals mapped out when the new democratic dispensation was ushered in twenty years ago?" This is a heavily loaded question that calls for robust and yet candid self-evaluation of how well or worse South Africa has done in the twenty years that have flown past as far as improvement of the quality of the lives of the ordinary people is concern, and concomitantly, as far as a sense of belonging to this 'new' nation is concerned. We might want to stretch the envelope even further and reflect on South Africa's competitiveness in the global community. Is the country doing well or worse than it did during the dark days of apartheid when it was a global pariah with a system of rule that was declared "a crime against humanity" by the international community? Former leader and founder of Agang South Africa [a then budding political party] Mamphela Ramphele (2013) publicly declared that South Africa's education system "was better before the advent of democracy". Ramphele lamented that "the irony is that the people who ignited the struggle for freedom in 1976 were protesting against poor education. If they were to come back today they wouldn't believe it – that what they had and what they were protesting [against] is much better than what our children in 80% of the schools get".

However, Ramphele's comments need to be taken with a pinch of salt. First, she was speaking as a leader of an insignificant opposition political party trying to cast aspersion at, and score valuable political points against the education policies of the ruling African

* letsem@unisa.ac.za.

National Congress (ANC). Second, we need to ask ourselves whether we agree with her that South Africa's current basic education is, in real terms worse than the education that was offered to Africans by the apartheid government. I have no hesitation in declaring that such a view is not only naïve, but it is far from the truth and misleading. First, apartheid education was offered by a separate and segregated department of education known at the time as the 'Department of Bantu Education'. Second, apartheid South Africa was a fascist state run by a minority white Afrikaner junta under the banner of the then conservative Nationalist Party (NP). The NP was not apologetic about its discriminatory and segregationist socio-political, economic and cultural stance. It was not a party for all South Africans, not even a party for all white people, but a party for a certain section of Afrikaners that shared and embraced its fascist inclinations. The apartheid government was unequivocal in its conviction that "the Bantu" [a derogatory term for the black, in particular African peoples] did not qualify as humans deserving of equal and dignified treatment as white people. To that end "the Bantu" did not deserve a better education because they would not have any use of it. Thus "the Bantu" were better off as "hewers of wood and drawers of water" for their Afrikaner masters and 'madams' who were, according to the Christian National Education (CNE) policy, called upon by God as "the senior trustee of the native" with a 'God-given' mission to "Christianize him and help him on culturally" (Rose and Tunmer, 1975: 128). The CNE declared the Afrikaners 'trustees' of "the natives", ironically on account of the "the natives" "cultural infancy". It went on to state: "we believe that it is the right and task of the state, in collaboration with the Christian churches, to give and control native education and training of the native teaching forces' (Rose and Tunmer, 1975).

South Africa's current political dispensation is a far cry from its apartheid predecessor. To start with, it is a democratic political dispensation that is based on a multi-party political system. The country's policies and laws are informed by the 1996 constitution, which has received praise globally for its liberal and egalitarian makeup. The constitution has been described as a model liberal democratic constitution that has few peers in the world community (Jordan, 1996); that "reflects the hallmarks of liberal democracy" (Dugard, 1998); is "widely seen and regarded as a 'state of the art' document (Mattes, 2002), and "is widely hailed as liberal and egalitarian" (Deveaux, 2003), because "it values human dignity and frames human rights at its heart" (Robinson, 2012). If there are failings within South Africa's education system, such failings should be resolved within the legal and constitutional framework provided by the constitution. Furthermore, such failings are not different from educational failings that are experienced in other parts of the world. For instance, the failings of the teacher preparation system of the Unites States (Richardson, 2014; Thorpe, 2014; Mehta, & Doctor, 2013), or of the failings of the national curriculum in the United Kingdom (UK) (Garner, 2013; McCormick, & Burn, 2011; Oates, 2011).

For many years Finland's education system was lauded as "a professional and democratic path to improvement that grows from the bottom, steers from the top, and provides support and pressure from the sides" (Sahlberg, 2011). Editor of *Phi Delta Kappan* Richardson (2013: 76) notes that the success of Finland's education is a result of "sweeping reforms that moved teacher education programs into universities and upgraded the standards for becoming a teacher". And yet in the 2013 Program for International Student Assessment (PISA) evaluation Finland was toppled from the top ranking by Shanghai-China, Singapore, Hong Kong (China), Chinese Taipei, Korea, Macao-China, Japan, and, Liechtenstein!! The decline of Finland education might elicited headline news in Helsinki such as "Finnish education is crumbling down", and "Golden Days where Finland's Education A Success are Over" (*Finnbay*, 2013).

The chapters that comprise this book engage with the challenges of open distance learning (ODL) in South Africa, with a focus on the University of South Africa (UNISA). South Africa is a nascent African liberal democracy, having just celebrated twenty years of existence. And yet South Africa holds so much hope for the larger part of the African continent, especially the vast portion of Africa commonly referred to as sub-Saharan Africa. Until recently South Africa was the leading African economy in terms of its GDP, its ability to attract foreign direct investment; perceptions of good governance; human rights track record; peace-keeping role on the African continent, and most importantly, due to that shining beacon known as the Truth and Reconciliation Commission (TRC). Of course South Africa has since surrendered its leadership of the African continent to Nigeria. Notwithstanding this minor glitch, the University of South Africa (UNISA) remains the biggest ODL institution on the African continent, providing higher education opportunities to an estimated 400 000 mature working students in South Africa and the rest of Africa.

THE STRUCTURE OF THE BOOK

What this book attempts to do is to generate debate on, and interrogate UNISA's ODL offerings. In this introduction I provide a brief roadmap of how the contributors that have been assembled share ideas on the areas in which they are not only deemed to be practitioners, but where they are also experts. There are eleven chapters in all, covering access to higher education through ODL; participation rates in higher education in general, and in ODL in particular; assessment in ODL and its related challenges; conceptions of best practices in ODL, pass rates and throughput rates; conception of success in ODL, and how success might be measured; critically though, the nexus between ODL and the labor market, especially in an emerging market like South Africa, and the all-important place of modern electronic technologies, which require a shift from ODL to open distance e-learning (ODeL).

In chapter two Mpine Makoe, who is head of the Open Distance Learning Institute at UNISA provides insights into our understanding of ODL's mission to provide wider access to higher education opportunities. She critiques UNISA mission statement as a document that defines and describes the purpose of the institution, and outlines related principles such as access, flexibility, affordability and student centeredness. She concludes that the extent to which these are realized can only be measured to the extent that the university's mission statement is critically interrogated. Closely linked to access through ODL is the burning issue of participation rates. Paul Prinsloo of the College of Economic and Management Sciences at UNISA takes up the issue of participation in chapter three. Prinsloo provides a socio-critical interrogation of the notion of participation in ODL in the specific context of South Africa. His take on participation in ODL is of a distinct notion different from access, and entailing a multi-dimensional and complex rite of passage consisting of mostly non-linear, multidimensional, interdependent interactions at different phases in the nexus between student, institution and broader societal factors. Prinsloo contends that participation in ODL in South Africa is influenced by international trends in higher education, and the increasing blurring of the boundaries between traditional residential face-to-face education and traditional distance education modes. Prinsloo's chapter is critical given that one of the major challenges of higher education in South Africa in general, and ODL in particular is that participation is skewed in favor of white students, in a country where, according to a recent national census the black African people constitute around 80% of the country's total population.

Ruth Mampane, of the Faulty of Education, University of Pretoria tackles the problematic area of assessment on ODL in chapter four. She starts from the premise that assessment is core to teaching and learning and its purpose is to measure student's knowledge, abilities, skills and attitudes. She is clear though that in ODL assessment is a multifaceted enterprise that should enable mature working adult students to evaluate their learning and for their lecturers to measure how well the study material is understood.. She contends that assessment should be an interactive process between the student and the lecturer that provides the much needed feedback to the lecture and student on learning and knowledge in place, and on learning and knowledge required to accomplish the learning goals. She concludes that to ensure that students are not prejudiced, multiple opportunities and forms of assessment should be provided to enable ODL students to continually assess their learning and knowledge. How do ODL practitioners ensure that their conduct in ODL complies with accepted notions of good practice? Victor Pitsoe and 'Matsephe Letseka take this up in chapter five where they argue that for assessment in ODL to be effective, efficient and have positive impact on teaching and learning, it should be underpinned by the notions of 'best practice', 'reflective practice' and 'culturally relevant pedagogy'. It is their contention that the appropriation of 'best practice', 'reflective practice' and 'culturally relevant pedagogy' is critical in the assessment of students' learning in the ODL context. They locate 'best practice' within Thomas Angelo's six steps to continuous improvement of learning.

In chapter six Moeketsi Letseka and Keleco Karel explore the notion of 'pass rates' with respect to UNISA. As mentioned throughout the book UNISA is the biggest ODL institution on the African continent with an estimated total headcount enrolment of 400 000. Given that the rest of the twenty-four universities share just around 1 million student headcounts, it follows that UNISA alone accommodates an estimated 40% of South Africa's entire university student headcount enrolments. And yet over the past years UNISA's pass rates, completion rates, graduation rates and throughput rates have remained the poorest. In some degree programs the official statistical reports of the Council on Higher Education (CHE) and the Department of Higher Education and Training (DHET) show that UNISA's pass rates are in single digits and below the national average while between 70% and 80% of student in some qualification will not graduate. Letseka and Karel's view is that UNISA needs to review its admission policies so that only those prospective students who qualify for admission, and have the potential to succeed are admitted. They also raise concerns on student support initiatives, which they do not discuss in detail given that the matter is a central theme of another chapter in this volume.

A throughput rate is the subject of chapter seven. Ruth Aluko, of the Unit for Distance Education at the University of Pretoria sheds light on throughput rates in ODL. She notes that even though distance education is recognized as having the potential to meet the rising demand for higher education globally, generally distance education is plagued by low throughput rate. In South Africa in particular, almost 50% of newly enrolled students drop out of the higher education system in the first and the second year. Aluko defines 'Throughput Rate' as "the calculation of how many students in a given cohort completed their degrees and graduated within the stipulated time, how many dropped out, and how many took longer than the stipulated time to graduate". She wants to see more commitment by governments through adoption of robust policies that ensure continuous quality improvement; she wants to see institutions taking responsibility through prompt acknowledgments of students' admission and enrolment, prompt material delivery and easy access to resources; prompt responses to students' queries; fast assignment turnarounds with positive, supportive feedback which are all directly linked to students' throughput rate. Finally, because most open and distance student learning occurs independently of the teachers' presence with students focusing primarily on engagement with the material they receive, Aluko also wants to see the students take more responsibility in their participatory co-production roles.

In chapter eight Victor Pitsoe and Gezani Baloyi unpack the issue of success in ODL. They argue that student support is a fundamental part of the delivery of quality distance education experiences and enhances students' success in a sustainable way. It is their contention that supporting students for success in a culturally diverse educational setting remains a complex challenge that calls for policy rethinking. While success and completion of studies are affected by numerous tenacious factors, it is their view that lack of appropriate support for ODL students can result in diminished student success and increased withdrawals. In chapter nine Shakila Dhunpath and Rubby Dhunpath grapple with the challenges of student support. They argue that the absence of a clear vision to embed student support in the mainstream curriculum can potentially relegate academic development practitioners as sub-contractors, further marginalizing a vital support function which can, regrettably be characterized as erratic and incoherent as staff providing this function are often on short-term contracts. Returning to some of the theories that advocate academic literacies support, Dhunpath and Dhunpath argue that academic development provisioning at UNISA should be significantly up-scaled and institutionalized for optimal impact.

In chapter ten Monaheng Sefotho of the Faculty of Education, University of Pretoria takes all the forgoing debates forward in his exploration of ODL and the labor market. Historically, continued labor market discrimination against previously disadvantaged groups, blacks, women and persons with disabilities in senior and executive management positions was a thorn in South Africa's employment sector. In recent years, recruitment and appointments have tended to be biased against blacks, especially graduates from historically black disadvantaged universities, with many experiencing extended waiting periods before being absorbed in the labor market, while their counterparts from historically white advantaged universities often secured jobs while they were still studying. The thrust of Sefotho's argument is that South Africa's labor market discriminates against black graduates who obtained their qualification from historically black and previously black disadvantaged higher education institutions. Concomitantly the South Africa's labor market privileges graduates from historically white advantaged universities who are already privileged by association with privileged city universities. In chapter eleven Sindile Ngubane-Mokiwa and Moeketsi Letseka explore the infusion and proliferation of modern electronic technologies such as computers, Tablets, WiFi, smart phones, the use of blue tooth, etc, and how these gadgets are changing the face of teaching and learning. They raise red flags on some of UNISA lecturers who are technophobic and resist the introduction of modern electronic technologies in teaching and learning. Ngubane-Mokiwa and Letseka are concerned that UNISA's younger generation of students, who are at home with modern electronic technologies will lose out on the benefits of proliferating digital technologies. In chapter twelve the editor provides his after thoughts.

REFERENCES

Deveaux, M. (2003) "Liberal constitutions and traditional cultures: The South African customary law debate". *Citizenship Studies*, 7 (2), 161-180.

Dugard, J. (1998) "The new constitution: a triumph for liberalism? a positive view", in R, W. Johnson and David Welsh eds. *Ironic Victory: Liberalism in Post-liberation South Africa*, Oxford University Press: Cape Town.

Garner, R. (2013) "Michael Gove has failed to 'engage and excite' teachers over national curriculum plans", *The Independent*, September 24.

Jordan, Z. P. (1996) "Harmony, an elusive objective", in *The Star and SA Times International*, June 12.

Mattes, R. (2002) "South Africa: democracy without the people". *Journal of Democracy*, 13 (1), 22-36.

McCormick, B., & Burn, K. (2011) "Reviewing the National Curriculum 5–19 two decades on", *The Curriculum Journal*, 22 (2), 109-115.

Mehta, J., & Doctor, J. (2013) "Raising the bar for teachers", *Phi Delta Kappan*, 94 (7), 8-13.

Oates, T. (2011) "Could do better: using international comparisons to refine the National Curriculum in England", *The Curriculum Journal*, 22 (2), 121–150.

Ramphele, M (2013) "Apartheid education was better", *City Press*, October 4.

Richardson, J. (2013) "The Finish way", *Phi Delta Kappan*, 94 (5), 76-77.

Richardson, J. (2014) "The Editor's Note: Stepping up to the profession", *Phi Delta Kappan*, 96 (1), 4-5.

Robinson, M. (2012) "Freedom, truth, democracy: citizenship and common purpose", Tenth Nelson Mandela Annual Lecture, delivered at Cape Town City Hall, August 5.

Rose, B., & Tunmer, R. (1975) eds., *Documents in South African Education*, AD. Donker/Publisher: Johannesburg.

Thorpe, R. (2014) "Residency: can it transform teaching the way it did medicine?", *Phi Delta Kappan*,96 (1), 36-40.

In: Open Distance Learning (ODL) in South Africa
Editor: Moeketsi Letseka
ISBN: 978-1-63463-890-6

Chapter 2

A FIT FOR PURPOSE MISSION FOR WIDENING ACCESS THROUGH OPEN DISTANCE LEARNING

Mpine Makoe*

Institute of Open Distance Learning

University of South Africa (UNISA), Pretoria, South Africa

ABSTRACT

The aim of the chapter is to examine the concept of access to higher education in relation to quality as espoused in the mission statement of the university. In an ODL context, what the institution does and how it does it is critical to understanding the university's purpose. The idea is to provide a critique of the University of South Africa (UNISA's) mission statement as a quality indicator. Given the importance of the mission statement in defining and describing the purpose of the institution, this chapter analyzes UNISA's mission statement in relation to the quality indicators as outlined in the Quality Assurance Criteria that were developed specifically for distance education institutions. To find out whether the UNISA is doing what it claims to do as an ODL institution mandated to widening access to higher education, three distance education Quality Assurance Toolkits developed by the Commonwealth of Learning (CoL), the African Council for Distance Education (ACDE) and the National Association of Distance Education Organisation of South Africa (NADEOSA) were analysed. Although mission statements are ubiquitous in higher education, very little attention is given to what the content of the statement means in relation to university's goals and objectives. This chapter analyzed the Quality Assurance criterion that purports to measure the mission of the university, that is, the general philosophy that guides the values, culture and ethos of an institution. The meaning found in the mission statement suggests that UNISA as an ODL institution should provide higher education guided by the open learning principles of access, flexibility and student centeredness.

* qakisme@unisa.ac.za.

INTRODUCTION

Most developing countries in the world are confronted with challenges of expanding access into higher education. These challenges are even more acute in places of limited resources and capacity to provide quality higher education for an ever increasing population. For many countries in Africa, distance education seems to be the only option that can play a role in widening participation to higher education provision. While acknowledging the necessity of distance education in widening access, it must also provide academically credible and quality education content at a low cost (Olcott, 2013). Due to this need, the number of Open Distance Learning (ODL) institutions has increased exponentially in the past 20 years. Even campus-based higher education institutions are now offering or considering distance education programs. The latest policy document on Post-School Education in Training has emphasized the need for distance education in expanding higher education skills development and training (Department of Higher Education & Training (DHET, 2014).

The government and policy makers identified ODL as a system that can "expand access to higher education to significantly larger number of students, and especially providing opportunities for social advancement for historically and socially disadvantaged social groups through equity of access, opportunity and outcomes", according to the 2001 National Plan for Higher education report. Since the inception of distance education in the 1800s, it was developed to address barriers that were often associated with classroom-based teaching and learning. These days, digital technologies have increased the possibilities of ODL, thereby removing barriers and widening access to higher education. Almost all institutions that adopted open distance teaching delivery mode did so to address the social mandate of encouraging and opening up access to education. Distance education institutions were driven by the need to provide higher education as a public good (Olcott, 2013). The main principle of openness in education is to address the fundamental right of access to education as outlined in the UNESCO's Universal Declaration of Human Rights. Open education, according to Olcott (2013:17), "is one of the great equalizers for higher education access".

Access to higher education for historically disadvantaged students has increased tremendously in the past 15 years and distance education accounted for almost a third of all higher education enrollments in South Africa. In reality, ODL has transformed higher education from an elite system to a mass system (Olakuhin and Singh, 2013). Although distance education has been credited with opening up access to higher education, it has also been criticized for the low output of students (CHE, 2004). Access to higher education without success is meaningless. According to the 2014 Policy for the Provision of Distance Education in South African Universities, distance education institutions should provide opportunities for reasonable chance of success while providing access" (DHET, 2014) For this to happen, the quality assurance processes of the Council for Higher Education (CHE) need to ensure that the expansion of access to study is "complemented by improved national and institutional planning, program design and support system for underprepared school – leavers" (DHET, 2014).

To establish if the institution is achieving what it is meant to do, quality assurance processes are critical in ensuring that the institution provides quality education to its students. Thus quality assurance processes are a set of activities that institutions undertake to ensure that set quality standards are followed. Menon (2007) draws a distinction between quality assurance and quality control. The former involves proactive measures taken to avoid faults while the latter is reactive measures taken to remove faults (Menon, 2007). However, both concepts are meant to measure quality as understood by stakeholders in education. Quality is a very important and the most complex component in education. What makes it even more complicated is that there are a variety of ways of giving meaning to the concept of quality sometimes inadequate or even inappropriate. "We all have an instinctive understanding of what it means but it is difficult to articulate" (Green, 1994, p.12). When people talk about quality in their day to day life, according to Alexander (2008), they usually mean or associate it with something good, excellent, exceptional or perfect. The assumption is that quality is something that can be measured or assessed according to a set of standards – that is – a set of agreed specification or other criterion used as a rule, guideline, or definition of a level of performance or achievement, according to the South African Qualification Authority Act (1995). As a result, people attach quality to what they see as quality standards. What is problematic about this description is that quality is used as an adjective rather than a noun. Alexander (2008) argues that in education, quality should be seen as a characteristic or an attribute which is a value-neutral noun. It is impossible that quality can be a value-neutral given that it takes place within the context of a society.

The other problem is that issues about quality are often assessed and described from the contact institutions perspective. While contact or traditional mode of education tend to be teacher-centered, ODL focuses on an individual student who is separated from the teacher and most of his or her learning is technologically mediated. ODL has processes, practices and systems in place to ensure the delivery of teaching and learning. In this context, the institution teaches an individual student sitting in a bus or in an office or at home while a teacher teaches a group of students in a contact institution (Guri-Rosenbilt, 2005). Despite these differences, Kirkpatrick (2005) argues that distance education quality needs to be assured in the same way as any other form of higher education. The primary purpose of ODL institutions is to widen opportunities for learning for those people who did not have a chance to study. It is therefore important that quality in distance education is measured in terms of how successful it has been in terms of access to quality higher education.

The purpose of this chapter therefore is to evaluate and identify quality issues that are fit for ODL purpose. Fitness for purpose equates quality with the fulfilment of a specification or stated outcomes_(Harvey and Stensaker, 2006); while fitness of purpose focuses on the stated goals and aims that are related to the universal task or purpose of the institution (Tjivikua, 2010). In a nutshell, according to Harvey and Green (1993), quality is something that fits the purpose if it does the job for which it is designed to do. Therefore quality in higher education should be assessed against the stated objectives of the institution, which are often found in the mission statement. The aim of the chapter therefore is to examine the concept of access to higher education in relation to quality as espoused in the mission statement of the university. The idea is to provide a critique of the University of South Africa (UNISA's) mission statement as a quality indicator. In an ODL context, what the institution does and how it does it is critical to understanding the university's purpose.

Mission Statements in Relation to Quality

The starting point in investigating the purpose of the institution is to analyze its mission statement. Almost every institution of higher learning has a mission statement that aims to articulate the "sense of purpose and has the capacity to inspire and motivate those within an institution and to communicate its characteristics, values, and history to key external constituents (Morphew & Hartley, 2006, p. 457). The role of a mission statement is to provide direction and give reasons of its own existence. Furthermore, mission statements present an" easily and publicly available window into the stated purpose" of the institution (Stemler and Bell, 1999). By so doing, they help to clarify the activities of the university to all its stakeholders. A clear mission statement helps organizational members distinguish between activities that conform to institutional imperatives and those that do not (Morphew & Hartley, 2006). Given the importance of the mission statement in defining and describing the purpose of the institution, this chapter analyzes UNISA's mission statement in relation to the quality indicators as outlined in the Quality Assurance Criteria that were developed specifically for distance education institutions. It is therefore important to look at what quality is in relation to the social mandate of distance education.

Since its inception in the 1800, distance education was meant to open up access to knowledge as a guiding core principle (Olcott, 2013). The most important aims of quality open distance education, according to Daniel (2004) is that it cuts across different societies and it is guided by the principles of flexibility, learner-centeredness and accessibility. If the concept of access is what guides openness in distance education provision, then what does quality mean in this context. Olakulehin and Singh (2013) argue that widening access is not only about enhancing access to higher education, it is also about providing opportunities for those "who have certain types of 'deficits' to develop to the required standards" (p.36). We therefore have to take this into consideration when we look at quality provision aimed at expanding access.

Many people have attempted to define quality in relation to 'fitness for purpose". For instance, Harvey and Green (1993) conclude that quality is slippery and value driven. On the one hand quality as a concept was borrowed from the industry and has been used interchangeably and in some instances with reference to education. The problem arises when accounts of educational quality are based on outcomes rather than processes and practices (Damme, 2002; Green, 1994; Kirkpatrick, 2005). On the other hand fitness for purpose in higher education is based on the ability of an institution to fulfil its mission or a program of study to fulfill its aims (Harvey and Stensaker, 2006). Looking at quality this way allows institutions to define their purpose in their mission statements. "This definition allows variability in institutions, rather than forcing them to be clones of one another" (Woodhouse, 1999, pp. 29–30). Thus fitness for purpose evaluates whether the quality-related intentions of an organization are adequate (Vlasceanu *et al.*, 2007).

Distance education institutions have been persistently criticized for their lack of quality because in the minds of many it is not possible to accommodate large numbers of students at low costs. The traditional concept of quality, according to Green (1994), is often associated with the provision of a product or service of extremely high standards which are defined in terms of low numbers and high costs in higher education. In other words, "an institution with tough admission requirements and high fees is a good institution, regardless of what happens within its walls" (Daniel et al. 2009). More often than not, the notion of exclusivity is implied (Green 1994). To debunk this myth, Daniel and colleagues (2009) developed an Iron Triangle where they argued that it is possible to have "scalable (wide access), academically credible (high quality) and affordable (low cost)" education. The ubiquitous growth and the use of technology in teaching and learning have shown that it is possible to "break open the iron triangle" (Daniel et al. 2009). What this means is that distance education institutions can increase access, improve quality and cut costs – all at the same time.

This argument shows that quality means different things to different people in different contexts and is therefore value laden. Any particular view of education, according to Stemler and Baibel (1999) is influenced by the organizational culture, systems and practices. Since the beginning of formal education, different societal demands influenced the mission– that is the purpose of the institution. In the British higher education, according to Singh (2001), quality is foregrounded on issues of value for money while in the Netherlands, quality is measured in terms of autonomy. Given the history of South Africa, it makes sense that quality should be centralized around transformation issues geared towards equity. Therefore, "what would quality look like that took equity and innovation as its central premise in the South African context" (Singh, 2001, p.147).

It makes sense therefore, that quality in South Africa, should be examined in terms of whether the systems and processes promote equitable practices. However, in distance education, according to Kirkpatrick (2005), quality is frequently judged in terms of learning materials. Success depends on how effectively course production, delivery and student support sub-systems operate, underpinned by academic standards and management processes. Assuring quality in distance education presents a challenge of design of the instruction. The development of study material goes through a series of steps that Pena-Bandalaria (2007), refers to as 'quality circle' that consists of the course writer (who is a subject matter expert); a subject matter specialist (another subject matter expert who peer reviews the soundness of the course and its contents); an instructional designer (who ensures the 'chunking of lessons' is appropriate and that the program/ course goals, contents, and assessments mesh logically with one another); a media specialist (who recommends appropriate delivery mediums); and a language editor (who performs copy and substantive editing). In sum, whatever the technology used to deliver instructional content, the 'quality circle approach' to course development should be standard practice (Pena-Bandalaria, 2007).

Unlike in contact institutions where a lecturer is responsible for the development and the delivery of the tutorial, in ODL there are many processes and people who are involved in both the development and the delivery of study material. What this means is that quality in distance education cannot be equated with quality in contact institutions. This viewpoint, however, is like comparing apples to oranges – both are fruit, but both are very different. The problem arises when issues of quality assurance systems do not take history and context into consideration. The traditional concept of quality, according to Green (1994), is associated with the provision of a product or service of extremely high standards. A high quality institution, according to Green (1994), is one that clearly states its mission (or purpose), and meeting the goals that it has set itself. Therefore this chapter will focus on "quality as fit for purpose" as encapsulated in its mission.

METHODOLOGY

To find out whether the UNISA's is doing what it claims to do as an ODL institution mandated to widening access to higher education, this chapter is going to critique the mission statement in relation to the quality indicators. Although mission statements are ubiquitous in higher education, very little attention is given to what the content of the statement mean in relation to university's goals and objectives. There are very few empirical studies, according to Morphew and Hartley (2006) that analyze the content of the mission statement in relation to the organizational reality. This chapter will look at the Quality Assurance criterion that purports to measure the mission of the university, that is, the general philosophy that guides the values, culture and ethos of an institution.

The starting point when analyzing the mission statement of an institution is to look at the Quality Assurance Toolkits that regulatory bodies in different countries use to assess and articulate what quality is in relation to the education provision. The tools that are used to measure quality help the authors to focus on specific schemas that are already set out for them (CHEA, 2007; Kirkpatrick, 2005). The problem arises when national regulatory and policy frameworks do not address issues that are uniquely ODL. Instruments used to measure or evaluate ODL programs are the same as the ones used in contact institutions yet the institutional mandate, systems and the delivery of programs are different. This creates a problem when ODL institutions are assessed the same way as contact-based institutions. In response to this concern, the Commonwealth of Learning (CoL), the African Council of Distance Education (ACDE), and the National Association of Distance Education Organizations of South Africa (NADEOSA) have developed toolkits aimed at assessing quality in a distance education context.

For the purposes of this chapter, three distance education Quality Assurance Toolkits developed by CoL, ACDE and NADEOSA were selected because they were developed by associations with specific interests in the development of distance education. CoL is an intergovernmental organization meant to develop capacity and sharing of open learning practices amongst commonwealth countries. The ACDE is the continental educational organization, committed to expanding access to quality education in Africa and NADEOSA is the forum for South African distance education organizations and individuals. These associations and organizations are committed to expanding access to quality education through distance education mode. The mandate of all of them, the international organization, the continental and national association is to provide a platform for distance education providers, supporters and other stakeholders to discuss and share knowledge about distance education practices, systems and processes.

QUALITY ASSURANCE TOOLKITS

Commonwealth of Learning Toolkit

In preparation for the development of the Quality Assurance Toolkit, CoL published a number of reports on quality issues in distance education. This was done to provide the rationale for the development of quality assurance systems for distance education (Koul,

2006). After a long reiteration process of engagements, 10 key areas which reflect the salient features of systems within the distance higher education were identified. The identified quality criteria include:

- Vision, mission and planning
- Management, leadership and organizational culture
- The learners
- Human resource and development
- Program design and development
- Course design and development
- Learner support
- Learner assessment
- Infrastructure and learning resources
- Research consultancy and extension services

All these identified criteria will assist institutions to quality assure, that is self-assess, instead of being assessed by regulatory bodies. In developing these criteria, CoL found out that experience from across the Commonwealth countries suggested that guided self-assessment is the most appropriate model in quality management.

African Council for Distance Education Toolkit

Although it is important to have regulatory bodies assessing quality, most African countries found that national regulatory frameworks are unresponsive and inadequate to address the unique requirements and demands of ODL (Barasa, 2006). On the other hand, regulatory agencies argue that ODL should be subjected to the same regulatory frameworks as that of conventional universities, or at worst seek for integration rather than differentiation (Kirkpatrick, 2005) while ODL institutions argue that ODL is significantly unique and should have distinct and even parallel quality assurance and accreditation frameworks, tools, procedures and even regulatory agencies separate from that of conventional universities (Barasa, 2006).

These arguments and counterarguments led to the development of the continental quality assurance toolkit for distance education in Africa. The ACDE developed the Quality Assurance toolkit in response to the credibility impediment of low quality of education provision, which is often associated with distance education. The Toolkit identified eleven (11) criteria which reflect the essential features/elements of distance Higher Education Institutions. Performance indicators were then developed for each criterion as tools that can be evaluated. To facilitate their use for evaluation, sources of evidence and performance measures on a five-point scale were identified for each performance indicator. The criteria included:

- Vision, Mission And Planning
- Organizational Management, Culture And Leadership
- The Learners

- Human Resource And Development
- Program Design And Development
- Course Design And Development
- Learner Support And Progression
- Learner Assessment And Evaluation
- Learning Infrastructure And Resources
- Research, Publication And Consultancy Services
- Collaboration And Partnership

National Distance Education Organizations' of South Africa Criteria

The process of the development of the quality assurance framework for distance education was initiated in 1996 by the Centre for Educational Technology and Distance Education in the Department of Education. After extensive comments from members of the newly formed National Association of Distance Education Providers of South Africa (NADEOSA), a policy statement was prepared, *Criteria for Quality Distance Education in South Africa. Draft Policy Statement* (DoE, 1998). After contextualizing quality assurance in distance education in South Africa, South African Institute for Distance Education (SAIDE) in consultation with the National Council of Distance Education (NADEOSA), developed 13 quality criteria that outlined the following:

- Policy and Planning
- Learners
- Program Development
- Course Design
- Course Materials
- Assessment
- Learner Support
- Human Resource Strategy
- Management and Administration
- Collaborative Relationships
- Quality Assurance
- Information Dissemination
- Results

Each of these quality criteria covers elements that are unique to distance education provision. This was done in order to infuse distance education concerns into the general criteria, whereas, in the Higher Education Qualification Council (HEQC) audit criteria, the approach was to separate out distance education concerns in separate tables (CHE, 2004). This difference in approach is justified, in that accreditation evaluations deal much more with concerns that are common to all educational provision – for example, program goals, learning materials, and assessment design are issues for all programs, regardless of mode of delivery, while audit evaluations focus on institutional systems. HEQC is concerned that higher education programs be transformative, rather than merely on fitness for purpose and they should also improve access and equity (CHE, 2004). These concerns fit in with the role of distance education in the South African context.

It is in this regard that we seek to analyze and to evaluate quality that fits the purpose of distance education. For the purposes of this chapter the mission statement of UNISA will be analyzed in relation to Criterion one of the Commonwealth of Learning Quality Assurance Toolkit and the ACDE Quality Assurance and Accreditation Toolkit because it the only criterion on the mission of the university. Although the Nadeosa criteria did not specifically refer to the mission statement in their Criterion one, which refers to Policy and Planning, it is suggested in some of the performance indicators.

According to the mission statement, UNISA is a comprehensive, open distance learning institution that produces excellent scholarship and research, provides quality tuition and fosters active community engagement. The university is guided by the principles of lifelong learning, student-centeredness, innovation and creativity. Its efforts contribute for the knowledge and information society, advance development, nurture citizenry and ensure global sustainability.

Criterion 1 - Vision, Mission and Planning

Scope - The institution determines its own mission and objectives that reflect its academic commitments and the needs of society.

To facilitate their application and use, Sources of Evidence and Performance Measures on a five-point scale were used, in which each level is given numerical weighting (points) and a descriptor:

Fails to meet the Criteria - 0
Unsatisfactory - 1
Satisfactory - 2
Good - 3
Excellent -4

Discussion on Findings

This statement "comprehensive, open distance learning institution" separates UNISA from other higher education institution in that it subscribes to open distance learning principles of flexibility and student-centeredness. The latter is important because it deals with enhancing student's autonomy through provision support services and learning programs that are geared towards helping students succeed (HEQC, 2009). UNISA identifies itself as comprehensive because it offers undergraduate and postgraduate vocational, professional and academic qualifications. By providing these academic and career-focused learning opportunities, the university is responding to the needs of the South African society. The ODL nature of the institution allows students to study wherever they are without restrictions of place and time. This makes higher education accessible to students who come from remote rural areas and who may not have the opportunity or access to study on campus.

Table 1.

Criteria Standards	Performance Indicators	Evidence	P/M	UNISA
1.1. The institution has a stated vision and mission that is supported by specific and clearly defined goals and objectives within the context of national development priorities and the latest international trends in education.	1.1.1. The vision and mission are relevant to national development priorities.	The vision and mission statements; Corporate/Strategic Plan; handbook of the institution; governing board/academic board meeting minutes; planning policy, framework; involvement of staff in the university plans.	0 1 2 3 4	"provides quality tuition and fosters active community engagement … contribute for the knowledge and information society, advance development, nurture citizenry"
	1.1.2. The vision and mission reflect the latest international trends in education	The vision and mission statements; Corporate/Strategic Plan; handbook of the institution; governing board/academic board meeting minutes; planning policy, framework; involvement of staff in the university plans.	0 1 2 3 4	"produces excellent scholarship and research … and ensure global sustainability"
	1.1.3. The vision and mission are made known to all stakeholders.	Handbook, brochures; other advocacy materials of the institution; circulation to all stakeholders through minutes, website, materials etc., interaction with staff, students and other stakeholders.	0 1 2 3 4	"is a comprehensive, open distance learning institution"
	1.1.4. The specific goals and objectives are clearly defined and relevant to the institutional context.	Handbook; Corporate/Strategic Plan; brochures; program information documents; website	0 1 2 3 4	"produces excellent scholarship and research, provides quality tuition and fosters active community"
1.2. The mission statement and objectives are regularly reviewed by the institution.	1.2.1. The institution has a process in place for obtaining feedback from stakeholders.	Feedback forms; documented feedback information; database; interaction with stakeholders, data on workshops, minutes of various committees dealing with feedback processes.	0 1 2 3 4	The vision and the mission statement was approved in 2004.
	1.2.2. The feedback is systematically analyzed and made available to the senior institutional decision makers to make the necessary revisions to the objectives and plans of the institution.	Feedback forms, documented feedback information, interaction with stakeholders, data on workshops, minutes of meetings of various committees dealing with feedback processes.	0 1 2 3 4	The vision, mission and values guide the decision making processes and planning.
	1.2.3. The senior management reviews the activities of the institution and their appropriateness and assesses their alignment with the needs of the stakeholders and the institution's mission and objectives. It makes necessary changes wherever appropriate.	Agenda and minutes of management meetings; details of review meetings of management with staff; appraisal data forms; incidences of changes made; interaction with staff, students and other stakeholders.	0 1 2 3 4	The mission statement is integrated into the implementation plan of the university.

As an ODL institution, UNISA gives expression to its identity through the characteristics that differentiate ODL from other South African institutions of higher learning. These are: 1. accessibility; 2. flexibility and 3. Student centeredness as described by the Commonwealth of Learning (Koul, 2006). Widening access is key to ODL. Therefore, methods and technologies that are used in this context should enhance not limit access. Most ODL institutions were established to provide access to quality education and equity to those who otherwise would have been denied access (Olakulehin and Singh, 2013).The HEQC (2009) report acknowledges that UNISA is accessible to a diverse student profile through addressing their needs by offering relevant learner support facilitated by appropriate learning resources. Secondly, as an ODL institution UNISA subscribes to the concept of flexibility. In the UNISA context, student can study anywhere, anytime and at anyplace. UNISA is flexible in terms of time, place of study and to some extent admission requirements. Finally, in ODL, students are at the center of the educational process. The aim is to develop in each student a sense of responsibility for his or her own learning by focusing on individual student's experiences, perspectives, background, interests, capabilities and needs.

In its mission statement, UNISA combines both the characteristics of distance education (method) and open (purpose or approach) of learning into open distance learning. In addition to this, UNISA is no different from any other university in terms of the three core elements of higher education: teaching, research and community engagement. From the mission statement, one can deduce that the purpose of the UNISA is to "produce excellent scholarship and research, provide quality tuition and foster community engagement."

In reviewing UNISA's mission, the HEQC, in its 2009 institutional audit, acknowledges the dangers of the revolving door syndrome, in which open access is not accompanied by success because student drop out without completing the course or qualification (HEQC, 2009, 17). Although it acknowledges that dropout rates are high in distance education, it was also found that UNISA throughput does not compare well with open distance learning institution in the world,. If UNISA has to "ensure global sustainability" and respond to this need, the time taken until graduation needs to be considered. If this is not addressed, "the social justice drive which defines UNISA's access mandate might not be realized if students cannot progress through their studies and the institution cannot produce a significant number of graduates to alleviate the country's skills shortage and contribute to social development" (HEQC, 2009, 17).

The fact that UNISA's mission stipulates that it needs "to nurture citizenry and ensure global sustainability", this means that UNISA's purpose is "to develop critical citizens capable of engaging with and committing to their societies (HEQC, 2009). ODL is a political and a moral choice which needs to be sustained through the development of educational processes geared to graduating students who have the necessary knowledge, skills and competencies to continue to learn.

Conclusion

Given this description of what UNISA is supposed to do as an ODL institution, is the mission congruent with its practice and in what way? Does it provide the possibility of a more flexible, accessible and student-centered end pedagogically sound education through technological mediation? How accessible is it? This can only be assessed and tested against the mission statement. The meaning found in the mission statement makes the statement a useful document for the empirical examination of the purpose of the institution. Assuring the quality of the key features of ODL provision will not only guarantee the distance learner the quality of the provision but will also establish connections between various activities, thereby informing and improving practice. Such a process should be an integral part of the overall functioning of each institution. Such institutions may operate within a larger, national framework and have the mandate to meet the expectations of a wide range of stakeholders in terms of equity and access to higher education. The idea was to find out if UNISA, as an ODL institution "has achieved its mission that values the character traits proscribed by the statement" (Davis et al. 2006). Criterion 1 of the Quality Assurance indicates that it does. However, this study examined the narrow view of the mission statement. It provides an overview of how UNISA presents itself in relation to its fitness for purpose. Further studies may be required to determine whether missions of the university influence practices and how different stakeholders both internally and externally view the mission statement.

REFERENCES

Alexander, R. (2008). *Education for All, The Quality Imperative and the Problem of Pedagogy, Create Pathways to Access: Research Monograph (20).* London: Institute of Education, University of London.

Barasa, F. S. (2011, May). Promoting Open and Distance Learning in Africa: A Critical Reflection on Rhetoric, Real and Ideal, paper presented at the Conference of Rectors, Vice-Chancellors and Presidents of African Universities.

Bart, C.K. & Baetz, M. C. (1998). The Relationship Between Mission Statements And Firm Performance: An Exploratory Study, Journal of Management Studies 35(6), 823-853.

Commonwealth of Learning (2009). Quality Assurance Toolkit: Distance Higher Education Institutions and Programs, Commonwealth of Learning.

Council for Higher Education Accreditation CHEA (2002). Accreditation and Assuring Quality in Distance Learning, Council for Higher Education Accreditation CHEA Monograph Series 2002, Number 1. Retrieved from http://www.chea.org/Research/Accred-Distance-5-9-02.pdf?pubID=246.

Council on Higher Education (CHE) (2004). Enhancing the contribution of distance higher education in South Africa, Pretoria, CHE.

Daniel, J. Kanwar, A. & Uvalic-Trumbic, U. (2009). Breaking Higher Education's Iron Triangle: Access, Cost, and Quality, *Change: The Magazine of Higher Learning, March/April 2009*

Davis, J.H.; Ruhe, J.A. Lee, M. & Rajadhyaksha, U. (2007), Mission Possible; Do school mission statements work? Journal of Business Ethics, 70, 99-110.

Damme, Van.Dirk. (2002). Trends and Models in International Quality Assurance and Accreditation in Higher Education in Relation to Trade in Education Services. OECD/US Forum on Trade in Educational Services, Washington, D.C.USA.

Department of Education (2001). National Plan for Higher Education, Pretoria, Government Printers.

Department of Higher Education and Training (DHET), (2013). *Statistics on Post-School Education and Training in South Africa*, Pretoria: DHET. Retrieved from http://www.saqa.org.za/docs/papers/stats2011.pdf.

Green, D. (1994). What is quality in higher education? Concepts, Policy and Practice, in What is Quality in Higher Education? Green D. (ed), Open University Press: SRHE.

Harvey L. & Green, D. (1993). "Defining quality", Assessment and Evaluation in Higher Education, 18: 8-35.

Harvey, L., Burrows, A. & Green, D. (1992). Criteria of Quality in Higher Education report of the QHE Project, The University of Central England, Birmingham.

Harvey, L. & Stensaker, B. (2007). Quality culture: Understandings, boundaries and linkages Paper presented to the 29th EAIR FORUM, Innsbruck, Austria.

Kirkpatrick, D. (2005). Quality Assurance In Open And Distance Learning, Commonwealth of Learning, Retrieved from, http://www.col.org/SiteCollectionDocuments/KS2005_QA.pd.

Kliebard, H.M. (2001). Curriculum theory as metaphor. *Theory Into Practice*, 26: 11–17.

Koul, B.N. (2006) Towards a culture of Quality in Open Distance Learning: Present Possibilities, in Koul, B.N. and Kanwar, A. (eds), Towards a Culture of Quality, Commonwealth of Learning, Vancouver.

Menon M.B. (2004). Networking for Quality Assurance in Teacher Education by Open Distance Learning in Rama K. and Menon, M.B. Innovations and Best practices in Quality Assurance for Teacher Education, NAAC-COL, Bangalore.

Morphew, C.C. & Hartley, M. (2006) Mission Statements: A thematic analysis of rhetoric across institutional type, *The Journal of higher Education*, 77(3), 456-471.

Olakulehin, F.Y. & Singh, G, (2013). Widening access through openness in higher education in the developing world; A Bourdieusian field analysis of experiences from the National Open University of Nigeria, pp.13-40.

Olcott, D. (2013). Access under siege: Are the gains of open education keeping pace with the growing barriers to university access? *Open Praxis*, 5(1), pp. 15-20.

Pena-Bandalaria, M (2007), Impact of ICTs Open and Distance Learning a developing country setting, The Philippine experience. International Review of Research in Open and Distance Learning. 8, 1-15.

Stemler, S. and Bebell, D. (1999) The empirical approach to understanding and analyzing the mission statements of selected educational institutions, a paper presented at the Annual Meeting of the New England Educational Research Organization (NEERO), Portsmouth, New Hampshire, April 9, 1999.

Tjivikua, U.C. (2010), An investigation of the Principal's leadership role in a successful rural school in Namibia, MA Dissertation, Rhodes University, available at http://eprints.ru.ac.za/934/1/Tjivikua-MEd-TR07-174.pdf, accessed 17 July 2012.

Vlăsceanu, L., Grünberg, L., & Pârlea, D., 2007, Quality Assurance and Accreditation: A Glossary of Basic Terms and Definitions (Bucharest, UNESCO-CEPES) Revised and updated edition. ISBN 92-9069-186-7, available at http://www.scribd.com/doc/84266002/A-Glossary-of-Basic-Terms, accessed 20 September 2012.

Understanding education quality, EFA Global Monitoring report (2005). http://www.unesco.org/education/gmr_download/chapter1.pdf.

Woodhouse, D. (1999). Quality and Quality Assurance' in Organization for Economic Co.

Young, S.F. (2008). Theoretical frameworks and models of learning: tools for developing conceptions of teaching and learning, International Journal for Academic Development, 13:1, 41-49.

In: Open Distance Learning (ODL) in South Africa
Editor: Moeketsi Letseka
ISBN: 978-1-63463-890-6

Chapter 3

PARTICIPATION IN OPEN DISTANCE LEARNING

Paul Prinsloo*

Department of Business Management
College of Economic and Management Sciences
University of South Africa (UNISA), South Africa

ABSTRACT

Increasing or widening participation has been a trend in international higher education since the 1990s. Not only was this in response to increased demand for access to higher education, but also due to a proliferation of different forms of delivery, open education becoming mainstream and, of course, the impact of technology. Distance education and open distance learning (ODL) in particular has been an integral part of the South African higher education landscape since 1873 when the University of South Africa (UNISA) was established. Until recently, UNISA was not only the only dedicated distance education provider in South Africa, but also the only ODL comprehensive institution, the biggest on the African continent and one of the mega universities in the world. To a large extent, participation in ODL is synonymous with UNISA. This chapter provides a socio-critical interrogation of the notion of participation in ODL in the specific context of South Africa. Participation in ODL with special reference to South Africa is, however, influenced by international trends in higher education, and the increasing blurring of the boundaries between traditional residential face-to-face education and traditional distance education modes. This chapter focuses on participation in ODL as a distinct notion different from *access*, and entails a multi-dimensional and complex rite of passage consisting of mostly non-linear, multidimensional, interdependent interactions at different phases in the nexus between student, institution and broader societal factors. I will firstly problematize participation in ODL and clarify a number of terms germane to the discourse. The next section in this chapter will then briefly discuss international trends in participation in higher education and ODL before addressing selected issues in the South African context with specific reference to "White paper for post-school education and training. Building an expanded, effective and integrated post-school system" (DHET, 2013) and the "Policy for the provision of distance education in South African universities in the context of an integrated post-school system" (DHET, 2014).

* Email: prinsp@unisa.ac.za

Against this background I will then discuss a number of theoretical constructs informing a socio-critical model of student participation in ODL.

INTRODUCTION

The present discourses on participation in (different forms of) open distance learning (ODL)[1] should be understood against the general current flux in higher education. Terms such as "disruption" and "innovation" (Christensen, 2008), "disaggregation" (Wiley & Hilton III, 2009), the "unbundling and unmooring" (Watters, 2012), "revolution" (Altbach, Reisberg & Rumbley, 2009), and "crisis" (Carr, 2012) have become endemic to discourses on the current and future states of higher education. Though many would propose that the higher education landscape is *irrevocably* changing (Staley & Trinkle, 2011), and that we are seeing the end of higher education as we know it; there are also sceptical voices warning against the many millennialist myths and eschatological language used to describe the current flux (see for example, Watters, 2013).

Amidst the different myths, claims and counter claims regarding the flux and/or permanency of current trends in higher education; the increase in participation rates in higher education is an accepted characteristic of the present higher education landscape (Altbach, 1999; Daniel, Kanwar & Uvalić-Trumbić, 2008, 2010a,b; Glennie, 2013; Lane, 2013a, 2013b; DHET, 2013, 2014; Lane, 2014; Osborne, 2004; Subotzky & Prinsloo, 2011). Referring to the growth and transformation of higher education in developing world contexts, and specifically *for-profit* higher education, Daniel, et al (2010b) refer to the impact of the rapid expansion of access to higher education as a "tectonic shift" (p. 17). There is furthermore agreement that traditional forms of higher education such as residential or face-to-face education cannot address the need for or cope with increasing participation rates. Distance education, and increasingly different forms of open and online education are seen as the panache to address the widening of participation in higher education (Altbach, 1999; Boeren, Nicaise & Baert, 2010; Daniel, 2012; Desjardins & Rubenson, 2013; Lane, 2013a; Lockwood, 1995; Moore & Kearsley, 2012; Peters, 2001; Zawacki-Richter, & Anderson, 2014).

Though the expansion of access to higher education has most probably increased, it is worthwhile to refer to Altbach (1999) who stated that the increases in access and participation in higher education result in the need for the "diversification of academic institution, less homogenous student populations, alterations in patterns of academic work and of the academic profession itself, an increase in managerial control of academic institutions, and recently, a reliance on distance methods of delivering instruction" (p. 107).

I acknowledge that there are many possible theoretical and analytical approaches to exploring participation in ODL. One could focus on a historical overview of the growth in participation in distance education in ODL, or focus on forces impacting on this growth. Another possibility is to approach participation in ODL against the increasing blurring of conceptual distinctions between different forms of education delivery such as MOOCs, hybrid models as the increasing use of technology continues to blur these distinctions.

[1] A clarification of the different layers or nuances of openness and distance education are crucial for a discussion of participation. A working definition determined by the scope of this publication is proposed later in the chapter.

Though this chapter addresses the notion of participation in ODL in the specific context of South Africa, participation in ODL should be seen against the broader context of international developments in higher education. I will engage with the notion of participation in ODL through a *socio-critical* lens – and firstly situate this chapter in the context of socio-political developments in South Africa post 1994; before exploring student participation through the lenses of a number of theoretical constructs informing a socio-critical model of student participation. I conclude the chapter by pointing to a number of issues that will continue to shape participation rates in ODL.

Problematizing Participation in ODL – A Clarification of Terms

Within the scope of this chapter, it is crucial to distinguish and clarify a number of terms that impact on my approach to participation in ODL. For example, what is the difference between participation in ODL from the notion of *access*, discussed in the previous chapter? What do we mean by the notion of participation? If by 'participation' we mean 'admission to register', the distinction from the previous chapter's focus on access may disappear or become problematic. And also, when we look at ODL in the context of South Africa, do we look at participation in all *distance education* programmes offered by a range of institutions (whether classified as a distance education institution or as a residential institution which happens also to offer distance education programmes) or do we specifically look at participation in ODL as a specific form of distance education? Do we also include programmes offered fully online, whether by residential institutions or by distance education institutions? (See for example Archer, Garrison & Anderson, 2013; Lane, 2013a; Zawacki-Richer & Anderson, 2014). Do we only investigate participation in formal education (certificates, diplomas and degrees, both undergraduate and postgraduate), or do we also include participation in continuing education or professional development through non-formal or informal learning, by public and/or private, and other forms of lifelong learning through, e.g. massive open online courses (MOOCs)?

In the general parlance terms such as access and participation, and distance education and open distance learning are used interchangeably. In the context of this chapter, I would like to justify a specific take on the issue of participation in the context of ODL, and it is therefore necessary to clarify these terms.

Access and Participation

In this chapter I explore the notion of participation as *distinct* from access while acknowledging that there are a number of linkages and overlaps in literature between the notions of 'access' and 'participation.' While access, in general, refers to issues such as admission requirements within the discourses of widening participation and the massification of higher education; I explore participation specifically as entailing not only issues of access, but more specifically participation in terms of the scope and different factors involved in the nexus between student and institution. Participation, in the context of this chapter, therefore explore issues surrounding student trajectories, dropout, stop-out and successful completion (Barnett, 1996; Subotzky & Prinsloo, 2011).

Participation in ODL – A Delimitation of Scope

In the scope of this chapter, what forms of ODL do I include or exclude? UNESCO (http://www.distance-learning.co.uk/whatis/dlvol.htm) acknowledges that the terms distance education and ODL are used interchangeably but indicate that there are also important differences. UNESCO proposes "open learning [as] an umbrella term for any scheme of education or training that seeks systematically to remove barriers to learning, whether they are concerned with age, time, place or space. With open learning, individuals take responsibility for what they learn, how they learn, where they learn, how quickly they learn, who helps them and when they have their learning assessed." In contrast to open learning, distance learning (as a form of open learning) specifically emphasizes the fact that "tutors and learners are separated by geographical distance."

In the context of this book dedicated to ODL in South Africa, it is important to note that the Policy (DHET, 2014) distinguishes between open distance learning (ODL) and open *and* distance learning. Therefore, ODL refers to "ALL distance programs offered are based on open learning principles" (DHET, 2014, p. 21). The open learning principles are described in the White Paper (DHET, 2013) as follows:

> Open learning is an approach which combines the principles of learner centeredness, lifelong learning, flexibility of learning provision, the removal of barriers to access learning, the recognition for credit of prior learning experience, the provision of learner support, the construction of learning programs in the expectation that learners can succeed, and the maintenance of rigorous quality assurance over the design of learning materials and support systems (p. p.48, referring to the White Paper, 1995).

Open learning is further described by the Policy (DHET, 2014) as typically involving "making provision to support a wider range of student choices regarding access, curriculum, pacing, sequencing, learning modes and methods, assessment and articulation" (p. 22). In the context of South Africa the definition by Chowdry, Dearden, Goodman and Vignoles (2013) is of particular interest. They specifically argue that 'participation' means "increasing the participation in HE [higher education] of pupils from lower socio-economic backgrounds and other under-represented groups" (p.431). This view resonates with the South African context where during the period 2005-2011, participation rates of Africans and Coloureds hovered between 10% and 14%, that of Indians between 44% and 47%, while that of whites were between 51% and 57% (CHE, 2013, p.41). The historical legacy of apartheid disenfranchising scores of youth from participation in higher education as well as the persistent impact of one's socio-economic status (SES) in either creating opportunities for success in higher education or hampering such opportunities; will continue to play a definitive role in participation rates in higher education (Subotzky & Prinsloo, 2011). This then gives rise to the question: what role should or can ODL play to enhance their active and optimal participation in HE?

There is also an increasing convergence between different forms of educational delivery as more and more traditionally campus-based or face-to-face institutions engage with and roll-out programs and offerings utilizing the affordances of technology for students who are not based on campus for whatever reason. Viewing the increasing convergence of different elements of educational delivery on a continuum ranging from fully campus-based to fully-distance education or remote delivery no longer suffices (DHET, 2014, p. 8). Figure 1 illustrates the different possibilities and scope of these possibilities on two axes – the extent to which an offering is online or offline, and the extent to which the same offering is campus-based or delivered remotely. As can be seen from Figure 1, while offering 'B' is fully online, it is also campus-based. It is also interesting to compare offering 'C' with offering 'B' that is also fully online but contains no campus-based element. For the sake of this chapter, it is important to note that offering 'B' therefore qualifies as a distance education offering and depending on the admission requirements, may actually also fit the description of an ODL offering.

Option 'A' illustrates the practice of offering an educational opportunity for learners through remote delivery in digitally supported ways. The Policy (DHET, 2014) therefore applies to offerings/practices "towards the right-hand side of Figure 1 in which it is assumed that students will rarely, if ever, be in the same physical location at the same time as their lecturer" (p. 9). In terms of the Policy (DHET, 2014) the term 'distance education' therefore refers to the "provision in which students spend 30% or less of the stated Notional learning hours in undergraduate courses at NQF levels 5 and 6, and 25% or less in courses and NQF level 7 and initial post-graduate courses at NQF Level 8, in staff-led, face-to-face, campus-based structured learning activities" (p. 9).

Of crucial importance for this chapter is therefore clarifying the relationship between distance education and open distance learning. The Policy (DHET, 2014) states that "Distance education provision is well-placed to give practical expression to open learning principles, *but in and of itself is not synonymous with open provision*" (p. 10; emphasis added). Therefore, all distance education offerings are therefore not, necessarily, open in an ODL sense.

Now that we clarified the distinction between distance education and ODL, it is also necessary to critically engage with the different nuances of 'open.'

Definitions of 'openness' in the context of ODL are bound to national legislation resulting in different gestalts of ODL depending on the geopolitical context. For example, ODL in the context of the Open University (UK) means that for enrolling in undergraduate courses students previous academic achievements are not considered. UNISA, on the other hand, is bound by national legislation that establishes the minimum admission requirements for enrolling in higher education, whether for certificate, diploma or degree purposes. While both the OU (UK) and UNISA are ODL institutions, the scope of their 'openness' differs.

When readers therefore engage with this chapter, it is crucial to take note of the different nuances and their implications when discussing participation in ODL or when comparing participation rates among, for example ODL institutions such as UNISA, the OU (UK), Athabasca University and Indira Gandhi National Open University (IGNOU).

In the context of this book that specifically focuses on ODL in South Africa, it is also important to note that while the Policy (DHET, 2014) refers to all distance education offerings as ODL, different South African higher education institutions may determine their own unique admission requirements for their distance education programmes *in addition to* the minimum national admission requirement of a matriculation certificate. As will be illustrated in the next section, there are a number of South African higher education institutions offering ODL (as defined by the DHET, 2014) courses and programmes. Participation, as defined earlier, may therefore have distinct characteristics as per institution.

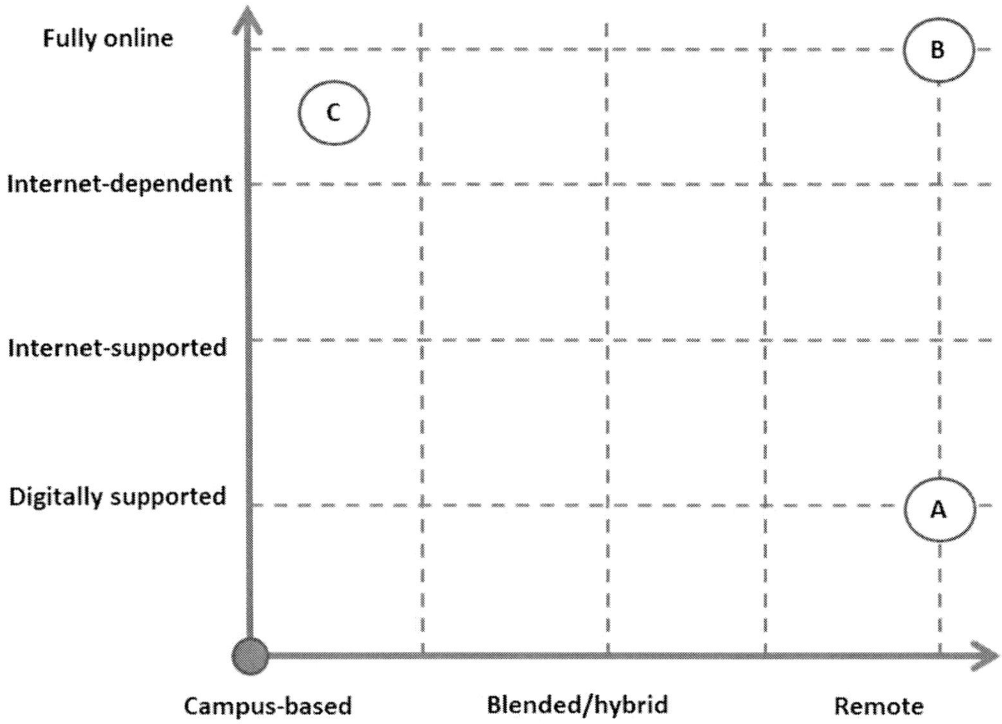

Figure 1. The provision grid (Adapted from DHET, 2014, p. 9).

I would therefore propose, for the sake of clarity, that I focus primarily on participation in the context of UNISA (as the largest ODL provider on the African continent)[2], but where appropriate, also refer to participation in other South African universities.

Situating Participation in ODL in the International Context

I would now like to disentangle participation from the broader discourses on *access* and situate participation in ODL using a socio-critical lens to engage with different elements of participation (see e.g. Badat & Sayed, 2014; Boeren, et al., 2010; Jansen, 2004; Subotzky & Prinsloo, 2011).

Already in 1999 did Altbach point to the fact that mass higher education "has become the international norm" (p. 107). One of the main drivers of the massification of higher education was the perception (often informed by policy) that "University degrees are … seen as important for social mobility" (p. 108).

---

[2] On 25 September 2014 UNISA had an enrolled student population of 351,502

Altbach (1999) states that it is difficult to generalize regarding the expansion of participation in higher education due to the fact that some contexts reached levels of maturity in participation rates, while in many developing world contexts, levels of participation are forecasted to grow exponentially. Of special interest for this chapter is Altbach's (1999) proposition of a number of characteristics that inform the "logic of mass higher education" (p. 110). These characteristics (pp. 110-122) are

- *The challenge of funding.* In the context of the debates surrounding higher education as public versus private good, and the increasing changes in funding regimes for higher education, the cost of participation – for students and institutions alike – is of increasing concern. Cost impacts directly on student fees (and rising student debt), the range of student support, quality, employee and program qualification mix (PQM) offered by institutions.
- *Growth of new sectors in higher education* – e.g. different combinations of public/private/for-profit/ not for profit. With the emphasis on increasing participation in higher education it is clear that current public higher education institutions will not be able to respond appropriately and effectively to the demand. This results in an increasing diversification of higher education providers as well as new forms of delivery (e.g. massive open online courses, Lane, 2013a), alliances and restricting or "unbundling" (Watters, 2012) (Also see Daniel et al, 2010).
- *Distance learning as a means for coping with the demand.* Though Altbach (1999) indicates that distance education is not a new idea, some of the traditional assumptions and beliefs surrounding distance education such as cost, effectiveness, and the role of technology should be questioned and explored. There is however no doubt that "distance higher education is an integral part of a mass higher education system" (Altbach, 1999, p. 115).
- The *diversification and complexity* of academic institutions. Responding to the massification of higher education has important implications for the size and complexity of the institutions and the way these institutions are governed.
- *Managerialism at academic institutions*, including the growth of the 'administrative estate'
- The *nature of the academic profession;* and
- *Students and student culture.* Altbach (1999) points to the fact that not only has the composition of the student population changed, "Students are also more varied in terms of their academic abilities and interests" impacting on the nature, scope, cost and effectiveness of student support.

Though Altbach wrote the above already in 1999, the above elements have been confirmed as continuing to shape the notion of participation in higher education (Boeren et al, 2010; Daniel et al, 2010b; DHET, 2014; Lane, 2013a; Whiteford, Shah & Nair, 2013)

It is therefore clear that increasing demands for participation in higher education, and more specifically through ODL, responds to the internal logic of mass higher education Altbach, 1999).

Situating Participation in ODL in the South African Context

A discussion of participation in ODL in the context of South Africa cannot and should not negate the complex and many mutually constitutive factors impacting on higher education post-1994 (Badat & Sayed, 2014; Subotzky & Prinsloo, 2011). Considering that at least 3.5 million youths between the ages of 18 and 25 are neither employed nor attending educational or vocational training (StatsSA, 2013), a discussion on participation in higher education does require a certain urgency and above all, critical engagement.

In the context of South Africa, distance education "has [always] formed a vital part of the university sub-system, contributing approximately 40% of headcount students and approximately 30 of FTE [full-time equivalent] students" (DHET, 2014, p. 10). The recently launched "White Paper for post-school education and training. Building an expanded, effective and integrated post-school system" (DHET, 2013) envisages a number of dramatic changes to the delivery of post-school education in South Africa. Of specific concern to this chapter on participation in ODL, is the opening up of distance education and blended learning provision to all higher education institutions in South Africa. Up to the promulgation of the White Paper (DHET, 2013), UNISA was the only dedicated, comprehensive distance education provider in South Africa. The White Paper (DHET, 2013) and the "Policy for the provision of distance education in South African universities" (DHET, 2014) now allows all higher education institutions to offer distance education programs within the context of a number of provisions. It is important to note (as pointed out earlier) that though these new providers may offer distance education programs, the admission requirements, pedagogy, and assessment will play a determining role to what extent these offerings can be classified as ODL.

Bunting, Sheppard, Cloete, and Belding (2010) state that of all the distance education providers, UNISA had the majority share of distance education students namely 262,000 in 2008 (p. 38), which was a "33% share of the total head count enrolment of 800 000 students in the public higher education system" with the majority of enrollments in undergraduate qualifications (90%) (p. 178). In the report by Bunting et al (2010) they state that the other role players in distance education were Nelson Mandela Metropolitan University (NMMU) (whose distance education enrollments sharply decreased from 2000 to 2008 (p. 131), impacting most dramatically on the amount of African students (p. 140). In 2008, North West University (NWU) had 21,300 distance education students (mostly in teacher education) which counted for 41% of NWU's enrollments.

At UNISA, from 2000 to 2010 there was an increase of 10% in enrollments from African students (53-63%), with female enrollment increasing from 50-56% for the same period (p. 179). Course success rates increased from 51% to 60%.

Up to 2014 when the "Policy for the provision of distance education in South African universities" (DHET, 2014) was promulgated, the majority of distance education students were enrolled at UNISA. With regard to participation rates it is also crucial to remember that participation does not only include those students who are registered for a full program or qualification, but also includes the provision of "discrete modules which have allowed students at contact institutions to complete their studies without needing to register for a whole semester or year of an additional campus-based study" (DHET, 2014, p. 10).

The increase in access and participation rates foreseen by the White Paper (DHET, 2013) and Policy (DHET, 2014) was provided impetus by increases in the availability and affordability of ICT in South Africa (DHET, 2014). While the new Policy (DHET, 2014) acknowledges that distance education, and implicitly ODL, can deliver high quality educational opportunities, in ways that may be more cost efficient and cost effective than traditional campus-based provision, issues such as access and quality will not be compromised.[3] Ensuring widened access *and* high quality provision necessitates

> investment in program design…; appropriate learning resources to support more independent learning; development of staff to enable effective teaching and learning through distance provisioning; ongoing proactive decentralized communication and support for remote and widely distributed students; and decentralized assessment strategies with a strong emphasis on formative feedback to encourage active engagement and retention (DHET, 2014, p. 11).

While the Policy (DHET, 2014) discusses distance education and not specifically ODL, it should be used as broad framework for contemplating the notion of participation in ODL. The issue of participation is therefore intertwined with issues of broadened access, the provision of "providing low enrollment niche programs that have a high impact and are required by small numbers of students across the country" the offering of opportunities for students who have outstanding modules in order to complete their qualifications, and opportunities to recognize prior learning (DHET, 2014, p. 12).

As Badat and Sayed (2014) indicate, despite the fact that post 1994 there was a commitment to equality of treatment and opportunity, this commitment was not sufficient "for eliminating systemic historical and structural educational inequalities that black South Africans experience as a result of the segregated (and underdeveloped and unequal) institutions that were reserved for them under apartheid" (p. 128). Providing equal access to higher education is therefore not enough due to the inherited, systemic and structurally produced nature of inequities. Participation in higher education and specifically in distance education and ODL continue to be shaped by inherited and prevailing economic and social structures. While higher education policy since 1994 attempted to address inequalities to access and participation through positive discrimination, in "the absence of far-reaching institutional transformation" (p. 129), the status quo remains unchanged. (Also see Scott, Yeld & Hendry, 2007).

Despite the "flurry of policy activity" (Badat & Sayed, 2014, p. 131) following 1994, resulting in a formal desegregation of higher education and an increase in access, "African and Colored South Africans continue to be underrepresented in higher education" (p. 134). Where race was the most important criterion for access prior to 1994, access and participation continue to be "conditioned by social class and geography" resulting in "new geographies of inequality" (p. 134). With regard to distance education, African students comprise 40.5 percent of the total student population compared to 33.3 percent of white students (Badat & Sayed, 2014). In general there is, however, an underrepresentation of African and female students at postgraduate level and in science, engineering, and technology.

---

[3] The issue of cost, quality and access – the so-called iron triangle (Daniel et al, 2010) – will be discussed later in this chapter.

While there were some changes with regard to access, Badat and Sayed (2014) point to persisting inequalities with regard to quality despite equal spending. In their analysis of educational outcomes post-1994, Badat and Sayed (2014) suggest that "the cleavages of race, while still noticeable, have become more muted; and inequities of class, gender, and geography have become more apparent" (p. 139).

The years 2013-2014 are seminal in our exploration of participation rates in open distance learning in the South African context.

In 2013 the expectation was that participation in higher education would increase from 17.3 percent to 25 percent with an expected enrollment in 2013 of 1.6 million enrollments (DHET, 2013, p. xiv). With the increasing emphasis on widening participation in higher education to specifically address issues of access and equity to erase the legacy of apartheid, there is an equal emphasis on increasing student success (DHET, 2013; Subotzky & Prinsloo, 2011). Widening participation in the South African context also means providing access and participation in a wide range of different possibilities for post-school education and training (DHET, 2013). "Differentiation is a way of ensuring a diverse system that will improve access for all South Africans to various forms of educational opportunities, improve participation and success rates in all higher education programs, and enable all institutions to find niche areas that respond to various national development needs" (DHET, 2013, p. 29). This differentiated system does not only refer to different types of institutions providing the education and training but also to accommodating "a variety of modes of learning, learning program, and methods of teaching and assessment for diverse student bodies, and should support both flexibility and innovation" (p. 29).

In July 2014 a dedicated policy on distance education (DHET, 2014) was promulgated. Despite and in the context of the increasing diversification of post-school education and training envisioned by the White Paper (DHET, 2013), the Policy (DHET, 2014) retains 'distance education' as "a distinct subset of provision" (p. 6) in the light of two factors namely (1) that many prospective students "cannot or ... choose not to attend traditional campus-based provision" and (2) the assumed "lower costs per student by amortizing curriculum design, materials development and some teaching costs across larger numbers of students and by obviating the need for continuing investment in physical infrastructure" (p. 6). While the DHET (2014) emphasize the institutional cost of providing access, Letseka and Pitsoe (2013) documented the comparative costs of access to *students*. In the South African higher education landscape, distance education is also the most affordable (Letseka & Pitsoe, 2013). The Policy (DHET, 2014) emphasizes, like the White Paper (DHET, 2013) that providing greater access and participation through distance education should offer "a reasonable expectation of turning access into success in courses or programs of proven quality… that are also affordable" (p. 6).

Situating Participation in ODL in the UNISA Context

In 2013, UNISA had 387,452 students (http://heda.unisa.ac.za/indicatordashboard/default.aspx) which shows a 30%+ increase to the enrollments in 2008. UNISA students carry, on average, half the course load per year compared to full-time students at residential universities, indicating that UNISA students may take double the time to complete their qualifications compared to residential students (Van Zyl, 2013, p. 9). Close to 90% of enrolled students are part-time students and female students constitute more than 60% of the total number of students (Van Zyl, 2013, p. 10). Black African students constitute more than 71% of the total of the number of registered students and Van Zyl (2013) reports that "Since 2008, the proportion of whites have decreased from 21,5% to 16,5%, that of Indians from 8,7% to 6,9% and coloreds from 5,8% to 5,2%" (p. 11). The proportion of students in the 25 to 39 year age group continues to grow year -on –year, with a decline of students in the younger-than-25 age bracket. In 2012 26,210 students graduated, of which close to 40% graduated with an undergraduate degree. "African graduates constitute 62,7% of all graduates in 2012, followed by white graduates (24, 4%)" (Van Zyl, 2013, p. 22). The proxy graduation rate for whites is 11,5 % followed by Indian students (9,4%) with Africans (6, 9%) and coloreds (6, 7%) reportingthe lowest rates (Van Zyl, 2013, p. 32).

Of particular concern is the dropout rate of students studying through distance education, in particular at UNISA. Close to 30% of students doing a three-year bachelor degree drop out at the end of the first year of registration, with about 2% of students graduating with a three-year bachelor degree in 5 years' time, with more than 30% still in process (Van Zyl, 2013, p. 36). In a CHE (2013) report it is noted that an estimated 72% of students in the 3 & 4-year degrees program at UNISA will not graduate; with an estimated 89% of all 3-year diplomas that will not graduate (See the full report, CHE, 2013). These statistics raise serious concerns regarding participation and success rates in ODL

THEORETICAL CONSTRUCTS INFORMING A SOCIOCRITICAL MODEL OF STUDENT PARTICIPATION IN ODL

Based on an extensive literature review (Prinsloo, 2009) on different models for understanding and predicting student success and dropout in higher education, and specifically in distance education contexts, Subotzky and Prinsloo (2011) state that student participation is characterized and shaped by "a complex, layered, and dynamic set of events" and that there is no "grand theory" that can fully explain student participation (p. 182). Subotzky and Prinsloo (2011) continue to moot a number of constructs that inform a sociocritical model for understanding and predicting student success. The constructs are:

Both the providing institution and students are situated agents. This construct emphasizes the agency of both students and the institutions, but acknowledges that this agency is situated and therefore constraint.

The student walk. As students and the institution engage in a social contract to not only make learning available but also possible, the nexus of this engagement is described as the "student walk" where the interactions are mutually constitutive and includes both planned (structured) and spontaneous (and mostly unforeseen) events that shape the participation of students. A crucial element of the student walk is the mutual responsibility both students and the institution have to ensure successful participation. At each of the different stages of the student walk (e.g., pre-registration, registration, formative assessment, etc.) the "fit" between students' expectations, life-worlds, and capital and those of the institution determines the depth of and outcome of the participation.

Capital. Not only do students and the institution bring to their joint participation different forms of capital, but "As situated agents, they acquire (or fail to acquire) these various forms of capital partly through the reproductive mechanisms embedded in their socio-economic and cultural contexts and partly through their own individual or institutional/organizational initiatives" (p. 186).

Habitus, of individuals and the institution constitute "the complex combination of perceptions, experiences, values, practices, discourses, and assumptions that underlie the construction of our worldviews" (Subotzky & Prinsloo, 2011, p. 186). As such habitus can either obstruct or enable successful participation.

The domains and modalities of individual and institutional transformation. Participation in ODL does not constitute a static environment, but is constituted, continuously, by inter and intrapersonal relations domains, as well as academic, administrative, and non-academic social domains. On both the side of students and institution, the modalities of attribution, locus of control and self-efficacy play a crucial role (Subotzky & Prinsloo, 2011).

A broad definition of success. In the context of this chapter, the construct suggested by Subotzky and Prinsloo (2011) defines the process and outcome of participation in higher education, and more specifically ODL. Crucial for our discussion on participation is the different nuances of participation such as course success and graduating in the minimum time allowed, a positive student experience throughout all the different phases of the student walk, a "successful fit between students' graduate attributes and the requirements of the workplace, civil society, and democratic, participative citizenship" and even "course success without graduating" (Subotzky & Prinsloo, 2011, p. 188).

From the above constructs it is clear that participation is much more than being limited to rates of participation. Participation, as such, is a complex phenomenon that constitutes a rite of passage consisting of mostly non-linear, multidimensional, interdependent interactions at different phases in the nexus between student, institution and broader societal factors. Participation entails therefore much more than access, and even notions such as retention, attrition and success. In following Subotzky and Prinsloo (2011), participation in ODL defies, to a certain extent, our spreadsheets, our statistics focused on narrow definitions. Due to the impact of technology, changing legislative and regulatory frameworks participation in ODL increasingly defies our clear-cut boundaries between those 'inside' and those 'outside' higher education(s).

CONCLUSION

This chapter opened up the notion of participation, by not only pointing to the (possibly) increasingly untenable distinctions between different nuances, definitions and practices of ODL. Even should we exclude the seeming impossibility to compare participation rates in international ODL due to different definitions, legislative and regulatory frameworks and context; the multiple forms of participation based on institution, formal or informal and different admission requirements infuse a discussion on participation in ODL in the South African context with complexity.

A number of different issues will continue to impact on participation rates in ODL such as the 'iron triangle' of cost, quality and access (Daniel, et al., 2008, 2010a); barriers to participation (including epistemological access, Morrow, 1992; also see Boughey, 2005); the discourses of "techno-solutionism" (Morozov, 2013) and "techno-romanticism" in education (Selwyn, 2013, 2014; Selwyn & Facer, 2013) in the context of the impact of technology on opening up participation or resulting in new gestalts of the digital divide (Czerniewicz, 2004; Czerniewicz & Brown, 2005; De Haan, 2004; Liebenberg, Chetty & Prinsloo, 2012); changing definitions of education provision (Butcher & Hoosen, 2014); the scope and impact of OER in opening up of educational opportunities and increasing participation (Kanwar & Balaji, 2011; Glennie, 2013) and the need for critical, theoretical and empirical interrogation on the notion of and practices regarding participation in ODL (see for example, Lane, 2013a, 2013b; 2014; Liyanagunawardena, Adams & Williams, 2013; Zawacki-Richter & Anderson, 2014).

Central to the South African discourse on participation in higher education and ODL is the need not only to continue to increase access, but also to provide reasonable chances for *successful* participation. Despite the proposal of Woodley (2004) that we should not pathologized student failure in ODL contexts, the 'revolving door' in higher education and specifically in distance education and ODL cannot leave us unaffected.

Reflecting on the possible interventions and pathways to increase successful and more representative participation in higher education, Badat & Sayed (2014) state that " carefully designed interventions are needed to ensure improvements in presentation" (p. 143). Of particular concern is the "unacceptably poor pass and graduation rates and high drop-out rates" which necessitate the urgent

> Enhancement of the academic capabilities of universities and rigorously conceptualized and designed academic development programs to support academics and students… to ensure equity of opportunity and outcome, especially for students of working-class and rural poor social origins (Badat & Sayed, 2014, p. 143).

With regard to successful participation in postgraduate higher education, there is a need to address funding regimes as well as infrastructure and availability of equipment, as well as inter-university collaboration. Of particular concern is the fact that "as a consequence of apartheid, knowledge production in South Africa has been predominantly the preserve of white men. The democratization of knowledge requires special measures to induct previously excluded social groups, such as blacks and women, into the production and dissemination of knowledge" (Badat & Sayed, 2014, p. 144).

REFERENCES

Altbach, P.G. (1999). The logic of mass higher education. *Tertiary Education and Management,* 5(2), 107—124.

Altbach, P.G., Reisberg, L., & Rumbley, L.E. (2009). Trends in global higher education: tracking an academic revolution. A report prepared for the UNESCO 2009 World Conference on Higher Education. Retrieved from http://graduateinstitute.ch/files/live/sites/iheid/files/sites/developpement/shared/developpement/cours/E759/Altbach,%20Reisberg,%20Rumbley%20Tracking%20an%20Academic%20Revolution,%20UNESCO%202009.pdf

Archer, W., Garrison, R., & Anderson, T. (2013). Adopting disruptive technologies in traditional universities: continuing education as incubator for innovation. *Canadian Journal of University Continuing Education*, 25(1), 13—44.

Badat, S., & Sayed, Y. (2014). Post-1994 South African education: The challenge of social justice. *The ANNALS of the American Academy of Political and Social Science,* 652, 127—148. DOI: 10.1177/0002716213511188

Barnett, R. (1996). Being and becoming: a student trajectory. *International Journal of Lifelong Education*, 15(2), 72-84, DOI: 10.1080/0260137960150202

Boeren, E., Nicaise, I., & Baert, H. (2010). Theoretical models of participation in adult education: the need for an integrated model. *International Journal of Lifelong Education,* 29(1), 45—61.

Boughey, C. (2005). 'Epistemological' access to the university: an alternative perspective. *South African Journal for Higher Education*, 19(3), 230—242.

Bunting, I., Sheppard, C., Cloete, N., & Belding, L. (2010). *Performance indicators in South African higher education, 2000–2008.* Wynberg, SA: Centre for Higher Education Transformation (CHET).

Butcher, N., & Hoosen, S. (2014). A guide to quality in post-traditional online higher education. Academic Partnerships. Retrieved from http://facultyecommons.org/wp-content/uploads/2014/04/A_Guide_to_Quality_in_Post-Traditional_Online_Higher_Education.pdf

Carr, N. (2012). The crisis in higher education. Technology Review. Retrieved from http://www.technologyreview.com/featuredstory/429376/the-crisis-in-higher-education/

Chowdry, H., Crawford, C., Dearden, L., Goodman, A., & Vignoles, A. (2013). Widening participation in higher education: analysis using linked administrative data. *Journal of the Royal Statistical Society*, 176(2), 431—457.

Christensen, C. (2008). Disruptive innovation and catalytic change in higher education. Forum for the Future of Higher Education. EDUCAUSE,[Online].Retrieved from https://net.educause.edu/ir/library/pdf/ff0810s.pdf

Council on Higher Education (CHE). (2013). *A proposal for undergraduate curriculum reform in South Africa: the case for a flexible curriculum structure.* CHE: Pretoria.

Czerniewicz, L. (2004). Cape of storms or Cape of Good Hope? Educational technology in a changing environment. *British Journal of Educational Technology. 35*(2), 145-158.

Czerniewicz, L. & Brown, C. (2005). Access to ICT for teaching and learning: From single artefact to interrelated resources. *International Journal of Education and development using Information and Communication Technology, 1*(2), 42-56.

Daniel, J., Kanwar, A., & Uvalić-Trumbić, S. (2008). The right to education: a model for making higher education equally accessible to all on the basis of merit. *Asian Journal of Distance Education*, 6(2), 5—11.

Daniel, J., Kanwar, A., and Uvalić-Trumbić, S. (2010a). Breaking higher education's iron triangle: access, cost, and quality. *Change: The Magazine of Higher Learning,* 41(2), 30—35. DOI: 10.3200/CHNG.41.2.30-35.

Daniel, J., Kanwar, A., & Uvalić-Trumbić, S. (2010b). A tectonic shift in global higher education. *Change: The Magazine of* Higher Learning, 38(4), 16—23. DOI: 10/3200/CHNG.38.4.16-23.

Daniel, J. (2012). Making sense of MOOCs: musings in a maze of myth, paradox and possibility. *Journal of Interactive Media in Education.* Retrieved from http://www-jime.open.ac.uk/jime/article/viewArticle/2012-18/html/

De Haan, J. (2004). A multifaceted dynamic model of the digital divide. *IT & Society 1*(7), 66-88.

Department of Higher Education and Training. (DHET).(2013). White paper for post-school education and training. Building an expanded, effective and integrated post-school system. Retrieved from http://www.che.ac.za/media_and_publications/legislation/white-paper-post-school-education-and-training

Department of Higher Education and Training. (DHET). (2014). Policy for the provision of distance education in South African universities in the context of an integrated post-school system. Retrieved from gov.za/documents/download.php?f=213796

Desjardins, R., & Rubenson, K. (2013). Participation patterns in adult education: the role of institutions and public policy frameworks in resolving coordination problems. *European Journal of Education,* 48(2), 262—280.

Glennie, J. (2013). Promoting open educational resources (OER). Keynote delivered at the Seventh Pan-Commonwealth Forum on Open, 5 December, International Conference Centre, Abuja, Nigeria. Retrieved from http://pcfpapers.colfinder.org/handle/5678/272

Jansen, J. (2004). Changes and continuities in South Africa's higher education system, 1994 to 2004. In *Changing class: Education and social change in post-apartheid South Africa*, ed. Linda Chisholm, pp. 293–314. Pretoria, SA: Human Science Research Council Press.

Kanwar, A., & Balaji, V. (2011). Three generations of open education: future implications. Inaugural address at the Institute of ODL, University of Mumbai, 24 February. Retrieved from http://www.col.org/resources/speeches/2011presentation/Pages/2011-02-24.aspx

Lane, A. (2014). Squaring the open circle: resolving the iron triangle and the interaction equivalence theorem. Paper presented at OER14, Building communities of open practice, *28-29 April, Newcastle. Retrieved from* http://oro.open.ac.uk/40092/7/Squaring%2520the%2520open%2520circle.pdf

Lane, A. (2013a). The social and economic impacts of open education. In Meiszner, Andreas; Squires, Lin and Husmann, Elmar (eds). *Openness and Education.* Advances in Digital Education and Lifelong Learning (1). Bingley: Emerald Publishing, pp. 137—172.

Lane, A. (2013b). The potential of MOOCs to widen access to, and success in, higher education study. Paper presented at *The open and flexible higher education conference,* 23-25 October, Paris, EADTU, pp. 189—203. Retrieved from http://oro.open.ac.uk/38881/

Lane, A. (2014). Squaring the open circle: resolving the iron triangle and the interaction equivalence theorem. Paper presented at OER14, Building communities of open practice, *28-29 April, Newcastle. Retrieved from* http://oro.open.ac.uk/40092/7/ Squaring%2520the%2520open%2520circle.pdf

Letseka, M., & Pitsoe, V. (2014). The challenges and prospects of access to higher education at UNISA, *Studies in Higher Education*, 39 (10). 1942-1954

Liebenberg, H., Chetty, Y., & Prinsloo, P. (2012). Student access to and skills in using technology in an open and distance learning context. *International Review of Research in Open and Distance Learning (IRRODL),* 13(4), 250—268. Retrieved from http://www.irrodl.org/index.php/irrodl/article/view/1303/2348

Liyanagunawardena, T.R., Adams, A.A., & Williams, S.A. (2013). MOOCs: a systematic study of the published literature 2008-2012. *International Review of Research in Open and Distance Learning (IRRODL),*13(3), 202—227.

Lockwood, F. (ed). (1995). *Open and distance learning today.* New York, NY: Routledge.

Moore, M.G., & Kearsley, G. (2012). *Distance education. A systems view of online learning.* (Third edition). Belmont, CA: Wadsworth.

Morrow, W. (2007). *Learning to teach in South Africa.* HSRC Press: Cape Town.

Morozov, E. (2013). *To save everything, click here.* London, UK: Penguin Books.

Osborne, M. (2003). Increasing or widening participation in higher education? – a European overview. *European Journal of Education,* 38(1), 5—24.

Peters, O. (2001). *Learning and teaching in distance education. Pedagogical analyses and interpretations in an international perspective.* New York, NY: Routledge.

Prinsloo, P. (2009). Modelling Throughput at UNISA: The key to the successful implementation of ODL. Retrieved from http://umkn-dsp01.unisa.ac.za/handle/10500/6035

Scott, I., Yeld, N., & Hendry, J. (2007). A case for improving teaching and learning in South African Higher Education. Higher *Education Monitor.* CHED: UCT. Retrieved from http://www.che.ac.za/media_and_publications/higher-education-monitor/higher-education-monitor-6-case-improving-teaching

Selwyn, N. (2013). *Education in a digital world. Global perspectives on technology and education.* New York, NY: Routledge.

Selwyn, N. (2014). *Distrusting educational technology. Critical questions for changing times.* New York, NY: Routledge.

Selwyn, N., & Facer, K. (Eds.). (2013). *The politics of education and technology. Conflicts, controversies, and connections.* New York, NY: Palgrave Macmillan.

Staley, D.J., & Trinkle, D.A. (2011). The changing landscape of higher education. *EDUCAUSE review*[online]. Retrieved from http://www.educause.edu/ero/article/changing-landscape-higher-education

StatsSA. (2013). Quarterly labor force survey. Retrieved from http://www.statssa.gov.za/publications/P0211/P02111stQuarter2013.pdf

Subotzky, G., & Prinsloo, P. (2011). Turning the tide: a socio-critical model and framework for improving student success in open distance learning at the University of South Africa. *Distance Education*, 32(2), 177-193.

Van Zyl, D. (2013). Institutional profile. UNISA facts and figures. HEMIS 2008-2012. Unpublished report.

Watters, A. (2012). Unbundling and unmooring: technology and the higher ed tsunami. *EDUCAUSE review,* [online]. Retrieved from http://www.educause.edu/ero/article/unbundling-and-unmooring-technology-and-higher-ed-tsunami

Watters, A. (2013, 24 May). The myth and the millennialism of "disruptive innovation" [web log post]. Retrieved from http://www.hackeducation.com/2013/05/24/disruptive-innovation/

Whiteford, G., Shah, M., & Nair, C.S. (2013). Equity and excellence are not mutually exclusive. *Quality Assurance in Education,* 21(3), 299-310. DOI: 10.1108/QAE-Apr-2012-0020.

Wiley, D., & Hilton III, J. (2009). Openness, dynamic specialization, and the disaggregated future of higher education. *International Review of Research in Open and Distance*

Learning, 10(5), 1—16. Retrieved from http://www.irrodl.org/index.php/irrodl/article/view/768/1414

Woodley, W. (2004). Conceptualizing student dropout in part-time distance education: pathologizing the normal? *Open Learning: The Journal of Open, Distance and e-Learning,* 19(1), 47—63 DOI:org/10.1080/0268051042000177845

Zawacki-Richter, O., & Anderson, T. (Eds.). (2014). Online distance education: towards a research agenda. Athabasca University Press. DOI:10.15215/aupress/9781927356623.0. Retrieved from http://www.aupress.ca/index.php/books/120233

In: Open Distance Learning (ODL) in South Africa
Editor: Moeketsi Letseka
ISBN: 978-1-63463-890-6

Chapter 4

ASSESSMENT IN OPEN AND DISTANCE LEARNING

Motlalepule Ruth Mampane*
Department Educational Psychology
Faculty of Education: University of Pretoria, South Africa

ABSTRACT

This chapter argues that assessment is core to teaching and learning and is used to measure student's knowledge, abilities, skills and attitudes. Assessment results give a measure of success or failure in subsequent work (a probability of subsequent performance). The purpose of assessment in open and distance learning (ODL) is multifaceted and educational. Feedback received through assessment activities enables students to evaluate their learning and for lecturers to measure their teaching. The chapter will demonstrate that as teaching and learning help to introduce, communicate, and expose students to skills, attitudes and new knowledge (local and global knowledge), and enables them to reflect and critically engage with module learning outcomes; assessment is used to evaluate, control and apply knowledge, skills and attitudes learned. Assessment helps to reaffirm the learning outcomes (as meaningful problem) and monitors the effect of teaching and learning (measures if learning outcomes have been achieved). Ultimately, assessment offers the student the opportunity to practically demonstrate their understanding of content learned and learning achieved (learning outcomes), to measure teaching success (determine if teaching was achieved), and to apply and demonstrate knowledge in place (problem solving skills).

INTRODUCTION

Theories of learning are interlinked and inform method and process of assessment. To assess the overall achievement of students through summative assessment, the lecturer can choose the level of questioning which is best suited to objectively measure student performance. With criterion-referenced assessment the objective of the lecturer is to evaluate each student on the 'basis of the quality of their work alone, uncontaminated by reference to

* Email: ruth.mampane@up.ac.za

how other students in the course perform on the same or equivalent tasks, and without regard to each student's previous level of performance' (Sadler, 2005:178). Accordingly, Sadler (2005) argues that the criterion that is mostly used in judging performance in assessment includes, achievement of learning outcomes, total score obtained, overall grade obtained, quality criteria or attributes of assessment (validity, relevance, presentation). While with the norm-referenced assessment criteria the grades are not rigidly fixed and 'includes some tolerance to allow for the characteristics of different student groups or other factors' (Sadler, 2005:186). Assigned grades help to determine 'where each student stands in relation to the others' (Sadler 2005:186). It is imperative that the form of assessment used does not adversely disadvantage students.

The interaction between the lecturer and student is important in teaching and learning and in determining and establishing the nature and value of their interaction. Self-directed learning (SDL) is core to the success of any distance student and requires students to acquire self-regulation skills. ODL learning environment is characterized by transactional distance, a separation between the student and lecturer can be managed by communication and use of information (Pereira, 2005). Pereira (2005) further dictates that distance education has specific expectations from the lecturer and student; students require specific skills of which self-regulation is core and the lecturer is required to design clear instructional material and to set learning support in place. Letseka and Pitsoe (2013:167) declare that open learning is broad and includes 'distance education, resource-based learning, correspondence learning, flexi-study and self-paced study'. Furthermore, distance learning environment acknowledges that although adult distance learners are far from their lecturers, they have the advantage to structure their own learning to meet their goals and needs as they might decide to form study groups (learn alone or in groups), they can even consult additional resources (e.g. audio-visual media); thus they reflect and ensure that they assume responsibility for their learning (Letseka & Pitsoe, 2013:197). However, Sampson (2003:104) warns that there is a clear distinction between the construct of open and distance learning. 'Open learning includes the notions of both openness and flexibility (whereby students have personal autonomy over their studies and where access restrictions and privileges have been removed) and distance (as in independence from the teacher)'. Thus, the use of open and distance learning is an assumption that students satisfy both constructs.

The teaching and learning rewards aligned to SDL are well encapsulated by Ni's (2013:62) acclamation of the independence and responsibility expected from the student which dictates that every student must take 'the initiative and the responsibility for what occurs. Individuals select, manage, and assess their own learning activities, which can be pursued at any time, in any place, through any means, at any age'. Letseka and Pitsoe (2012:221-224) outline the various strategies ODL students can engage in to self-direct their learning such as: learning alone or in small groups; learning at their own pace and in their own time; using a variety of learning materials including the use of audio-visual media; they need less frequent help from their teachers; they learn from other people beside their teachers; are capable of doing self-assessment.

Based on the responsibility and directedness of distance students, assessment is important in directing student's learning and achievement of learning outcomes. Accordingly, Gibbs and Simpson (2004:3) concur that 'assessment has an overwhelming influence on what, how and how much students study'.

With contact and face-to-face students, the physical presence establishes the sense of being and belongingness (Picciano, 2002). While with open and distance learning students, the physical distance between the lecturer and the student remains vast (Okonkwo, 2010; Terblanche, 2010) and the sense of presence and belonging is established by the learning content and the participation in the module; which makes assessment significant in maintaining consistent interaction and providing feedback to both the lecture and student. Thus, the quality of feedback is equally critical. Price (1997) concludes that distance education students should receive reliable and accurate feedback with clear explanation and justification of the grade received. Accordingly, Kearsle, Anderchek and Mugridge (2004, p.1) argue that, 'increased interaction potentially improves student achievement, attitude towards learning, and course effectiveness core to teaching and learning'.

This chapter aims to argue that ODL assessment cannot be considered in isolation, but is integral to the curriculum. Assessment is embedded into the scholarship of teaching and learning with clearly outlined learning objectives and assessment outcomes. Assessment is a process and multifaceted and can present as criterion-referenced and norm referenced assessment. This chapter will present that ODL assessment is a form of feedback to students, and interactive process which aims to improve and inform student performance.

The Purpose of Assessment in ODL

Assessment is feedback for students and a measure for their development, knowledge and abilities. Hatzipanagos and Warburton (2009:47) argue that, 'nature and form of assessment have a significant impact upon the student learning experience, approaches to learning, motivation, and retention rates'. Thus, feedback is a developmental tool which is more objective when based on assessment instruments. Assessment tools provide students with the platform to demonstrate their learning and to apply their knowledge; similarly, student performance during assessment activities provide lecturers with the opportunity to assess how the learning outcomes have been achieved. Letseka and Pitsoe (2013:199) applied the framework of Angelo to argue that assessment is about 'finding what and how much (or how little) students have learned between points A and Z, that is, to establish accountability and improve efficiency'. Assessment serves to monitor and evaluate teaching and learning. Lectures are able to gauge their teaching through student's performance and assessment results. Lagowski (1986:461) concurs that assessing the improvement of skills, knowledge and ability of students in achieving educational outcomes is a good measure to evaluate the student and to 'gain a better understanding of the educational processes'.

To ensure that assessment is valid and reliable, quality assurance is core in assessment (Okonkwo, 2010) and this is achieved by maintaining the reliability and consistency of markers and the ability to provide feedback to students. Lagowski's (1986:461) conceptualization of assessment denotes that, 'assessment involves different goals than the process known as "testing". Assessment usually denotes a procedure that has been designed to provide information about the teaching and learning process in an effort to help improve the effectiveness with which students, faculty, and the institution carry out their work. Ideally, assessment is an internal part of education'.

Extensive training of markers and feedback providers in open distance learning institutions is important to promote consistency and depth of feedback. It is further encouraged that a balance between positive and negative feedback should be maintained; the strengths and weaknesses of student performance should be included in the feedback to promote feedback receptivity. In dyad relationship between supervisor/ lecturer and student (unequal relationship) receptivity of feedback is high. Students rely on communication and feedback to improve, succeed and progress with their educational goals. Feedback provides direction and should be directive, objective, fair, valid, reliable and specific to promote student satisfaction, guide towards achieving educational success and module objectives, increase throughput rate and add value to the qualification the intuitional vision and mission and aim to increase financial income of the institution through increased enrolment of students.

Students in open distance learning rely heavily on feedback for measuring and validating the quality, depth and breadth of the learning process. The result of assessment gives the probability of success in subsequent performance. Accordingly Nicol and Macfarlane-Dick (2006:205) declare that a good feedback encourages self-regulated learning and assists in achieving the following objectives of assessment; 'to clarify good performance (goals, criteria, expected standards); facilitates the development of self-assessment (reflection) in learning; delivers high quality information to students about their learning; encourages teacher and peer dialogue around learning; encourages positive motivational beliefs and self-esteem; provides opportunities to close the gap between current and desired performance; provides information to teachers that can be used to help shape teaching'.

WHY DO WE ASSESS?

Summative and formative assessment can be used for purposes of teaching and learning. It is however important to note the purpose of formative and summative assessment is different. Summative assessment is used for grading, certification, evaluation of progress of students at the end of a term, module, course, or program; lecturers further use this form of assessment to investigate and research on the effectiveness of a curriculum, module, qualification, program course of study, or educational plan (Bloom et.al., 1981). Thus, summative assessment gives evidence (statistics) for reporting on overall achievement; it aims to measures the status of learning. Formative assessment highlights the strengths and weaknesses of students, provides feedback on students and opportunity to learn more. Accordingly, Bloom (1971) emphasizes that, formative assessment is to improve the curriculum and teaching and learning; this form of assessment is achieved by using systematic evaluation in the process of curriculum construction, teaching and learning. Terblanchè (2010) concurs that formative assessment is consistent with learning and aims to maintain learning and guide student regarding the learning process. Ultimately, formative assessment serves the purpose of identification of strength and weaknesses of students; it aims to identify strengths and achievement of students so that appropriate steps can be planned (Harlen & James 1997).

Both summative and formative assessments are core to teaching and learning. Nicol and Macfarlane-Dick (2007) declare that summative assessment encourages students to regulate their learning (as informed by the feedback received) and to set goals on how to achieve the learning outcomes. Self-regulated learning is defined as 'the degree to which students can regulate aspects of their thinking, motivation and behavior during learning' (Nicol & Macfarlane-Dick 2007:200). Race, Brown & Smith (2005:5-7) and Brown (1999:6) in (Medland n.d:5) emphasize the significance of assessment for students and lectures as summarized below in figure 1:

Assessment benefits on students	Assessment benefits on Supervisor / Lecturer
Provide feedback to students & opportunity to improve	Give us feedback on effectiveness of promoting learning
Provide context to translate learning outcomes into reality.	Help to structure teaching & constructively align learning outcomes to assessment
Provide opportunity to apply abstract principles to practical contexts	Estimate students' potential to progress to other levels or courses
Provide motivation and focus on achievement	Provide statistics for internal and external agencies
Provide opportunity to reflect on learning and to identify weaknesses and rectify mistakes and to consolidate learning	Form basis for assessing throughput rate; enable classification of grades and student achievement

Figure 1. Characteristics of assessment.

The Core Principles of Assessment

Learning outcomes should be aligned to assessment strategies. Thus assessment is valid, reliable, fair and relevant if it assesses what it purports to measure. Nyoni and Segoe (2013) emphasize that institutions should take steps to secure and ensure that the integrity of examinations is protected against unauthorized access (especially summative assessments). Similarly with formative assessments, students should be monitored against plagiarism and measures should be in place (policy) to address any process that can invalidate the assessment process.

As much as formative and summative assessments are highly used in teaching and learning, how the students and lecturers interpreted assessment and feedback (performance) is important. In ensuring that principles of assessment are adhered to and applied accordingly, Letseka and Pitsoe (2013:198) recommend 'transformative assessment' model which rests on four pillars as a-culture-change-model. This model, according to the authors allows for students to experience deeper or higher learning. The four pillars provide guidelines to the lecturer to ensure that assessment benefits them (effective feedback) as much as it benefits students. The four pillars are explained as an emphasis in building core principles and promoting an interactive process between lecturer and students which will result in assessment as a process that can maintain shared: *trust, motivation, language and guidelines* (Angelo, 1999 in Letseka & Pitsoe, 2013:198). These four pillars can be realized if the principles of assessment as discussed in figure 2 are adhered to in the design of the course, module, program and qualification.

The principles and practices of assessment that guide the program design can best be operationalized if the four pillars of transformative assessment are applied by the lecturer when designing assessment activities. The following principles and practices of assessment are core and should align with module, course and program and inform the assessment process (University of Pretoria, 2006a:788).

1. Learning program and module should have clear outcomes and consistent assessment criteria
2. Assessment should be integrated into the learning program and module design process and be matched to learning outcomes
3. Assessment should promote desirable educational results
4. Students' competence should be judged on quality evidence
5. Credible assessment is valid, reliable, consistent and fair. Credibility is maintained through moderation. The use of various assessment methods assist in reflecting an authentic environment
6. Assessment should be transparent with expectation and assessment criteria being clearly communicated in advance
7. Student should have access to feedback on assessment which is timely so as to promote learning and facilitate improvement
8. Assessment should be efficiently managed. The practicality and feasibility of assessment, the volume or magnitude and the timing of assessment, student and staff workload, available resources, security arrangements and time provided to student to reflect should be efficient

The assessment framework is a good guide to designing assessment tools and formulating criteria. Bloom's taxonomy of assessment provides a clear framework to guide assessment and to ensure that assessment is in line with teaching and learning. Learning occurs in three domains, cognitive, skills, affective or value domain. According to Bloom et al., (1956 in University of Pretoria, 2006b:4) Bloom's taxonomy of learning centers on the cognitive domain (see Figure 2) and clearly outline how each learning outcome can be assessed.

WHAT DO YOU ASSESS?

We assess 'learning in place' and learning can be deep or surface; deep learning is recognized as 'real' learning because it leads to understanding and internalization of knowledge and linking new knowledge with previous one, thus creating links (Harlen & James, 1997). The important aim of education is to bring about learning and understanding, which is referred to as learning as an interpretive process (Harlen & James, 1997). According to Harlen and James, (1997:369), learning is characterised by the following:

- Progressive development of big ideas, skills for living and learning, attitudes and values
- Contraction of ideas on the basis of previous ideas and skills
- Ability to apply in context other than those which it was learned

Cognitive domain learning outcome	Evidence of outcome: align to learning outcomes	Terms / verbs used for measuring outcome in assessment questions	Level / Hierarchy
Knowledge Recall & remember facts	Know terms, facts, methods, procedures, basic principles	Define, describe, label, list, match, name, outline, reproduce, select, state, tabulate, show, arrange	1
Comprehension Understand & interpret learned information	Understands facts & principles, interpret and translate material, differentiate between constructs, explain the effects, classify concepts, demonstrate, estimate	Convert, defend, distinguish, estimate, explain, extend, solve, translate, generalize, infer, summarize, predict, recognize, differentiate, discriminate, discuss, report, contrast, convert	2
Application Use learned materials in new situation	Apply concepts, theories & principles to new situations; solve problems, construct framework, graphs, charts; demonstrate correct use of method and procedure, construct timeline; select and employ techniques	Apply, assess, calculate, relate, complete, compute, construct, demonstrate, develop, find, discover, employ, examine, experiment, illustrate, interpret, manipulate, modify, operate, organize, practice, predict, prepare, produce, schedule, select, show, sketch, solve, transfer, use.	3
Analysis Break information into components	Recognize unstated assumptions & logical fallacies, distinguish between facts & inferences; evaluate relevance of information; analyze the organizational structure of work	Break down, diagram, differentiate, discriminate, distinguish, identify, illustrate, infer, outline, point out, relate, select, separate, subdivide, classify, calculate, categorize, differentiate, compare, order, relate, investigate,	4
Synthesis Ability to put parts together	Recognize and formulate problems, propose solution, summarize causes, effects, principles; write a well-organized theme, write a creative short story;	Categorize, combine, compile, compose, create, devise, design, explain, generate, modify, organize, plan, rearrange, reconstruct, relate, reorganize, revise, rewrite, summarize, tell, write, generalize, integrate, explain, formulate	5
Evaluation ability to judge the value of material for a given purpose	Assess importance of concepts; evaluate strategies/ principles; summarize information; judge the logic/ facts/ information; judge the value & adequacy	Appraise, compare, conclude, contrast, criticize, describe, discriminate, explain, justify, interpret, relate, summarize, support,	6

Figure 2. Framework of Assessment from the Bloom's Taxonomy of Learning Outcomes (arranged from low hierarchy to high).

- It's owned by the learner in the sense that it becomes a fundamental part of the way he/she understands the world. It is not simply ephemeral knowledge that may be memorized for recall in examination but subsequently forgotten.

Using Bloom's taxonomy framework when planning assessment, the lecturer can decide which 'learning in place' can be assessed. Harlen and James (1997) refer to 'deep learning'; 'surface learning' approach and 'strategy learning'. The three approaches distinguish between learning with understanding (deep learning), rote learning (surface learning) and 'strategic learning' (efficient learning, a combination of the two). Some questions assess deep learning while others surface learning, thus how questions are formulated during assessment guides the relevance and purpose of assessment. Their analogy of these approaches of learning is that even though reading in-depth (deep learning approach) is time consuming, it is characterized by (Harlen & James, 1997:368):

- an intention to develop personal understanding
- an active interaction with content particularly in relating new ideas to previous knowledge and experiences
- linking ideas together using intergrading principles and relating evidence to conclusions

The disadvantage of surface learning approach is that it does not lead to long-term retention of knowledge and is characterized by (Harlen & James, 1997:368):

- an intention to reproduce content as required
- passive acceptance of ideas and information
- lack of recognition of guiding principles or patterns
- focusing learning on assessment requirement

Assessment is an integral part of teaching and learning and it is linked to how the lecturer understands the learning outcomes and demonstrates learning competencies required for the module, course, program or qualification.

Figure 3 below illustrates the alignment of assessment to the curriculum, the scholarship of teaching and learning (pedagogy, methodology), and assessment as a process (continuous action with the purpose of achieving learning outcomes) and the (quality / type and relevance of the learning content assessed). When lecturers assess for subject-matter knowledge, assessment tends to be separated from instruction (Shepard, 2000). This includes summative assessment for grading purposes (where standardization and uniformity are encouraged to maintain fairness) and which falls within the category of criterion-referenced assessment tools. The social-constructivist conceptual framework of Shepard (2000) argues that assessment (classroom) is intertwined with vision of curriculum and informed by cognitive and constructivist learning theories. The framework uses cognitive theories to argue that 'existing knowledge structures and beliefs work to enable or impede new learning, that intelligent thought involves self-monitoring and awareness about when and how to use skills, and that expertise develops in the field of study as a principled and coherent way of thinking and presenting problems, not just as an accumulation of information' (Shepard, 2000:6-7).

The work of Vygotsky (zone of proximal development) shows the role of context, ecology and culture in learning. Social constructivists view learning as a social and cultural phenomenon (Geduld, 2014). Thus social constructivists argue that 'cognitive abilities are developed through socially supported interactions' (Shepard 2000:7). With ODL, learning is self-directed. Assessment becomes core in supporting learning and enabling students to assess their knowledge. Thus, assessment cannot be the end product of learning but the process in learning. Rust, Price and O'Donovan (2003) argue that assessment processes and methods

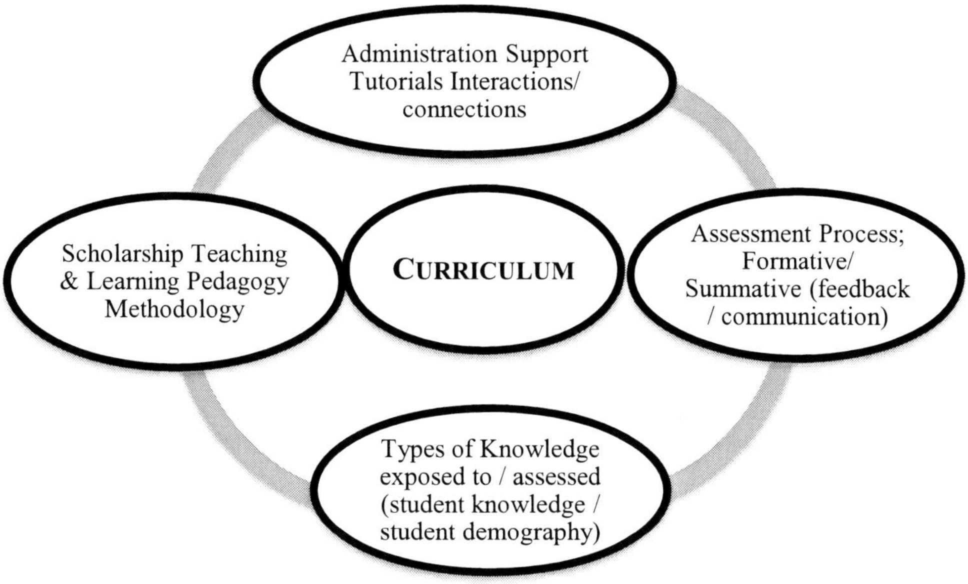

Figure 3. Alignment of curriculum, teaching and assessment.

need to be clearer and accessible to students (transparency in assessment). This form of assessment is a move towards using rubrics in assessment which enables and empowers students to operationalize the learning and assessment objectives.

How Can We Assess?

What kind of skills, knowledge and attitude should be assessed? The answer to the question will direct the methods of assessment which can be used. Based on the principles of assessment, the learning outcomes, assessment strategies and the framework of assessment (Bloom's taxonomy of assessment) lecturers have a broad scope and guidelines on how to assess learning. Various methods of assessment exit. Similarly, when providing feedback rubrics are more relevant to use because they are fair and efficient; they can be used to enhance feedback and promote preparation for future performance. The assessment principles and practices discussed above clearly dictate that the assessor should:

- Ensure that assessment is aligned with learning outcomes
- Ensure that all the learning outcomes are assessed
- Ensure that low and high order learning is assessed (Bloom's taxonomy of assessment)

Method	Ability measured	Application of assessment
Examination: Unseen exam- might seem unreliable for summative assessment (good to know what is being assessed) Take-away paper – student have opportunity to deliver product/ practical activity; OR/ Case study as preparation for exam/ reading before exam Open book exam	Consolidate work; Cognitive ability Easy to set-can assess varied skills e.g. retention & comprehension of knowledge; and can be reliable (know what is being assessed) Enable students to have 'real world problem solving opportunity'; more thoughtful performance / assess for synthesis, evaluation and research skills; More authentic, assess what students can do with information	Problem solving Essays: integrate knowledge; communicate understanding, support argument with evidence; Multiple-choice questions (MCQs) –cope with student numbers- assess trivial knowledge Case study- assess problem solving, analysis and evaluative skills;
Projects and reports- ensure students reflect (give critical reflection of process)	Authentic context; report on own learning; can require research (use of other resources)	Assess applied competence; knowledge application, understanding and skills.
Portfolios (collection of evidence to demonstrate that learning outcomes have been achieved)	Include range of evidence, self-assessment, checklist, personal reflections on learning development, outcomes achieved, evidence trail (audio-visual)	Assess own design, theory, practice, applied competence, knowledge application, critical analysis of information
Assignment	Include written work in paragraph to address a question; a cases study can be provided; practical application of theory	Ability to reflect, critical thinking, interpret information academically, synthesize information, writing skills
Self-assessment activities in learning materials (exercises; quizzes)	It's a method of learning, provide opportunity to assess own learning process; assess knowledge of content; provide	Revision activity, providing performance feedback, diagnosis and prescription recommendations

Figure 4. Examples of methods of assessment.

CONCLUSION

The university or college policy informs the processes of assessment. To ensure that students are not prejudiced, multiple opportunities and forms of assessment are provided per module. Thus, formative and summative assessment activities become paramount to ensure that students experience multiple opportunities to demonstrate their knowledge. Assessment is an interactive process between the student and the lecturer. Ensuring that assessment activities are included in the learning guide and text books, it assists the ODL students to continually assess their learning and knowledge. Assessment is important in the teaching and learning and it provide feedback to the lecture and student on learning and knowledge in place and learning and knowledge required to accomplish the learning goals.

REFERENCES

Bloom, B. (1971). *Handbook on the Formative and Summative Evaluation of Student Learning*. London: McGraw-Hill.

Bloom, B.S., Madaus, G.F. & Hastings, J.T. (1981). *Evaluation to Improve Learning.* London: McGraw-Hill.

Chaudhary, S.V.S. & Niradhar, D. (201, July-September). Assessment in Opien and Distance Learning System (ODL): A challenge. *Open Praxis, 5*(3), 207-216.

Dhunpath & Renuka Vithal (eds) *Access to Higher Education: Under-prepared Students or Under-prepared Institutions?* Pearson: Cape Town,

Geduld, B. (2014). Self-directedness in open distance learning: twists and turns. *Instructional Technology.*

Gibbs, G. & Simpson , C;. (2004). Conditions under which assessment supports student's learning. *Learning and Teaching in Higher Education, 1*(1), 3-31.

Harlen, W., & James, M. (1997). Assessment and learning: differences and relationships between formative and summative assessment. Assessment in Education, 4(3), 365-379.

Hatzipanagos, S. & Warburton, S. (2009). Feedback as dialogue: Exploring the Links Between Formative Assessment and Social Software in Distance Learning. *Learning, Media and Technology, 34*(1), 45-59.

Kearsle, G., Anderchek, P. & Mugridge, I. (2004). The nature and value of interaction in Distance Learning., (pp. 1-7).

Lagowski, J. (1986, June). Assessment and feedback. *J.Chem.Edu., 63*(6), 461.

Lave, J. (1996). Teaching as learning in practice. *Mind, Culture and Activity, 3*(3), 149-164.

Letseka, M., & Pitsoe, V. (2013) "Reflections on assessment in Open Distance Learning (ODL): the case of the University of South Africa (UNISA)", *Open Praxis*, 5 (3), 197-206.

Letseka, M., & Pitsoe, V. (2012) "Access to higher education through Open Distance Learning (ODL): reflections on the University of South Africa (UNISA)", in Rubby Dhunpath & Renuka Vithal (eds) *Access to Higher Education: Under-prepared Students or Under-prepared Institutions?* Pearson: Cape Town.

Medland, E. (n.d.). *Assessment and Feedback.* Retrieved July 7, 2014, from surrey.ac.uk: http://www.surrey.ac.uk/dhe/programmes/cpd/Assessment%20and%20Feedback.pdf

Ni, L. (2013). Self-directed Learning: Teacher and computer technology assist. *International Journal of Computer Networks and Wireless Communications, 3*(2), 60-66.

Nicol, D.J., & Macfarlane-Dick, D. (2006). Formative assessment and self-regulated learning: A model and seven principles of good feedback practice. Studies in Higher Education, 31(2), 199-218.

Nyoni, J., & Segoe, B. A. (2013). Critical Spective Reflectivity on Open and Distance Learning (ODL) Assessment Rigidity: Keeping Pace with Security Measures of Assessment Modalities. Mediterranean Journal of Social Sciences, 4(3), 101.

Okonkwo, C. A. (2010, November 11). PhD. *Turkish Online Journal of Distance Education-TOJDE, 11*(4 Artilcle 6), 121-129.

Pereira, A. (2005). Pedagogical issues in ODL. Getting started with ODL. Antwerpen: Ed. Garant Publishers.

Picciano, A. (2002, July). Beyond student perceptions, Issues of interaction, presence, and performance in an online course. *JALN, 6*(1), 21-40.

Price, B. (1997). Defining quality student feedback in distance learning. *Journal of Advanced Nursing, 26*(1), 154-160.

Race, P., Brown, S., & Smith, B. . (2005). *500 tips on assessment.* Psychology Press.

Roblyer, M. D., & Wiencke, W. R. (2003). Design and Use of a Rubric to Assess and Encourage Interactive Qualities in Distance Courses. *The American Journal Of Distance Education*, 77(2), 77-98.

Rust, C., Price, M., & O'Donovan, B. (2003). Improving students' learning by developing their understanding of assessment criteria and processes. *Assessment & Evaluation in Higher Education*, 28(2), 147-164.

Sadler, D.R. (2005). Interpretations of criterion-based assessment and grading in higher education. *Assessment & Evaluation in Higher Education*. 30(2):175-194.

Sampson, N. (2003). Meeting the needs of distance learners. Language learning & technology, 7(3), 103-118.

Shepard, L.A. (2000). The role of assessment in a learning culture. *Educational Researcher*, 29(7), 4-14.

Terblanche, E.J. (2010). Portfolios: An alternative to traditional assessment in ODL. *Progressio, 32*(2), 117-133.

University of Pretoria. (2006a). *Planning and organising a learning opportunity*. Pretoria: Department of Education Innovation.

University of Pretoria. (2006b). *Principles of the UP'S Educational Model (S6144/06)*. Pretoria: University of Pretoria.

In: Open Distance Learning (ODL) in South Africa
Editor: Moeketsi Letseka
ISBN: 978-1-63463-890-6

Chapter 5

BEST PRACTICES IN OPEN DISTANCE LEARNING ASSESSMENT

***Victor Pitsoe*[1] *and Matsephe M. Letseka*[2*]**
[1]Department of Leadership and Management College of Education, University of South Africa, South Africa
[2]Department of Educational Foundation, College of Education, University of South Africa, South Africa

ABSTRACT

In this chapter we argue that, given the complex and culturally diverse nature of students in ODL, for assessment in ODL to be effective, efficient and have a positive impact in teaching and learning, it should be underpinned by the notions of 'best practice', 'reflective practice' and 'culturally relevant pedagogy'. We note that these notions in ODL assessment have gained serious attention from higher education institutions, stakeholders, and scholars. For us, assessment methods should be appropriate to the students, the level and the material to be tested, and embrace the cultures of the students. Notwithstanding the fact that there are pockets of excellence in ODL assessment theory and practice, our take is that with the increase of ICT in higher education there is tangible evidence that assessment of learning in ODL in the 21st century is not free and immune to challenges. We are convinced that the appropriation of 'best practice', 'reflective practice' and 'culturally relevant pedagogy' is critical in the assessment of students' learning in the ODL context. Among others, we consider that best practice account offers unique value, not only by extending the descriptive knowledge base in ODL assessment, but in uncovering significant cognitive and socio-cultural adjustments which are critical to the theory and practice of ODL assessment. This chapter begins with a brief overview of thoughts on the best practice in ODL assessment. The second section explores Reflective Practice and Best Practice in ODL Assessment. In the third section we briefly sketch Culturally Relevant Pedagogy as a tool for measurement. The forth section reflects on assessment in ODL through the lens of the emerging paradigms. Finally, we provide some concluding remarks.

[*] Corresponding author: Email: Pitsovj@unisa.ac.za.

INTRODUCTION

Assessment of learning, both as a topic in higher education discourses and as a matter of public policy, has been around from time immemorial. The question '*what is best practices in Open Distance Learning (ODL) assessment?*' is critical in the discourses around assessment policy issues and its implementation. Hence, we start this chapter by asserting that best practices in ODL assessment lead to positive outcomes for students. However, it is widely accepted that best practices in the assessment of learning must be guided by clear principles and firm belief that students' learning will improve. Our point of departure is that best practices in assessment in the ODL context should focus less on '*do they (students) have the right or wrong answer?*', and more on making students' thinking visible to both teacher and student. It is reasonable to conjecture that best practices in assessment are not limited to tests of factual and procedural knowledge, but that assessment should help develop understanding of the strategies and patterns students have constructed in order to make sense of the world. Notwithstanding that ODL has become the globally desired label for innovative non-traditional modes of delivery of learning that aims to overcome hurdles to access, a shift towards best practice assessment, both as a topic in higher education circles and as matter of public policy, remains a challenge. Among others, it presents practitioners with an intricate set of challenges and calls for a need to develop new skills, embrace changes in the nature of their role and then reassess the pedagogies they employ in assessing students learning.

As some scholars (Deyle & Wiedenman, 2014; Ermeling, 2014; Aguinis & Vandenberg, 2014; Kanwar, 2012; Applegate & Irwin, 2012; Martell & Calderon, 2005; Angelo, 1995) point out, "assessment is an ongoing process that involves planning, discussion, consensus building, reflection, measuring, analyzing, and improving based on the data and artifacts gathered about a learning objective." For Orlich, Harder, Callahan and Gibson (2004), assessment encompasses a range of activities including testing, performances, project ratings, and observations. Given the complex and diverse nature of students in ODL, it is necessary to indicate that for assessment in ODL to be effective, efficient and have positive impact in teaching and learning, it should be underpinned by the notion of 'best practice', 'reflective practice' and 'culturally relevant pedagogy'. Like quality assurance, the notion of best practice in ODL assessment has gained serious attention from higher education institutions, stakeholders, and scholars. Though assessment is not an end in itself but a vehicle for educational improvement, best practice assessment sustains and encourages student learning. For us, assessment methods should be appropriate to the students, the level and the material to be tested, and embrace the cultures of the students. Some scholars see assessment as an integral piece to assuring that an educational institution achieves its learning goals (Haken, 2006; Hersh, 2004). It is appropriate to perceive best practice assessment not as a 'once in a lifetime' undertaking. Quite often, ODL practitioners review and revise the content, structure and teaching methods of a course, whilst leaving assessment unchanged.

Despite pockets of excellence in ODL assessment theory and practice, with the increase of Information Communication Technologies[1] (ICTs) in higher education there is tangible evidence that assessment of learning in ODL in the 21st century is not free and immune to challenges. While the concept 'best practice' is often considered by skeptics as a business

[1] In this chapter we take ICTs to refer to all forms of modern digital technologies – computer, ipads, smartphone, faxes, internet, wifi, etc.

buzzword, used to describe the process of developing and following a standard way of doing things that multiple organizations can use, we are convinced that its appropriation is critical in the assessment of students' learning in the ODL context. We believe that 'best practice' account offers unique value, not only by extending the descriptive knowledge base in ODL assessment, but by uncovering significant cognitive and socio-cultural adjustments which are critical to the theory and practice of ODL assessment. In line with the above-mentioned view, we begin with a brief overview of thoughts on the 'best practice' in ODL assessment. In the second section, we explore Reflective Practice as a fundamental element in 'best practice' in ODL Assessment. In the third section we briefly sketch Culturally Relevant Pedagogy (CRT) as a tool for measurement in ODL. Fourthly, we reflect on assessment in ODL through the lens of the emerging paradigms. Finally, we provide some concluding remarks.

Thoughts on the "Best Practice" in ODL Assessment

It is not our intention to dwell on the pedantics in an effort to understanding the concept of 'assessment' given that there are various definitions of assessment in the literature. It is our view though that it is essential to have a shared understanding of what assessment might entail. Thus our definition of assessment is adapted from the work Thomas Angelo, North Arizona University education theorist and researcher. Angelo's work emphasizes assessment as a continuous, systematic process, the goal of which is to improve the quality of student learning. The process calls for planning, discussion, consensus building, and reflection in addition to measuring, analyzing, and improving performance. As an integral component of teaching and learning, assessment requires a considerable amount of faculty involvement, particularly at the beginning when learning goals are established, and at the end where the data are used to improve the curriculum. These tasks may also require participation, in varying degrees depending on a program's mission, from external stakeholders such as employers and key alumni. Reflection is a necessary part of assessment—it is an essential element of each phase of the assessment process. It is through reflection that; (1) faculty, administrators, and key external stakeholders consider contextual and background information from multiple sources; (2) utilize specific data and information about their students learning experiences; paint a holistic picture of what's going on; and (3) ask difficult questions, and find creative solutions to improve learning and close the gap.

While assessment is an ongoing process aimed at understanding and improving student learning, in ODL it has evolved over the years. The 21st century imperatives have far reaching implications for the dominant ODL assessment theory and practice. Notwithstanding that assessment measures student' knowledge, skills, and values, the emerging paradigm widely accepts that assessment of student academic achievement is fundamental to all organizations that place student learning at the center of their educational endeavors. For us, assessment should be used for both improving the quality of the student learning process as well as evaluating a program's success in meeting its educational goals. As Angelo (1995:11) observes, "assessment is a means for focusing our collective attention, examining our assumptions, and creating a shared culture dedicated to continuously improving the quality of higher learning".

Assessment requires making expectations and standards for quality explicit and public; systematically gathering evidence on how well performance matches those expectations and standards; analyzing and interpreting the evidence; and using the resulting information to document, explain, and improve performance. With this in mind, best practices in assessment are consistent with Thomas Angelo's framework. For Angelo and Cross (1993), assessment is "first and foremost about improving student learning and secondarily about determining accountability for the quality of learning produced." Thus we hold that best practices should be guided and informed by Thomas Angelo's six steps to continuous improvement of learning (see Figure 5.1).

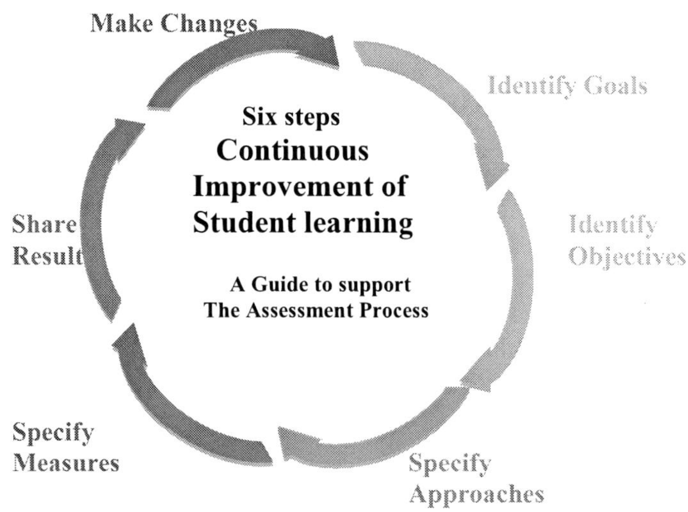

Source: Adapted from AAHE Bulletin (1995:7).

Figure 5.1. Thomas Angelo's six steps to continuous improvement of learning.

To briefly sum up this section, the systematic and formal assessment of student learning should provide the evidence to support and guide excellence in teaching, curriculum development, and achievement of program goals. The process of seeking, evaluating, reflecting upon data, and making changes should foster continuous improvement of student academic learning and achievement. Angelo's work ensures the alignment between goals and teaching methods and guides in modifying assessments. While there is a growing public dissatisfaction with the quality of ODL graduates, Angelo's six steps to continuous improvement of learning have the potential to give ODL assessment practitioners an account of how they know what (or if) students are learning - Learning Goals, Objectives and Traits are the product of reflection on the skills, attitudes, and knowledge. In short, Angelo's work can be said to be consistent with reflective practice – student learning outcomes/course objectives are the knowledge, skills, attitudes, and values that students gain from a learning experience; and student learning outcomes/course objectives define what students know, are able to do, and value by the end of a learning experience. Hence, reflective practice is a necessary part of assessment—it is an essential element of each phase of the assessment process.

Reflective Practice and Best Practice in ODL Assessment

It could be argued that 'best practice' in ODL assessment and reflective practice have a symbiotic relationship, and that they negate model of technical rationality. At a philosophical level, the dominant ODL assessment theory and practice is underpinned by technical rationality, behaviorist and banking education principles. The dominant ODL assessment theory and practice, as practice of hegemony, flows from the theoretical frameworks of mechanistic (bureaucracy, Taylorism, Fordism, etc.) and behaviorist worldviews. As Bottery (1993:35) observes, "the functions of bureaucracy are: (a) to impose upon society the kind of order which perpetuates its domination; and (b) to conceal this domination by means of unending flow of form-filling, task division and constant supervision".

In addition, at the heart of bureaucracy are four primary mechanisms of social influence and control, namely: authority, power, persuasion and exchange. In particular, these mechanisms of social influence and control represent the fundamental tools for the dominant ODL assessment theory and practice. While dominant ODL assessment fits through Foucauldian lens, power in 'best practice' in ODL assessment must be analyzed as something which circulates, or as something which only functions in the form of a chain. It is employed and exercised through a netlike organization. The ODL practitioners could be considered as the vehicles of power, not its points of application. They are not just the objects of power, but they are the locus where the power and the resistance to it are exerted.

With this in mind, the fluid nature of the ODL practitioner training demands a revitalized framework of effective best practice assessment consistent with reflective practice and Kolb's theory, focusing not only on the mastery of static content but rather on the construction of meaning within a collaborative environment. In this chapter, we depart from the assumption that assessment in ODL should be approached from a reflective practice perspective. Our thesis is that the dominant assessment approach in ODL is trapped in banking education and technical-rationality model of assessment. For us, there is a need to shift from technical-rationality model towards a model that encourages internalization. We view reflective practice, as alternative pedagogy, fit to be recognized as a central tenet of the assessment process – it is at the very heart of effective emerging paradigms of assessment theory and practice. Through reflective practice ODL practitioners are able to rethink the methods and practices they use in their teaching and learning. Reflective practice has a considerable number of benefits for best practice assessment in ODL.

Perhaps, we should consider the following questions: 'What is reflection?' and 'How do we conceptualize reflective practice for the purpose of helping ODL practitioners to become reflective practitioners?'. Reflective practice is a very old concept – it has an extensive history that dates as far back as the Greek philosophers. For example, it can be traced back to the Socratic method of enquiry - in which questioning and exploration of the implications of another's viewpoint are employed to enlighten the enquirer. Reflection as a slogan for educational reform also signifies recognition that no matter what we do in our teacher education programs and how well we do what we do, at best we can only prepare teachers to begin teaching (Zeichner, 2008). In addition, when embracing the concept of reflective teaching, there is often a commitment by ODL practitioners to help students internalize during their initial training the dispositions and skills to learn from their teaching experience and become better at it throughout their teaching careers.

Reflection is perceived as a critical attribute of competent practitioners who are prepared to address these challenges (Boud et al., 1985; Moon, 2004; Schön, 1983, 1987; Larrivee & Cooper, 2008; Osterman & Kottkamp, 2004). It is an important human activity in which people recapture their experience, think about it, mull over and evaluate it (Boud, Keogh & Walker, 1985: 43). It is this working with experience that is important in learning. Proponents of reflective practice hold that reflective teachers have the capacity to reflect on their teaching practices and their actions by taking wider historical, social and political contexts into consideration; to make informed decisions; to change their practices accordingly; thus, they can take the responsibility of their teaching. On the other hand, Braun and Crumpler (2004:60) maintain that "to be unreflective...results in a practitioner who is merely a skilled technician, i.e. one who has limited ability to make good decisions; to consider the consequences of their actions; and, to alter their actions."

Reflective practice is a term that carries diverse meaning. Central to reflective practice is the assumption that the quality of our actions is not independent of the thinking we are able to do before and in the process of the action. For Reid (1993:305), reflection is "a process of reviewing an experience of practice in order to describe, analyze, evaluate and so inform learning about practice." Reflective practice is more than thoughtful practice. It is that form of practice that seeks to problematize many situations of professional performance so that they can become potential learning situations and so the practitioners can continue to learn, grow and develop in and through practice (Jarvis, 1992:180). Moon (1999) defines reflective practice as "a set of abilities and skills, to indicate the taking of a critical stance, an orientation to problem solving or state of mind". In essence, it is a readiness to constantly evaluate and review your practice in the light of new learning (which may arise from within the context of your professional practice).

Reflective practice can also be defined in terms of action research, whereby specific problems (in specific settings) are targeted and a continuous feedback mechanism established in order to inform on-going development of practice (Hopkins & Antes, 1990). Action research, in turn, is defined as a tool of curriculum development consisting of continuous feedback that targets specific problems in a particular school setting (Hopkins & Antes, 1990). As such, it has become a standard concept in teacher education programs. Reflective practice is self-regulated, and engages the student in a process of relating theory and practice (Pavlovich, 2007).

Although the term reflective practice is interpreted and understood in different ways, within this discourse it is about: (1) the awareness of the knowledge we use, how that use is and how we can improve our action in real time; (2) how our minds work and how we use and create theories in practical situations; (3) invisible and visible, tacit and explicit, blindness and sight; and (4) flexibility, adaptation and effectiveness. Also, reflective practice focuses on the relationship between action and thinking; the kind of thinking that shapes our actions – before, during and after the action; and deals with the interaction between practice, reflection, thinking, learning and performance. Outstandingly, reflective practice is driven by questions, dialogue, narratives and stories; fundamentally structured around inquiry; and is a mode that integrates or links thought and action with reflection. It involves thinking about and critically analyzing one's actions with the goal of improving one's professional practice (Imel, 1992:8).

In the light of the above, it can be argued that Schön's reflective practice framework has a critical role to play in the designing of assessment policies in ODL. Among others, Schön's work provides a framework that not only addresses cognitive and organizational barriers, but distinctly illuminates the practice of reflectivity as well. Reflective practice is a beneficial process in assessment policy development, both for ODL practitioners and policy developers. As Schön (1983b) writes, "the capacity to reflect on action so as to engage in a process of continuous learning was one of the defining characteristics of professional practice." His work supports a shift from what he termed 'Technical Rationality'. Technical-rationality is a positivist epistemology of practice. It is "the dominant paradigm which has failed to resolve the dilemma of rigor versus relevance confronting professionals" (Schön, 1983b). Schön looks to an alternative epistemology of practice in which the knowledge inherent in practice is to be understood as artful doing.

Culturally Relevant Pedagogy As a Tool for Measurement

It is perhaps best to start with a radical assertion that assessment, as both social and political construct, is not fixed. Instead it is shaped by the context in which the ODL practitioner practices. Thus assessment is strongly influenced by the wider culture and the community and society in which the learning takes place. With today's ODL environment becoming so ethnically diverse, it would seem appropriate to begin this discussion by highlighting that the design of ODL assessment policy should draw from many educational philosophies, learning theories, and pedagogical methods compatible and consistent with culturally relevant pedagogy (CRP). We hold that educational programs must be aligned with students' needs, interests, values, student perceptions, communication styles, and desired learning outcomes that apply within a particular cultural context. It is noteworthy that culturally responsive ODL practitioners develop intellectual, social, emotional, and political learning by using cultural referents to impart knowledge, skills, and attitudes. We observe CRP in ODL context as all about using culture and experiences of different ethnic groups as a way to assess more effectively. A culturally relevant assessment must provide a way for students to maintain their cultural identity, while succeeding academically. Thus, the question '*What is culturally responsive pedagogy (CRP)?*' becomes critical.

A great deal of research has been conducted in the area of CRP. CRP, also known as culturally sensitive pedagogy, is not a new concept and has a rich history. Literature suggests that the concept CRP is used interchangeably with several terms, such as culturally responsive, culturally appropriate, culturally congruent and culturally compatible, to describe effective pedagogy in culturally diverse classrooms. It is a pedagogy that empowers students intellectually, socially, emotionally, and politically by using cultural referents to impart knowledge, skills and attitudes (Ladson-Billings, 1992a, 1992b, 1994a, 1994b, 2001). Gay (2000:29) defines CRP as "using the cultural knowledge, prior experiences and performance styles of diverse students to make learning more appropriate and effective for them; and it teaches through the strengths of these students." Among others, CRP has had an immense influence through the works of Gloria Ladson-Billings, Geneva Gay, Elizabeth Moje, Kathleen Hinchman and Coffey Heather. The proponents' works perhaps offer important theoretical considerations in the development of culturally sensitive teaching approaches.

Central to CRP is the postulation that culture is fundamental to learning and assessment. Culture refers to the system of shared beliefs, values, customs, behaviors and artefacts that members of society use to interact with their world and one another – it drives values development and binds people together (Bourdieu, 1973; Bourdieu & Passeron, 1977). CRP is a pedagogy that empowers students by using cultural referents to impart knowledge; and it moves between two cultures but recognizes each as legitimate. Interestingly, Ladson-Billings (1992a; 1992b; 1994a; 1994b; 2001) asserts that "culture plays a role not only in communicating and receiving information, but also in shaping the thinking process of groups and individuals." For Bourdieu (1973), cultural capital is a form of cultural transmission that individuals acquire from their given social structure. Cultural capital embodies the norms, social practices, ideologies, language and behavior that are part of a given context (Bourdieu, 1973; Bourdieu & Passeron, 1977).

Gay (2000:29) describes CRP as having these characteristics: (a) it acknowledges the legitimacy of the cultural heritages of different ethnic groups, both as legacies that affect students' dispositions, attitudes, and approaches to learning and as worthy content to be taught in the formal curriculum; (b) it builds bridges of meaningfulness between home and school experiences as well as between academic abstractions and lived sociocultural realities; (c) it uses a wide variety of instructional strategies that are connected to different learning styles; (d) it teaches students to know and praise their own and each other's cultural heritages; and (e) it incorporates multicultural information, resource, and materials in all the subjects and skills routinely taught in schools.

A plethora of literature indicates that CRP recognizes respects and uses students' identities and backgrounds as meaningful sources for creating optimal learning environments. Ladson-Billings (1992a, 1992b, 1994a, 1994b, 2001) suggests that CRP acknowledges, responds to and celebrates fundamental cultures, as well as offering full, equitable access to education for students from all cultures; consequently recognizing the importance of including students' cultural references in all aspects of learning. Hence, Bourdieu (1973) argues that education systems often institute 'pedagogic action', which requires a familiarization with the dominant culture and all its beliefs, behaviors and ideals.

In its most general sense, the purpose of CRP is the maximization of learning for racially and ethnically diverse students. It is important to recognize, however, that all students, regardless of race or ethnicity, bring their culturally influenced cognition, behavior and dispositions with them to school. Thus the efficacy of CRP is not limited to students of color even though the term is most often used to describe effective teaching of racially and ethnically defined learning environments (Villegas, 1991; Villegas & Lucas, 2002). CRP builds on the premise that "how people are expected to go about learning may differ across cultures. To maximize learning opportunities, teachers must gain knowledge of the cultures represented in their classrooms, then translate this knowledge into instructional practice" (Villegas, 1991; Villegas & Lucas, 2002). However, student achievement is not the only purpose of a CRP. Teachers must also assist students to change society not simply to exist or survive in it.

For us, CRP facilitates and supports the achievement of all students. Richards et al. (2007) contend that in a culturally responsive classroom, effective teaching and learning occur in a culturally supported, learner-centered context, whereby the strengths students bring to school are identified, nurtured, and used to promote student achievement. CRP comprises three dimensions: (a) institutional, (b) personal and (c) instructional. The institutional dimension reflects the administration and its policies and values. The personal dimension refers to the cognitive and emotional processes teachers must engage in to become culturally responsive. The instructional dimension includes material, strategies and activities that form the basis of instruction. All three dimensions significantly interact in the teaching and learning process and are critical to understanding the effectiveness of culturally responsive pedagogy. While all three dimensions are important, because of space limitations only a few points will be made about the institutional dimension. This brief focuses on the two most relevant for teachers' work: the personal and instructional dimensions (Richards et al., 2007).

The poststructuralist trinity (Lacan, Derrida and Foucault) note that culture as a category of social life has itself been conceptualized in a number of different ways. Among others, they see culture as: (1) creativity or agency, (2) a system of symbols and meanings, and (3) practice. Culture is neither a particular kind of practice nor practice that takes place in a particular social location. It is rather the semiotic dimension of human social practice in general (Sewell, 2005:48). As Ladson-Billings (1992a, 1992b, 1994a, 1994b, 2001) puts it, culture is central to learning. It plays a role not only in communicating and receiving information, but also in shaping the thinking processes of groups and individuals. A pedagogy that acknowledges, responds to, and celebrates fundamental cultures offers full, equitable access to education for students from all cultures (Ladson-Billings, 1994a, 1994b, 2001).

Some scholars see CRT as liberating, transformative, comprehensive, validating, empowering, emancipatory and transformative (Ladson-Billings, 1994a, 1994b; Asante, 1991; Au, 1993; Erickson, 1987; Gordon, 1993; Smith & Ayers, 2006; Lipman, 1995; Gay, 2000; Pewewardy, 1994; Philips, 1983). In addition, it guides students in understanding that no single version of 'truth' is total and permanent. It does not solely prescribe to mainstream ways of knowing. CRT infuses family customs—as well as community culture and expectations—throughout the teaching and learning environment (Ladson-Billings, 1994a, 1994b; Gay, 2000). In addition, by providing instruction in a context meaningful to students and in a way that values their culture, knowledge, and experiences, CRT fosters student motivation and engagement. Central to CRT, as Gay (2000:37) notes, is making authentic knowledge about ethnic groups accessible to students.

Following on from the above, it is worth noting that CRP qualifies to be viewed as a tool for measurement. Among others, CRT is "using the cultural knowledge, prior experiences, and performance styles of diverse students to make learning more appropriate and effective for them. It lifts the veil of presumed absolute authority from conceptions of scholarly truth typically taught in schools; and helps students realize that no single version of truth is total and permanent" (Gay, 2000:38). Just as the teaching and learning environment is constantly changing, so must the ODL practitioners adapt their roles and responsibilities - ODL practitioners are no longer teaching in isolation – culture and generational divide play a critical role. For this reason, best practices ODL assessment should match the students' generational culture and should be compatible with practices which speak to culturally diverse students.

REFLECTIONS ON ASSESSMENT IN ODL THROUGH THE LENS OF EMERGING PARADIGMS

In the previous sections we emphasized the importance of assessment for learning, in open distance learning (ODL). We showed how best practice, reflective practice and culturally relevant pedagogy (CRP) can aid ODL practitioners in improving the way they assess ODL students. In this section we reflect on whether or not the current assessment strategies in ODL adhere to reflective practice and culturally relevant pedagogy. Regarding best practice, we have highlighted in the section above that this requires assessment to be an integral component of teaching and learning, involving planning, discussion, consensus building, and reflection by all involved – practitioners and students – particularly at the beginning when learning goals are established, and at the end where the data are used to improve the curriculum. Best practice in assessment also means that the process "should be a collaborative endeavor between lecturers and students" (Letseka & Pitsoe, 2013: 202). This aspect of quality assessment is usually ignored when compiling assessment materials. For instance, Ngara, Ngwarai and Mhute (2012:176), report on the research they conducted at the Zimbabwe Open University (ZOU) that some students complained about not being provided or familiarized with the criteria for assessment of assignments. According to the principles of best practice, these criteria should have been planned and discussed with the students. An example of best practice in ODL is evident in India, where interaction between practitioners and students has been improved by using self-instructional study materials, interactive technologies and counseling services (Ansari, 2002:221). A study conducted in an ODL institution in Pakistan revealed that when there is no interaction between ODL practitioners and the students, about marking, content material and the nature of questions for assignments learners do not get the full benefit of this assessment strategy (Hussein & Jumani, 2008:37).

As we have argued above best practice in ODL assessment and reflective practice have a symbiotic relationship. Best practice in ODL assessment should be characterized by reflective practice. But does this really happen in ODL institutions? Davis (2003:243) argues that although reflective practice is seen as the way forward for both students and academics alike and is supposed to lead to better learning, it is still not universally accepted, because of the many challenges it encounters. ODL encounters challenges such as plagiarism, because students do their assessment tasks away from the presence of the tutors, where there is no guarantee of the originality of their work (Ngara et al, 2012:171). This is where reflective practice for students would be effective. Davis (2003:253) suggests that for thorough reflective practice, "the curriculum given to students … must be flexible and open to compromise (while) teaching and assessment must encourage and allow all students to demonstrate that they have achieved the objectives of their course of study". Other challenges brought about by the changing nature of higher learning are the belief in lifelong learning, accreditation for prior learning and simplifying access to higher education. Governments are encouraging higher learning institutions to admit students without formal qualifications, resulting in the student body with diverse educational backgrounds and qualifications (Davis, 2003:244). This scenario does not only occur in conventional universities, but also in ODL institutions which often "market themselves as open, accessible, flexible, supportive and affordable" (Letseka & Pitsoe, 2013:197) in order to attract students. ODL institutions should recognize that by marketing themselves in the above manner they will attract students from diverse backgrounds who will require that "curriculum, student support, teaching practices and assessment methods are relevant" (Davis, 2003:244) to their diversity. Reflective practice recognizes that students do not only differ in terms of their academic achievement, but also in their "ability, disability, age, maturity, experience, commitment, motivation, study mode, class, sex, race, religion and the like" (Davis, 2003:245). Besides a diverse student body, ODL assessment has to take cognizance of these diversities.

Student diversity brings us to another component of ensuring best practice in ODL assessment; culturally relevant pedagogy (CRP). Ngara et al. (2012: 171) note that most ODL institutions cater for very diverse groups of learners in terms of age, race, socio-economic status and special needs, but assessment in these institutions fails to address this learner diversity. This diversity could be addressed through the adoption of CRP. Howard (2003:196) argues that "the most important goal of culturally relevant pedagogy is to increase the academic achievement of culturally diverse students". As we have argued above, literature indicates that CRP recognizes, respects and uses students' identities and backgrounds as meaningful sources for creating optimal learning environments. Thus ODL practitioners have to be able to "critically reflect on their own racial and cultural identities and to recognize how these identities coexist with the cultural compositions of their students" (Howard, 2003:196). ODL practitioners will be able to recognize that their students will perform well if they are treated competently. In order to be culturally relevant, ODL practitioners "need to engage in honest, critical reflection that challenges them to see how their positionality influences their students in either positive or negative ways (Howard, 2003:197). This is where reflective practice comes in. Howard (2003:198) argues that "in order to become culturally relevant pedagogues, teachers must be prepared to engage in a rigorous ... reflection process about what it means to teach students who come from different racial and cultural backgrounds than their own".

CONCLUSION

In this chapter, we reflected on how best practice, reflective practice, and culturally relevant pedagogy can help ODL practitioners to improve the way they assess. We showed that in addition to the usual processes of measuring, analyzing and improving performance, best practice also involves planning, discussion, consensus building and reflection. We argued that best practice and reflective practice have a symbiotic relationship. In other words, best practice should be characterized by reflective practice. We also argued that because of the diverse student body in ODL institutions, best practice and reflective practice should go along with CPR. The CRP recognizes that ODL students are not only different in their academic abilities, but they also differ in their "ability, disability, age, maturity, experience commitment, motivation, study mode, class, sex, race, religion and the like" (Davis, 2003:245). We have also shown that in order for best practice to prevail in ODL assessment, practitioners have to be reflective and culturally relevant pedagogues. In the same vein, culturally relevant pedagogy can only be effective in the presence of reflective practice.

REFERENCES

Aguinis, H. & Vandenberg, R. J. (2014). An ounce of prevention is worth a pound of cure: Improving research quality before data collection. *Annual Review of Organizational Psychology and Organizational Behavior*, *1*, 569-595.

Angelo, T. (1995). Reassessing (and defining). assessment. *The AAHE Bulletin*, *48*(2), 7-9.

Angelo, T. A. & Cross, K. P. (1993). *Classroom Assessment Techniques: A Handbook for College Teachers*, 2nd Edition, San Francisco, CA: Jossey-Bass.

Angelo, T. (Ed.). (1998). *Classroom Assessment and Research: An Update on Uses, Approaches, and Research Findings*, San Francisco, CA: Jossey-Bass.

Asante, M. K. (1991). Afrocentric curriculum. *Educational Leadership*, *49*(4), 28-31.

Ansari, M. M. (2002). Best practices in open distance learning systems in India: An assessment. *Indian Journal of Open Learning, 11*(2), 219-228.

Applegate, R. & Irwin, M. (2012). Learning outcomes assessment via electronic portfolios. In Woodsworth, A. & Penniman, W.D. (Eds.). *Advances in Librarianship.* Volume *35*, *Contexts for Assessment and Outcome Evaluation in Librarianship*, Bingley, UK: Emerald.

Au, K. H. (1993). *Literacy Instruction in Multicultural Settings*, New York: Harcourt Brace.

Boud, D., Keogh, R. & Walker, D. (1985). *Reflection Turning Experience into Learning*, London: Kogan Page.

Bourdieu, P. (1973). Cultural reproduction and social reproduction, in Brown, R. (ed). *Knowledge, Education and Cultural Change,* London: Tavistock: 71-112.

Bourdieu, P. & Passeron, J. C. (1977). *Reproduction in Education, Society and Culture*, London: Sage.

Braun, J. A. & Crumpler, T. P. (2004). The social memoir: An analysis of developing reflective ability in a pre-service methods course. *Teaching and Teacher Education*, *20*(1), 59-75.

Davis, M. (2003). Barriers to reflective practice. *Active Learning in Higher Education, 4* (3), 243 – 255.

Deyle, R. E. & Wiedenman, R. E. (2014). Collaborative Planning by Metropolitan Planning Organizations: A Test of Causal Theory. *Journal of Planning Education and Research, 34*(3), 257– 275.

Ermeling, B. (2014). Learning to learn from teaching: A first-hand account of lesson study in Japan. *International Journal for Lesson and Learning Studies*, *3*(2), 170- 192.

Erickson, F. (1987). Transformation and school success: the politics and culture of educational achievement. *Anthropology and Education Quarterly*, *18*(4), 335-383.

Gay, G. (2000). *Culturally Responsive Teaching: Theory, Research & Practice*, New York: Teachers College Press.

Gordon, B. M. (1993). African American cultural knowledge and liberatory education; dilemmas, problems, and potentials in a postmodern American society. *Urban Education*, *27*(4), 448-470.

Haken, M. (2006). *Closing the Loop-learning from Assessment.* Presentation made at the University of Maryland Eastern Shore Assessment Workshop. Princess Anne: MD.

Hersh, R. (2004). Assessment and accountability: Unveiling value added assessment in higher education. A paper presented at the AAHE National Assessment Conference. June 15, 2004. Denver: Colorado.

Hopkins, C. D. & Antes, R. L. (1990). *Educational Research: A Structure for Inquiry*, 3rd Edition, Itasca, Illinois: FE Peacock.

Howard, T. (2003). Culturally relevant pedagogy: Ingredients for critical teacher reflection. T*heory into Practice*, *42* (3), 195 -202.

Hussein, M. A. & Jumani, N. B. (2008). Students' tensions and attitudes towards formative assessment in open distance learning. *Progressio*, *30*(1 & 2), 31-42.

Imel, S. (1992). Reflective Practice in Adult Education. *ERIC Digest*, *122*, 1-7.

Jarvis, P. (1992). Reflective practice and nursing. *Nurse Education Today*, *12*, 174-181.

Kanwar, S. (2012). Assessment - An Important Facet of Learning. *Literacy Information and Computer Education Journal* (LICEJ), *1*(2), 825-831.

Kolb, D. A. (1984). *Experiential learning: Experience as the Source of Learning and Development*, New Jersey: Prentice Hall.

Ladson-Billings, B. (1992a). Reading between the lines and beyond the pages: A culturally relevant approach to literacy teaching. *Theory into Practice*, *31*(4), 312-320.

Ladson-Billings, G. (1992b). Liberatory consequences of literacy: A case of culturally relevant instruction for African American students. J*ournal of Negro Education*, *61*(3), 378-391.

Ladson-Billings, G. (1994a). *The Dream Keepers: Successful Teaching for African-American Students*, San Francisco: Jossey-Bass

Ladson-Billings, G. (1995a). But that's just good teaching! The case for culturally relevant pedagogy. *Theory Into Practice*, 34(3), 159-165.

Ladson-Billings, G. (1995b). Multicultural teacher education: Research, practice, and policy. In J.A. Banks & C.A.M. Banks (Eds.), *Handbook of Research on Multicultural Education*, New York: Macmillan: 747-759.

Ladson-Billings, G. (2001). *Crossing Over to Canaan: The Journey of New Teachers in Diverse Classrooms*, San Francisco: Jossey-Bass.

Larrivee, B. & Cooper, J. M. (2006). *An Educator's Guide to Teacher Reflection*, Boston: Houghton Mifflin Company.

Letseka, M. & Pitsoe, V. (2013). Reflections on assessment in open distance learning (ODL): the case of the University of South Africa (UNISA). *Open Praxis*, *5* (3), 197 – 206.

Lipman, P. (1995). Bringing out the best in them: The contribution of culturally relevant teachers to educational reform. *Theory Into Practice*, *34*(3), 202-208.

Martell, K. & Calderon, T. (2005). Assessment of student learning in business schools: What it is, where we are, and where we need to go next. In K. Martell & T. Calderon, Assessment of student learning in business schools: Best practices each step of the way (Vol. *1*, No. 1, 1-22). Tallahassee, Florida: Association for Institutional Research.

Moon, J. (2004). *Reflection in Learning and Professional Development: Theory and Practi*ce, London: Kogan Page.

Moon, J. (1999). *Learning Journals: A Handbook for Academics, Students and Professional Development*, London: Kogan Page.

Ngara, R., Ngwarai, R. & Mhute, I. (2012). Assessment in ODL: Practices, opportunities and challenges. *International Journal of Social Sciences and Education*, *3* (1), 166-177.

Orlich, D. C., Harder, R. J., Callahan, R. C. & Gibson. H. W. (2004). *Teaching Strategies: A guide to Better Instructio*n, New York: Houghton Mifflin.

Osterman, K. F. & Kottamp, R. B. (2004). *Reflective Practice for Educators*, Thousand Oaks, CA: Corwin Press.

Pavlovich, K. (2007). The development of reflective practice through student journals. *Higher Education Research and Development*, *26*(3), 281-295.

Pewewardy, C. D. (1994). Culturally responsive pedagogy in action: An American Indian magnet school. In ER. Hollins, J.E., King, & WC. Hayman (eds), *Teaching Diverse Populations: Formulating a Knowledge Base*. Albany: State University of New York Press, 77-92.

Philips, S. U. (1983). *The Invisible Culture: Communication in Classroom and Community on the Warm Springs Indian Reservation*, Long Groove, IL: Waveland Press.

Phillips, P. (2008). Professional Development as a critical component of continuing teacher quality. *Australian Journal of Teacher Education*, *33* (1), 1-9.

Reid, B. (1993). 'But we're doing it already!' exploring a response to the concept of reflective practice in order to improve its facilitation. *Nurse Education Today*, *13*, 305-309.

Richards, H., Brown, A. & Forde, T. (2007). Addressing diversity in schools: culturally responsive pedagogy. *Teaching Exceptional Children*, *23*(3), 64-68.

Schön, D. A. (1983a). *Reflective practitioner: From Technical Rationality to Reflection-in-action*, New York: Basic Books.

Schön, D. A. (1983b). *The reflective Practitioner: How Professionals Think in Action*, New York: Basic Books.

Schön, D. (1987). *Educating the Reflective Practitioner: Towards a New Design for Teaching in the Professions*, San Francisco: Jossey-Bass.

Sewell, W. H. (2005). The Concept(s). of Culture. In Spiegel, GM (ed). *Practicing History: New Directions in Historical Writing after the Linguistic Turn*, New York: Routledge. (770-800).

Smith, D. R. & Ayers, D. F. (2006). Culturally responsive pedagogy and online learning: implications for the globalized community college. *Community College Journal of Research and Practice*, *30*, 401- 415.

Villegas, A. M. (1991). Culturally Responsive Pedagogy for the 1990's and Beyond, Trends and Issues Paper No. 6. Washington, DC: ERIC Clearinghouse on Teacher Education.

Villegas, A. M. & Lucas, T. (2002). *Educating Culturally Responsive Teachers: A Coherent Approach*. Albany, NY: State University of New York Press.

Zeichner, K. (2008). A critical analysis of reflection as a goal for teacher education. *Campinas: Education & Society*, *29* (103), 535-554.

In: Open Distance Learning (ODL) in South Africa
Editor: Moeketsi Letseka
ISBN: 978-1-63463-890-6

Chapter 6

PASS RATES IN OPEN DISTANCE LEARNING (ODL)

***Moeketsi Letseka*[1,*] *and Keleco Karel*[2]**
[1]Department of Educational Foundations, College of Education,
University of South Africa (UNISA), South Africa
[2]Adult Basic Education and Training and Youth Development College of Education,
University of South Africa (UNISA), South Africa

ABSTRACT

This chapter interrogates the challenges of poor pass rates at UNISA and the associated trend by which students do not graduate within the specific duration required to complete their designated study program. It briefly describes the ODL framework with a view to providing readers with some understanding of how a distance education institution like UNISA operates. In a country like South Africa, which is marked by high levels of unemployment, adult illiteracy and socio-economic inequalities, an optimally functioning higher education sector that delivers good pass rates and good throughput rates is *sine qua non* to global economic competitiveness and a sense of well-being among its citizenry. Thus the imperative to sufficiently deal with the twin issue of equity and redress in a country that has only just emerged from a system of rule that privileged the white minority while marginalizing, disadvantaging and excluding the vast majority of the African peoples from socio-economic opportunities cannot be overemphasized. The chapter briefly describes the open distance learning (ODL) mode that UNISA operates. By its very nature as an ODL institution UNISA targets mature working adults who do not have the time to pursue higher education qualification at full-time contact institutions. At the time of writing UNISA's student headcount enrollments were estimated to be close to 400 000 in a country where national headcount enrollments are close to 1 million. This puts UNISA's share of South Africa's headcount enrollments at just over 40%. The chapter grapples with the challenges of UNISA's pass rates, which have been described as "shocking". A recent authoritative government report on post-school education and training statistics shows that UNISA's percentage of graduation rates in undergraduate, masters and doctoral degrees during 2010 were well below national averages of 16%, 18% and 12%. In fact UNISA's averages in the three categories above were in single digits. The chapter proposes a review of the university's

* Corresponding author: Email: letsem@unisa.ac.za.

admission policy; a coordinated and sustained student support program, and a tightening of the tracking system of 'at-risk' students.

INTRODUCTION

Student pass rates in open and distance learning (ODL) institutions are typically low compared to pass rates in full-time contact higher education institutions (HEIs). One of the major problems facing HEIs in South Africa today is the policy imperative to be responsive to open and equitable access, quality education and high throughput rates. Through policies of open and equitable access, large numbers of students, some well-prepared, partially prepared, and others under-prepared and without the requisite skills either for higher education teaching and learning or for open distance learning are enrolling in large numbers at South Africa's HEIs, in the process compounding the sector's pass rates and throughput rates. The University of South Africa (UNISA) is the largest ODL institution on the continent of Africa, with student headcount enrollments at close to 400 000. UNISA offers higher education opportunities to mature working adults who would otherwise not be able to obtain a higher education qualification if their only choice of HEIs were to be full-time contact institutions.

South Africa's HEIs are under pressure to transform their plans, policies and procedures in order to accommodate the ever increasing number of students. Enrollments in distance education are on the rise. South Africa in particular experiences swelling enrollment numbers in both the schooling and higher education sectors. The higher education sector itself has grown by over 80% with a total enrollment of close to 1 million . We should hasten to mention that UNISA's enrollment figures above constitute an estimated 40% of the entire national enrollment figures. The increase in enrollments is in part in response to the pressure exerted on HEIs by government to redress the race and gender inequalities in admissions and in participation. As a result of this pressure South Africa's higher education participation rates increased from 15% in 2000 to 18% in 2010.The widening of access has resulted in the issue of low pass rate becoming the Achilles heel of most HEIs. The growing enrollments have the unintended consequence of resulting in low pass rates, poor throughput rates and concomitantly poor uptake of graduates by the labor market (Letseka, 2009; Pauw, Oosthuizen, and van der Westhuizen, 2008; Bhorat and Oosthuizen, 2005). According to the Department of Education (DoE) (2001)'s *National Plan for Higher Education* (NPHE), the university pass rate of 15% is one of the lowest in the world. This was echoed by Letseka's (2010, 2009, 2008a, 2007) research at the Human Sciences Research Council (HSRC) which probed the reasons why university students drop out without obtaining the qualification for which they are registered. The NPHE set out required HEIs' graduation benchmarks as indicators of access with success. The benchmarks distinguished between the full-time contact institutions and open distance learning institutions. As things stand ODL institutions like UNISA are struggling to meet the stipulated national graduation benchmarks and the pressure is on to design policies and procedures that create a conducive environment for its students to succeed. One important area where change is no doubt necessary is in the number of modules for which the students may be allowed to register and succeed.

UNISA is by far the biggest ODL institution on the African continent catering for mature and diverse working students who do not have the time to enroll in full-time contact HEIs, but the desire and ambition to pursue a range of generic bachelor's degrees or work-oriented certificates, diplomas and degrees (Pityana, 2009; Subotzky, 2009; UNISA, 2008). The programs that students register for are of different durations with different minimum and maximum periods for completion. Students that enroll at UNISA are only allowed to graduate if they complete and pass the modules for which they are registered. The expected duration of a qualification is indicated by the formal time allocated to it in the funding framework: a diploma and a general formative Bachelor's degree should take three years to complete while a professional Bachelor's degree should take a minimum of four years, and only after the student has completed the maximum duration prescribed for the course. Distance learning students are typically older, do their studies part-time, and often juggle full-time jobs along with family responsibilities (Fjortoft, 1995; Galusha, 1997; Holmberg, 1995; McGivney, 2004). Ostman and Wagner (1987) found "lack of time" to be the single most commonly cited reason for dropping out offered by distance learners. Other factors attributed to students' low pass rates include general institution preparation, lack of guidance and information prior to enrollment, poor student support structures, and difficulties in contacting them (Brown, 1996; Frew & Weber, 1995; Pierrakeas, Xenos, Panagiotakopoulos, and Vergidis, 2004; Tresman, 2002). According to Simpson (2003-2004) students can leave during the course or leave the institution altogether. Some students do not complete the modules or programs due to unavoidable reasons.

The chapter is divided into five sections. First, we briefly touch on the ODL framework with a view to providing some understanding on how a distance education institution like UNISA functions. Second, we tease out the issue of pass rate, noting in particular that in a country like South Africa, which has only just emerged from a system of rule that privileged the white minority while marginalizing and disadvantaging the majority of the Africa peoples, the imperatives of equity and redress rank high on government policies. Third, and mainly as a result of years of systematic and institutionalized exclusion from educational opportunities, we look into the extent of under-preparedness for university teaching and learning and how it impacts poor pass rates. Fourth, we touch on completion rates, some of which are admittedly "shocking" (CHE, 2013; Macfarlane, 2006). In the fifth and final section we offer some concluding remarks. We now turn to a brief sketching of the ODL framework.

The ODL Framework

The accepted mandate of ODL institutions is to provide access to higher education to adult working students who neither have the time nor the means to study for a higher education qualifications at full-time contact higher education institutions. By its very nature, ODL has a dispersed organizational structure. As former Vice Chancellor and Principal of UNISA Professor Barney Pityana (2009:7) cogently points out, in the developing world ODL is a promising and practical strategy for addressing the challenges of widening access, and in the process, for increasing participation in higher education. Pityana contends that on the African continent where resources are scarce and higher education provision is poor, ODL comes across as the only viable and cost effective means of expanding provision of higher education without costly outlay in infrastructure. ODL has been defined in different ways by ODL practitioners. But there is consensus among ODL practitioners that distance learning is a teaching and learning scenario in which the teacher and the student are physically separated in space and possibly time, and yet are able to interact, engage and make progress that results in the student obtaining the necessary skills and qualifications (Greenberg 1998; Teaster and Blieszner 1999; Heydenrych and Prinsloo 2010). Thus ODL provides access to higher education to different kinds of students with no restrictions on age, social status, marital status and distance away from the host institution.

The notion of ODL suggests an educational mode of delivery that is designed to reach learners anywhere: in their homes, in their offices, or while travelling, through the use of modern electronic technologies and to provide them with teaching and learning experiences to qualify and obtain higher education qualification without the requirement to attend formal classes in person. Against this backdrop it can be reasonably argued that the ODL mode of teaching and learning provides the space and opportunities for lifelong learning. This is critically important in the specific case of South Africa where there are high levels of unemployment, adult illiteracy and enduring socio-economic inequalities. Add to this the salient reality that the price tag of formal university education is extremely high and beyond the reach of many poor households, then ODL is, to reiterate Pityana (2009), a viable and cost effective means of expanding access to higher education. In the next section we mull over whether access to higher education opportunities provided by the ODL mode translates into quality in terms of pass rates and or notions of success.

Conceptualising Pass Rates at UNISA

An important indicator of the efficiency of the higher education system is students' success rates (Subotzky, 2003). And yet, as Fiske and Ladd (2004) point out, as a result of apartheid policies and legislation, repetition and drop-out rates among black students are high and matriculation pass rates low. In full-time contact universities about one in three students drop out, which raises serious questions about the sector's ability to generate a viable throughput rate (Letseka and Maile, 2008b). While UNISA is committed to intervening in this sector by expanding affordable access to higher education, especially to the vast majority of blacks and Africans who were previously disadvantaged by apartheid policies and legislation, the true measure of its commitment will be the success of its students to exit the system with qualifications and requisite skills within stipulated durations of their chosen fields of study. This is necessary given that the then Department of Education (DoE) set specific graduation benchmarks, as indicators of success, that all HEIs were expected to meet. The DoE (2001) observed that there are wide disparities in the graduation rates of black and white students. For instance, the average graduation rate for white students tended to be more than double that of black student. From the point of view of government these disparities were unacceptable. They require urgent and sustainable plans and policies to redress them. The DoE's (2001) *National Plan for Higher Education* (NPHE) set clear and specific policy targets with respect to increasing the participation, graduation, and overall success of blacks in general, and of women in particular (DoE, 2001: 30). Cognizant of the differentiated nature of the country's higher education sector the DoE set different graduation targets for full-time contact institutions and different graduation rates for open distance education institutions. For example, in the 3-year undergraduate degree program at full-time contact institutions the

NPHE set the graduation benchmark at 25%, while for a similar program in ODL the target benchmark was set at 15% (See Table 1).

Table 1. Benchmarks for graduation rates

	Graduation Rate	
	Contact	**Distance**
Up to 3 years undergraduate	25%	15%
4-year or more undergraduate	20%	10%
Postgraduate up to honors	60%	30%
Masters	33%	25%
Doctoral	20%	20%

Source: DoE (2001) *National Plan for Higher Education*.

A critical question we grapple with in this chapter is whether UNISA has been able to meet the above graduation benchmarks as set out in, and required by national policy. An Achilles heel for UNISA remains poor pass rates. We will come back to this point in more detail below when we broach the issue of completion rates. Notwithstanding that the university has been experiencing rapid and unanticipated increases in student enrollments, it is marked by persistent poor success and throughput rates, which are attributed to, among others, underpreparedness of some of the students gaining admission. We should clarify that underpreparedness may mean different things, as in lack of 'academic literacy' as a distinctive phenomenon (Bradbury and Miller, 2011), or lack of 'epistemological Access' to knowledge (Lotz-Sisitka, 2009; Boughey, 2005; Morrow, 1992). We explore some of these issues in a bid more detail below where we sketch factors that influence under-preparedness.

Factors Influencing Under-Preparedness and Low Pass Rates

Under-preparedness is one of the major problems that hampers success in higher education for most students. Under-preparedness manifests in different ways; from struggling with the concepts one needs to succeed in their respective fields of study - 'lack of epistemological access', to failure to cope with one's study environment - 'institutional cultures' (Jansen, 2004). Most of the students enrolling in South African universities are first generation university entrants in their families and lack access to the social networks with reservoirs of experience of university study (Slonimsky and Shalem 2006). A view that has been advanced by some South African scholars to try and understand the challenges of university first entrants has been to suggest that such students lack the necessary "epistemological access" or forms of knowledge that one requires to cope with the complex nature of teaching and learning in higher education (Lotz-Sisitka, 2009; Boughey, 2005; Moll 2004; Nyamapfene and Letseka 1995; Morrow, 1992). One of the reasons for this lack of epistemological access is that public schooling in South Africa is characterized by dysfunctionality (Development Bank of Southern Africa 2008; South African Human Rights Commission 2006; Taylor 2006; van der Berg, 2007; Taylor, Muller and Vinjevold, 2003;

Fedderke, de Kadt and Luiz 2000; Case and Deaton 1999). According to the South African Human Rights Commission (2006) many schools in township and rural areas are characterized by dysfunctionality, vulnerability, alienation and lack of social cohesion. Drawing on the study of seven HEIs involving 34 548 respondents (20 353 dropouts and 14 195 graduates) which he conducted for the Human Sciences Research Council (HSRC) on why university students drop out, Letseka (2010, 2009, 2007) argues that an estimated 70% of the students who dropped out of university had no siblings with university experience. They therefore lacked the kind of information and guidance to navigate the maze of fields of study for which they had to choose and register.

Education policy and legislation in South Africa emphasize equity of access and fair chances of success to anyone who seeks to realize their potential through opportunities offered by higher education. We want to argue that it is reasonable to expect that the schooling system, which serves as a feeder pipeline to higher education should be supported in order to improve the quality of teaching and learning that adequately prepare school leavers to exit the schooling system with the requisite knowledge and skills to succeed in higher education. We want to make a case for the link between schools and HEIs. Consequently HEIs need to reform their policies and programs to allow them to forge mutually beneficial collaborative partnerships with schools with a view to linking teaching and learning in schools with teaching and learning in HEIs. This way the transition from schooling to post-schooling will be eased and not appear as a shock to most first year university entrants as is currently the case.

Students who are admitted into ODL are expected to be prepared for the challenges of distance education or to have more realistic expectations of ODL teaching and learning given their age and levels of maturity as adult learners. It is expected that they will be prepared to take responsibility for their learning by acquainting themselves with their study material early, and putting in place structured plans, schedules and time-tables to be able to efficiently manage their study portfolios, work on, and submit their assignments on scheduled deadlines. Often though, such expectations are misplaced. As Warren (2002:88) reminds us, not all students enter higher education at the same level of preparedness. As such additional guidance to familiarize them with the distinctive culture and approaches to teaching and learning becomes necessary.

For ODL institutions to improve their pass rates hard choices and decision with respect to admission requirements have to be made. Admission without specific requirements might be the norm at international ODL institutions such as, for example, the Open University of the United Kingdom (OU UK). The OU UK describes itself as open to people; open as to places, open as to methods and open to ideas (Gourley and Lane, 2009; Johnson and Barrett, 2003). Should this also be the norm for UNISA? While UNISA might not be equated with the OU UK which prides itself with no admission requirements, its admission requirements are too relaxed compared to full-time contact universities. And herein lies the rub. In South Africa most of the students who are admitted into the ODL mode of teaching and learning come from disadvantaged backgrounds or are products of the public schooling system that has been described by the South African Human Rights Commission (2006) above as ‘dysfunctional’. They do not have the necessary study skills to engage with the concepts in a guided contact university, let alone study in the ODL environment where they are expected to take responsibility for their studies. To curb the low pass rates the type of students that are admitted into UNISA need to be thoroughly screened to ensure they are the right material with the necessary ODL-aligned learning skills and mental dispositions to succeed in their studies. Koch and Foxcroft (2003) rightfully remind us that although selection procedures are not the only culprits for poor pass rates and lack of throughput, they are often regarded as one of the major factors that increase the problem. It is a well-documented phenomenon that selection should identify students with potential to succeed (Louw, 1996; Miller, 1992; Nunns and Ortlepp, 1994; Zaaiman, 1998). Selection criteria that are used should be acceptable and fair to all parties. Jackson and Young (1998) encourage us to use a variety of admission criteria instead of a single criterion. One of the major attributes to low pass rates is the mismatch between the demands of higher education and the preparedness of students for higher education.

There is no doubt that people's identities are shaped by participation in various systems of learning (Wenger, 2000; Northedge, 2003), and that schooling background does influence, even determine, the values and attitudes (the culture of "not learning" and lack of vision) that students bring with them to higher education. It is therefore imperative that the skills that students gained during schooling are transferable to their intended plans for further studies (Astin, 1993). In the next section we briefly touch on UNISA's completion rates.

COMPLETION RATES AT UNISA

According to Council on Higher Education (CHE, 2013), South Africa's higher education system generally produces too few graduates. The CHE further notes that there is a mismatch between graduates' attributes and the broader needs of labor market and society in general. The nexus between higher education and the labor market is the theme of Maximux Sefotho's chapter in this volume and we shall therefore not dwell on it. Fisher and Scott (2011) argue that South Africa's higher education can at best be described as "low-participation, high attrition system". For Berg and Huang (2004), completion rate in distance education have been investigated and vigorously debated over the last seven decades. In South Africa poor completion rates have been attributed to low numbers in the proportion of the student body that succeed. It should be noted that ODL students in particular take more time to complete their studies given that distance learning by its nature means students need more time to complete their modules given that the system regulates registration to a limited and manageable number of modules. Consequently distance education students can be expected to take longer than full-time contact university students to complete their studies. Two authoritative reports have highlighted the seriousness of UNISA's poor pass rates, low completion rates and poor throughput rates (CHE, 2013; DHET, 2013). The CHE (2013) report shows that in the 3-year degrees only 9% graduated within five years, while an estimated 72% will never graduate. In both 4-year degrees and all 3 and 4 year qualifications only 8% graduated within 5 years while again 72% will never graduate. The most shocking statistics is in the 3-year diplomas where a miserly 2% graduated within five years while a whopping 89% will never graduate (see Table 2).

The above data are confirmed by the DHET (2013) report, which shows that UNISA's graduation rates in 2010 were not only the lowest of all South Africa's twenty-three universities, but that UNISA's rates in all the three categories were in single digits, below the national average, and way off the national policy benchmarks of 15%, 25% and 20% set by the DoE's (2001) *National Plan for Higher Education*.

Our suggestion for remedying the above situation should be seen in the light of some of the recommendations we have above vis-à-vis UNISA's admission requirements. It is our contention that for UNISA to deliver the best pass rates, completion rates, and throughput rates its admission requirements should be explicit about admitting only those students who have the potential to succeed in their chosen fields of study. Another critical area which we shall only mention in passing here is the area of student support. This is dealt with in detail by Shakila Dhunpath and Rubby Dhunpath in chapter nine and we shall therefore not belabor it here.

Table 2. Cohort completion rates of first-time entering student, 2006 cohort

		Graduated within 5 years (%)	Estimated % that will never graduate
UNISA	3-year degrees	9	72
	4-year degrees	8	72
	All 3- & 4-year degrees	**8**	**72**
	3-year diplomas	2	89
	All 3- & 4-year qualifications	**6**	78

Source: Council on Higher Education (CHE) (2013).

Table 3. Summaries of graduation rates in public Higher Education institutions, 2010

Institution	Undergraduate Degrees and Diplomas (%)	Master's Degree (%)	Doctoral Degrees (%)
UNISA	8	9	5
National average	16	18	12

Source: Department of Higher Education and Training (DHET) (2013).

CONCLUSION

What we have attempted to do in this chapter is to open the debate on pass rates and completion rates in ODL, with particular reference to UNISA. We have acknowledged that while UNISA has a national and constitutional mandate to provide access to higher education, especially to the majority black and African students who were excluded from such opportunities during apartheid, open admission without success is merely a revolving door that perpetuates the development of mediocre human resources. Such access can only result in 'certificated' graduates and not 'educated' graduates who possess the knowledge and skills that equate to 'graduateness'. We demonstrated with raw statistical data from reputable sources that UNISA's pass rates, completion rates, graduation rates and throughput rates fall extremely short of the national policy benchmarks set out by the former Department of Education (DoE) in the *National Plan for Higher Education*. UNISA rates are in single digits and way below even the national average. This situation calls for deeper and candid dialogue by the relevant stakeholders at UNISA on how to formulate robust and sustainable strategies to remedy the enduring but shocking poor performance. As far back as 2004 former Vice Chancellor and Principal of UNISA Professor Barney Pityana lamented the 'appalling pass rates' and expressed concern that such 'shocking' dropout rates put the university in danger of ruining whatever academic reputation UNISA has ever had. The 2013 reports by the Council on Higher Education (CHE) and the Department of Higher Education and Training (DHET) suggest that 'it's business as usual' at UNISA, and that ten years later, there are no tangible lessons learned from the 2004 revelation of the institution's then 'shocking dropout rates'.

REFERENCES

Bhorat, H. & Oosthuizen, M. (2005). The post-apartheid South African labor market. Working Paper, Development Policy Research Unit (DPRU), University of Cape Town.

Boughey, C. (2005). Epistemological access to the university: An alternative perspective. *South African Journal of Higher Education*, *19* (3), 230–42.

Bradbury, J. & Miller, R. A. (2011). A failure by any other name: The phenomenon of underpreparedness. *South African Journal of Science*, *107*(3/4), 112-119.

Brown, K. (1996). The role of internal and external factors in the discontinuation of off-campus students. *Distance Education,* 17 (1), 44-71.

Case, A. & Deaton, A. (1999). School inputs and educational outcomes in South Africa. *Quarterly Journal of Economics*, *114* (3), 1047–84.

Council on Higher Education (CHE). (2013). *A Proposal for Undergraduate Curriculum Reform in South Africa*: *The Case for a Flexible Curriculum Structure*, Pretoria: CHE.

Council on Higher Education (CHE). (2000). *Towards a New Higher Education Landscape: Meeting the Equity, Quality and Social Development Imperatives of South Africa in the 21st Century*, Pretoria: CHE.

Department of Higher Education and Training (DHET). (2013). *Statistics on Post-School Education and Training in South Africa: 2010*, Pretoria: Department of Higher Education and Training.

Department of Education (DoE). (2001). *National Plan for Higher Education*, Pretoria: Department of Education.

Development Bank of Southern Africa (DBSA). (2008). *Education Roadmap: Focus on Schooling System*, Midrand. Johannesburg: DBSA.

Fedderke, J. W., de Kadt, R. & Luiz, J. M. (2000). Educating South Africa: The failure to address the 1910–1993 legacy. *International Review of Education*, *46* (3/4), 257–81.

Fiske, E. B. & Ladd, H. F. (2004). *Elusive equity: Education reform in post-apartheid South Africa*, Washington, D.C: Brookings Institution Press.

Fjortoft, N. (1995). Predicting Persistence in Distance Learning Programs, paper presented at the Annual meeting Mid-Western Educational Research Meeting, Chicago, IL, 12th October.

Frew, E. & Weber, K. (1995). Toward a higher retention rate among distance learners. *Open Learning,* 10 (2), 58-61.

Galusha, J. (1997). Barriers to learning in distance education. *Interpersonal Computing and Technology: An Electronic Journal for the 21st Century,* 5 (3-4), 6-14.

Gourley, B. & Lane, A. (2009). Re-invigorating openness at The Open University: the role of Open Educational Resources. *Open Learning: The Journal of Open and Distance Learning, 24* (1), 57-65.

Holmberg, B. (1995). *Theory and practice of distance education,* 2nd Edition, New York: Routledge.

Jansen, J. D. (2004). Race and education after ten years. *Perspectives in Education*, *22*(4), 117-128.

Jackson, I. M. & Young, D. A. (1988). "Student selection using a model which could predict success in first year biological studies at university", *South African Journal of Education*, *8* (3), 170-175.

Johnson, M. & Barrett, C. (2003). Addressing the learning skills needs of students at a distance: a dual medium approach. In Alan Tait and Roger Mills (eds), *Rethinking Learner Support in Distance Education: Change and Continuity in an International Context*, New York: RoutledgeFalmer.

Letseka, M., Cosser, M., Breier, M. & Visser, M. (eds). (2010). *Student Retention and Graduate Destinations: Higher Education and Labor Market Access and Success*, Cape Town: HSRC Press.

Letseka, M. (2009). University drop-out and researching (lifelong). learning and work. In Shirley Walters & Linda Cooper (eds), *Learning/Work: Turning Work and Lifelong Learning Inside Out*, Cape Town: HSRC Press, 88-105.

Letseka, M. & Breier, M. (2008a). Higher education dropout and poverty. In Simeon Maile (ed) *Education and Poverty Reduction Strategies: Issues of Policy Coherence, Colloquium Proceedings*, cape Town: HSRC Press, 83-101

Letseka, M. & Maile, S. (2008b). *High University Drop-out Rates: A Threat to South Africa's Future*, HSRC Policy Brief, Cape Town: HSRC Press.

Lotz-Sisitka, H. (2009). Epistemological access as an open question in education. *Journal of Education*, *46*, 57-79.

Louw, A. D. (1996). The use of confidential reports for the selection of prospective students for the Cape Technikon. *South African Journal of Education*, *16*(4), 194-204.

Louw, A. D. (1993). Keuring van voornemende student. *South African Journal of Higher Education*, *7* (3), 156-161.

Macfarlane, D. (2006). Shock varsity dropout stats. *Mail & Guardian*, September 22–28.

McGivney, V. (2004). Understanding persistence in adult learning. *Open Learning*, *19* (1), 33-46.

Miller, R. (1992). Double, double, toil and trouble: The problem of student selection. *South African Journal of Higher Education*, *6* (1), 98-104.

Moll, I. (2004). Curriculum responsiveness: The anatomy of a concept. In Hanlie Griesel (ed). *Curriculum Responsiveness: Case Studies in Higher Education*, Pretoria: SUAVCA, p–19.

Morrow, W. (1992). Epistemological access in university. *AD News*, *1*, 3-5.

Nunns, C. & Ortlepp, K. (1994). Exploring predictors of academic success in psychology I and WITS University as an important component of fair student selection. *South African Journal of Psychology*, *24* (4), 201-207.

Nyamapfene, K. & Letseka, M. (1995). Problems of learning among first year students in South African Universities. *South African Journal of Higher Education*, *9* (1), 159-167.

Ostman, R. & Wagner, G. (1987). New Zealand management students' perceptions of communication technologies in correspondence education. *Distance Education, 8* (1), 47-63.

Pauw, K., Oosthuizen, M. & van der Westhuizen, C. (2008). Graduate unemployment in the face of skills shortages: a labour market paradox. *South African Journal of Economics, 76* (1), 45-57.

Pityana, B. (2009). Open distance learning in the developing world: trends, progress and challenges, keynote address given at the M-2009 23rd ICDE World Conference on open Learning and Distance Education, Maastricht, The Netherlands, June 7-10.

Pierrakeas, C., Xenos, M., Panagiotakopoulos, C. & Vergidis, D. (2004). A comparative study of dropout rates and causes for two different distance education courses. *International Review of Research in Open and Distance Learning,* 5 (2).

Slonimsky, L. & Shalem, Y. (2006). Pedagogic responsiveness for academic depth. *Journal of Education*, *40*, 35–58.

South African Human Rights Commission (SAHRC). (2006). Report of the Public Hearing on the Right to Basic Education. Johannesburg: South African Human Rights Commission.

Subotzky, G. (2009). Strategic discussion forum, modeling throughput at UNISA: the key to the successful implementation of ODL. Unpublished presentation, Pretoria: UNISA.

Subotzky, G. (2003). Public higher education. In Andre Kraak & Helene Perold (eds). *human Resource Development Review 2003: Education, Employment and Skills in South Africa*, Cape Town: HSRC Press, 353-379.

Taylor, N. (2006). Schools, skills and citizenship. *JET Bulletin*, *15*, 2-3.

Taylor, N., Muller, J. & Vinjevold, P. (2003). *Getting Schools Working: Research and Systematic School Reform in South Africa*. Cape Town: Maskew Miller Longman.

Tresman, S. (2002). Toward a strategy for improved student retention in programs of open, distance education: A case study from the Open University UK. *International Review of Research in Open and Distance Learning, 3* (1), 1-11.

UNISA. (2009). *UNISA Open Distance Learning Policy,* Pretoria: UNISA Press.

Van der Berg, S. (2007). Apartheid's enduring legacy: Inequalities in education. *Journal of African Economies*, *16* (5), 849–880.

Warren, D. (2002). Curriculum design in a context of widening participation in higher education. *Arts & Humanities in Higher Education*, *1* (1), 85-99.

Zaaiman, H. (1998). Selecting students for mathematics and science: the challenge facing higher education in South Africa, unpublished Ph.D. thesis, VrijeUniversiteit, Amsterdam.

In: Open Distance Learning (ODL) in South Africa
Editor: Moeketsi Letseka
ISBN: 978-1-63463-890-6

Chapter 7

THROUGHPUT RATES IN OPEN DISTANCE LEARNING: TOWARDS UNDERSTANDING AND MANAGING THE 'REVOLVING DOOR' SYNDROME

Folake Ruth Aluko[*]
Unit for Distance Education
Faculty of Education, University of Pretoria, South Africa

ABSTRACT

The 'revolving door' syndrome is a term that has been used to describe the low throughput rate in higher education. Even though distance education has been recognized as having the potential to meet the escalating demand for higher education all over the world, the mode is plagued with low throughput rate. This is especially true in South Africa, where almost 50% of newly enrolled students drop out of the higher education system in the first and the second year. In this chapter, the author attempts to provide possible succinct reasons for low throughput rate in distance education in the country; discuss the challenge with calculating throughput rate, and the need to understand the intricacies involved, especially given the historical past and the social context of the country. As well she proffers suggestions on possible ways to stem the tide from the governmental, institutional and student angles. It is hoped that even though scholars have been making attempts to understand the phenomenon and to recommend solutions for it for decades, this chapter would help to move distance education providers closer to answering some of the myriad of questions that confront the phenomenon.

INTRODUCTION

Higher education has been tipped as being a panacea for economic woes of nations because the strength of every nation lies in its educated workforce and populace. Nonetheless, it has been argued that nation leaders are only interested in educating their populace for

[*] Corresponding author: Email: Ruth.Aluko@up.ac.za.

selfish reasons (Dhanarajan, 1997). However, this argument is beyond the scope of this chapter. Given the shrunken economic strength of nations especially in developing countries and the continuous higher demand for university education, nations have turned to distance education as a means of meeting these needs. There is no gain saying the fact that distance education has immensely contributed to access, not only in South Africa, but as well as in other parts of the world. For instance in South Africa, distance education accounts for about 40% of the headcount enrollment (Department of Higher Education and Training [DHET], 2012). According to the Grobler (2013), distance education institutions have also reached the tipping point where demand outstrips capacity due to the exponential growth in the demand for this mode of delivery. However, irrespective of its potential benefits, this mode of delivery is not devoid of its challenges. These include: high dropout rates thereby leading to low throughput rate.

Though the aim of the South African government in its White Paper document in 1997 (Department of Education [DoE], 1997) was to avoid equity of access with high failure and dropout rates leading to a "revolving door" syndrome for students (due to the historical background of the country), yet this trend has persisted. Recent government documents attest to this (DHET, 2012; National Planning Commission [NPC], 2011). It is also a fact that dropout is higher in open and distance higher education institutions than in contact or face-to-face institutions, even in recent times (Kotsiantis, 2009). Nonetheless, In South Africa, as elsewhere, access and success are profoundly linked to the social and political context within which universities operate, and must be understood in historical terms (Lewin & Mawoyo, 2014).

This chapter is divided into six sections. In section one, I made an attempt to define the term 'throughput rate' – an elusive term; section two focuses on the phenomenon in the South African context followed by possible reasons for it in section three. In section four, I dwell on the challenge of calculating throughput rates, not just in South Africa, but with examples from other countries. Section five looks into how the tide of low throughput rates could be stemmed at the governmental, institutional, and student levels. In the final section, I provide some concluding remarks.

What Is a Throughput Rate?

Scott, Yeld and Hendry (2007) define 'Throughput Rate' as "the calculation of how many students in a given cohort completed their degrees and graduated within the stipulated time, how many dropped out, and how many took longer than the stipulated time to graduate". In essence, the question would be 'To what extent has an institution of higher education achieved its goal irrespective of the mode of delivery?' The goal of an education system should always be to graduate as many students in a cohort as possible. This to a large extent determines the success or failure of the education system to meet its goal. It also determines value for money. In order to better understand the term, there might be the need to juxtapose an opposite term – drop-out rates. Higher education institutions and researchers use the latter term differently, and it is sometimes manipulated to reduce dropout statistics (University of Cape Town, 2012; Dreyer 2010).

Though there is no consensus on the definition of the term, scholars (Dreyer 2010; Parker 1999; Peters 1988; Bartels 1982) have used 'Throughput Rate' to refer to all students who have discontinued their studies; non-completers data; nonstarters (students who did not submit any work); dropouts (those who did submit some work but did not gain entry to the examinations); no-shows (those allowed to write examinations but did not do so); and those who failed (i.e. wrote examinations but did not pass). In essence, throughput rate would indicate students who have successfully completed their studies.

THROUGHPUT RATES IN SOUTH AFRICA

In South Africa, the higher education system has been described as a relatively poor performing and highly unequal system, with low participation (Lewin & Mawoyo, 2014). According to the National Plan for Higher Education (DoE, 2001), South Africa's graduation rate of 15% is one of the lowest in the world. For example, this is in comparison to Norway where forty-two per cent of new students who began a tertiary education in the school year 2001/2002 did not complete their degree within 10 years (Norway Statistics, 2014). With regard to South Africa, Letseka and Maile (2008) assert that a system in which about 50% of the students enrolled in higher education dropped out within the first and second year alone raises serious questions about the sector's ability to generate a viable throughput rate. Unfortunately, the situation for distance education is worse. For instance, the throughput rate of the mode in 2007 in the country was 15%. Almost a decade down the line, the situation appears to remain unchanged.

As earlier indicated, throughput and drop-out rates in higher education are closely related to social and political context. Therefore, there are diverse reasons for low throughput rates. In an earlier study, citing various research findings, Yorke (1999) groups reasons for student non-completion of courses as: course factors, institutional factors, study environmental factors, personal blame and motivational factors. These have been substantiated by diverse scholars (Reneland, 2003; Biswas and Mythili, 2004; Yukselturk & Inan 2006; Ngoma, 2006; Dreyer, 2010). Ironically, reasons for non-completion in South Africa are similar to those at open and other distance higher education institutions worldwide (Dreyer, 2010). Some of these are briefly elucidated below.

REASONS FOR LOW THROUGHPUT RATES

In South Africa given the social context of the majority of students involved in distance education, reasons for the trend include: poverty (which is more common, but not limited to the Black community (Letseka & Maile, 2008; Breier, 2008; Lewin & Mawoyo, 2014); a lack of academic 'preparedness' in terms of both social class and the high school curriculum (Scott et al., 2007: 42-3; Mays 2007); and high school fees because universities rely on government subsidy, third-stream income and student fees for their financial viability (DHET, 2010; Aluko 2011; Lewin & Mawoyo, 2014). Others include language barrier in verbal and written communication, a lack of attention to teaching practice by distance education providers or not thinking actively about teaching practice which leads to poor assessment practices, a lack of contact time with lecturers, and the importance of students' own attitudes towards learning (Lewin & Mawoyo, 2014).

As well, South Africa's Council on Higher Education (2010) citing the case studies of three universities in the country gave the notion of "under-preparedness" or students not being academically "strong enough"; issues of students' prior learning and language skills; students' approach to learning, and their attitude and expectations; a diminished learning culture or students taking less responsibility for their learning; and issues of the students' life and other pressures such as personal, social, financial or family matters as student related aspects affecting success.

Of great importance in the country is the notion of "under-preparedness" or students not being academically "strong enough" (CHE, 2010:30) due to the education legacies of the past apartheid system. Though many attempts have been made to address this through for example recognition of prior learning (RPL), the challenge is still persistent. According to Grobler (2013), the diversity in student abilities often means that the resources of institutions are stretched as diverse and individualized support is most often required to ensure student success. This links to the fact that some scholars in the country have laid the blame for low throughput rates at the feet of institutions. For instance in a recent study, Ravhudzulo (2012) concluded that the large number of courses at a distance teaching institution shares the following characteristics:

- content driven
- very little reflection and metacognition
- not always contextually relevant
- do not encourage critical and independent reflection and do not empower the learner to critically reflect on the "what" and the "how" of learning
- do not constitute a learning experience characterized by dialogue, research and application to authentic real-life scenarios
- student engagement is seen as an add on and is not embedded in the design of the learning experience.

In other words, providers of the distance mode of delivery need to critically look into improving the design of their courses. Other challenges facing higher education institutions in the country include the need to retain and continuously improve quality (Grobler, 2013). Though the recently drafted policy on distance education in the country is expected to address these challenges, one cannot but agree with Scott's (2012) view on the Green Paper on Education and Training that the policy has been largely silent on analyzing the main factors constraining success and efficiency in the sector, and hence on what it would take to effectively realize the vision of higher education that the DHET espouses.

In the first two sections, I have attempted to provide the definition of the term 'Throughput Rate' followed by the possible reasons for the phenomenon in section two.

THE CHALLENGE WITH CALCULATING THROUGHPUT RATES

Throughput rates have been described as a measure of evaluating a university's level of efficiency, and regardless of how they are calculated, is a source of contention (Paterson & Gordon, 2010). In the recently published policy on distance education in South Africa (DHET 2013), the department declares its firm intent to use the throughput rates of cohorts of students as a measure of the efficiency and effectiveness of distance education. However, Lewin and Mawoyo (2014) assert that throughput rate is a complex terrain, given that it is popularly misunderstood. Measures of the efficiency of the teaching and learning process from the point of view of access, retention and throughput are problematic and most indicators can be seen only as proxies that might serve as warnings about the existence of problems with this process (Council on Higher Education [CHE], 2010). From the point of view of the monitoring of institutions' efficiency, it is difficult to produce simple measures for throughput (Lewin & Mawoyo, 2014).

Discussion on how best to calculate throughput rates have been going on for decades and are diverse. However, three main methods of calculating throughput rates have been highlighted in this chapter. First is the graduation rate, which is measured as the proportion of the students enrolled (headcount enrollments) for a particular degree in a particular year who graduate in that year (Watson, 2008). Also in the United States of America (USA), the method adopted by the National Centre for Education Statistics (NCES), is to report graduation rates as the percentage of full-time, first-time, degree/certificate seeking freshmen who complete their program within six years of entering an institution. However, this method has been criticized because it does not present a complete or true picture of the state of things. For instance, scholars are of the opinion that part-time students are excluded, while the method misrepresents the experience of transfer students (Brier 2009; Akst, 2007; Scott et al., 2007: 12; Capaldi, Lombardi & Yellen, 2006; Reindl and Russell, 2004). Thus, the method has been criticized for not taking into account fluctuations in enrollment or the different durations of various programs or students, who though they may not finish a program, they still benefit from the skills and insight they will have received from participating in the program (CHE, 2010; Steyn & De Villiers, 2006; University of the Witwatersrand, 2003). In the recently published policy framework on distance education, the South African government has declared its firm intent to discontinue use of the global 'graduation rates' as a proxy for proper analysis of the throughput of cohorts of students (DHET, 2013).

The second method is the success rate, which is determined by calculating Fulltime Equivalent (FTE) passes in a particular category of courses as a proportion of the FTE number of enrolled students for each category of courses (DHET, 2013). However, according to Watson (2008), since this method operates at course level and is not linked to degree registrations or to retention, this indicator does not by itself provide an adequate measure of student throughput. As well, Ramsden and Dodds (1989) have earlier warned that evidence from research into tertiary student learning, indicates that pass rates of students may not necessarily prove the quality of learning of students because inappropriate assessment encourages students to adopt learning strategies aimed narrowly at anticipated examination questions and it is not surprising that students may graduate with fundamental misconceptions of physical and social phenomena.

The third is the cohort studies, which refers to tracing a group of students from first year to graduation, which more often provide an accurate picture of the throughput rate, (Cosser & Letseka, 2009). It could thus be regarded as a longitudinal study of student success (Watson, 2008). As well, one of the benefits of cohort studies is that it allows for comparison with the earlier cohort studies (DHET, 2013). Nonetheless, Watson (2008) has warned that it is useful for throughput purposes to know the number of students who, without having obtained the original degree, have transferred to another degree (as opposed to those who have simply left the system), the number of students who, having successfully graduated from one degree, have proceeded to register for another. It has been suggested that tracing individual student might help in this regard (Paterson & Gordon, 2010).

Nevertheless, this writer is of the opinion that all the methods briefly discussed above only provide quantitative data on throughput rates without necessarily reflecting the intricacies of social conditions and the teaching and learning process (Aluko, 2007; Lewin & Mawoyo, 2014). It has been advised that students' drop-out rates should not be taken out of context, especially in the case of distance education given its peculiar context. One could therefore surmise that stakeholders in higher education institutions should still be on the hunt for the best method.

This section focuses on the challenge with calculating throughput rates, while it highlights three main methods of calculating the phenomenon.

Stemming the Tide of Low Throughput Rates

In view of the growing demand for university education coupled with international evidence that this mode of delivery can, under certain conditions, provide high quality educational opportunity (DHET, 2013); it becomes paramount to keep finding ways to stem the tide of low throughput rate. Thus, this chapter suggests that stemming the tide of low throughput rates should be addressed from three angles: governmental, institutional and student.

Governmental

The recently approved policy on distance education practices in the country is a welcome relief. This is because previously, the standards that applied to conventional practices as in most places have been applied to distance education. Though scholars are of the opinion that there appears to be a growing consensus on using the same basic methodology for both traditional and distance education, nevertheless, there is disagreement on the extent of modification needed (Antony & Gnanam, 2004). Welch and Reed (2005) are of the opinion that such an approach does not sufficiently meet the needs of distance education. There is no gainsaying the fact that having a national policy in place will help to align practices of distance education providers. However, this can only be possible where they (providers) are made accountable to the government. One hopes that the formal commitment made by the government in the policy document to ensure continuous quality improvement, especially in distance education and large enrollment modules and programs would be carried out (DHET, 2013).

Though the importance of the distance mode of delivery has been recognized by the government, an area of concern is funding. Ensuring quality can be expensive. Institutions need to put structures in place to support students, which mostly require funding interventions as well as attention from universities (MacGregor, 2012). As indicated by Grobler (2013), the large number of students enrolling for distance education put strain on the support structures provided by institutions. Related to this is that the funding made available to conventional students is not available to distance education students, who often bear hidden costs of programs. Examples of the ‘hidden’ costs for distance education students are purchase of computers and bandwidth, textbooks not included in study packages, work-time lost to attend practicals, contact-sessions and/or work integrated learning sessions as well as the direct transport and accommodation costs that may be attendant on these (DHET, 2013). This trend has to change especially due to the demographic changes taking place in the student enrollment for distance education. For instance at the University of South Africa (UNISA), younger students now enroll for distance education programs than previously (UNISA, 2012). Letseka et al. (2010) in a study on why university students drop out demonstrate that lack of finance was the most important reason for students leaving higher education prematurely. They conclude that poverty was “the most important issue” to be addressed in remedying student dropout rates. Therefore, scholars have indicated that addressing student poverty and funding needs are essential to improving access, retention and success in university (van der Berg, 2013; Letseka et al., 2010; Chisholm et al., 2009).

Institutional

Management provides the framework for the policies, procedures, practices and leadership of an organization (Mizikaci, 2010). At the institutional level (in a recent paper), the author (Aluko, 2014) provides evidence through a case study that distance education programs can benefit a lot from good management by its providers. The author identified six important areas. First, there is the need for a clear institutional policy on quality assurance because quality is a major concern in distance education, thereby perpetuating negative perception about it. With the promulgated policy on distance education in the country, the institutional policy of the provider should be clearly linked to the national policy. According to Lomas (2004) the two major approaches to quality improvement are quality assurance and quality enhancement. Thune (2005) asserts that quality assurance within higher education institutions include policy and procedures for quality assurance; approval, monitoring and periodic review of programs and awards; assessment of students; quality assurance of teaching staff; learning resources and student support; information systems and public information. Also, writing on this in an earlier report, Perraton and Hulsmann (1998) suggest the following aspects of quality assurance: ‘Policy development and management’, ‘Staff development’, ‘Service provision’, and the ‘Process of distance education’. As well, it is important to involve all stakeholders - faculty members and students in assessing the quality of programs. This will also inadvertently help students to be aware of their rights regarding distance education (DHET, 2013).

Second, having a policy in place is not enough. There should be plans for its implementation. Practices guided by policy are essential. It is possible for an institution to have a policy in place, but it may not necessarily adhere to the stipulated practices. Third, of importance is an ongoing monitoring of the distance education students' profiles. According to Pulsipher (2009), university policy-makers need quality data in order to make data-driven decisions regarding program improvement to accomplish their stated mission, among other things. For instance, keeping track of students' technology profile will help management to decide on the most relevant technology to its student context. It will be a fruitless effort to adopt a type of technology that students cannot relate to. Although modern technology has taken over the delivery of distance education programs, most countries in Africa are still trapped in the first-generation mode of delivery.

Fourth is an effective student support structure system. Simpson (2000: 6) has defined student support structures in the broadest terms as 'all activities beyond the production and delivery of course materials that assist in the progress of students in their studies', which can include both academic and non-academic services. The lack of coherent student support systems causes a low throughput rate because of a high dropout rate (Ravhudzulo, 2014), and suggests inefficiency and not enough support at the foundational and entry level (MacGregor, 2012). Unfortunately, most students who enroll for distance education programs from traditional learning backgrounds are ill-equipped to handle the unique demands of studying at a distance (Lowe, 2005). It is paramount that providers develop support structures that are relevant to students' contexts (Aluko & Hendrikz, 2012; Richards, 2005)). Though distance learning institutions often claim that they provide a comprehensive student support system, but students often complain of individual isolation and loneliness (Ravhudzulo, 2014). Ironically, the quality and scope of the support that students are given is a determinant of student's success and the success of the institution (Louw, 2005). In South Africa, due to the historical past of the country, universities clearly need to continue assisting underprepared students, which could involve foundation programs, intensifying tutorial-driven models or increasing the length of degrees (Macgregor, 2012). According to Scott (2003) educational development work in South Africa has produced substantial evidence that the generally poor performance of students from disadvantaged groups is not due to shortage of talent, but has to do with the incapacity of the existing higher education structures and approaches to cater for diverse educational background.

Fifth, is the issue of program design, which Fresen and Hendrikz (2009) indicate should consider the purpose of the program, its structure, the articulation between modules in the program, the learning activities, the support material and the assessment strategy. While the quality of distance education has improved over the last decade, quality issues remain, with examples being found of poor didactic, de-contextualized course materials, irrelevant and out-dated curricula, lack of sequencing or pacing, course materials not arriving on time, inadequate support for learning to maintain motivation and engage with student difficulties, inadequate formative assessment, lack of meaningful feedback, and inadequate practical work or exposure to work integrated learning especially in light of the changing student profile (DHET, 2013). According to Louw (2005), interactive study packages take the distance out of learning. On this, Duval (2005) asserts that quality is not so much a characteristic of a learning object, but rather a characteristic of how that subject is used in a particular context.

In the recently published Green Paper on Post-school Education, the South African government admits that challenge to turn access into success requires substantial upfront investment in curriculum design and materials development, including attention to issues of structure, pacing and meaningful formative assessment, as well as considerable investment in decentralized student support (DHET, 2012). Another area of assistance on this could be in the area of collaboration among universities with similar programs, which has been recommended for managing cost and improving the quality of such materials (Rockwell, Furgason and Marx, 2000; CHE, 2004).

Sixth is research focused on programs. According to Mizikaci (2006), research focused on programs situated within the delivery mode helps providers to obtain detailed information about the program activities and the effectiveness of the program from the viewpoint of various stakeholders. Research in distance education has passed the level of *no significance difference*; providers need to diversify research into aspects that will add quality to their programs. As well, it is important that researchers should move beyond using only the quantitative approach. Therefore, scholars have suggested more use of the mixed-methods approach that provides detailed information about a phenomenon (Dreyer, 2010; Aluko, 2009; Fahy, Spencer and Halinski, 2007; Mizikaci 2006). Such studies must also be grounded in sound theoretical and conceptual frameworks (Saba 2000), which should be used as a guide for action (Magagula, 2002).

Other factors on the institutional level that have been identified include: prompt acknowledgments of students' admission and enrollment, prompt material delivery and easy access to resources, as well as fast responses to queries, fast assignment turnarounds with positive, supportive feedback which are all directly linked to students' throughput rate (SAIDE, 1999). Lending their voice to the discussion, students in a study by Dreyer (2010) have suggested the following among others: better administration; availability of administrative staff/better communication with administrative departments; availability of lecturers/better communication with lecturers; more contact sessions/support; and bursaries/financial support.

On some of the above, unfortunately, many students have low expectations of distance education (for example they do not expect to get feedback on an assignment before they write the next one) and, given the dispersed nature of the student body, they find it difficult to make their demands heard (DHET, 2013). Lastly, the new distance education policy in South Africa requires that institutions establish systems that make provision for student tracking, the identification and support of at-risk learners and the monitoring of throughput cohort analyses differentiated by level, type and classification of educational subject matter (CESM) category (DHET, 2013).

Student

University teachers are of the opinion that the most important student characteristic associated with successful studies, are attitude, motivation, and genuine interest (Berg, 2005). These become necessary because most open and distance student learning occurs independently of the teachers' presence with students focusing primarily on engagement with the material they receive (Evans, 1997). According to Knowles (1975), most of us only know how to be taught; we have not learned how to learn. Therefore, most distance education students are often ill-prepared for studying at a distance because they are often not taught the essential skills of self-directed learning which is so critical for academic success in this mode of delivery (Lowe, 2005). Even though providers need to continually improve on their program design, unless students perform their participatory co-production roles effectively, the desired outcomes of the service provision are unlikely to be realized (Telford & Masson, 2005). The success of any program depends on the students effectively playing their part (Aluko & Hendrikz, 2009).

In this chapter, I have proffered suggestions on possible ways of stemming the tide of low throughput rates at three levels: governmental, institutional and student.

Conclusion

Globally, distance education is often considered to be the solution to the ever-increasing demand for higher education as more students require access for further study (Grobler, 2013). South Africa also faces similar situation. In this chapter, the author has made an attempt to shed more light on understanding the term 'throughput rate' and has provided some suggestions on how to better improve on this phenomenon. It is the author's belief that the former is important to the latter. It is not possible to improve on a situation in the absence of understanding or by ignoring the context in which the problem is situated. Though the newly published policy is a welcome relief yet, it will do no one any world of good if its intentions are not carried out. Related to this is the need for all distance education providers to put in place their policy on this mode of delivery that is closely linked to the national policy, and that is also adhered to. As well, the student populace has to play their part with the help of providers, who sensitize them to their responsibilities and their rights. It is hoped that the plan of the government to raise university enrollments from a current 900,000 to 1.5 million by 2030, in order to achieve a participation rate of 23%, in higher education (DHET, 2012), will not become a mirage due to the revolving door syndrome

References

Akst, G. (2007). Postsecondary Attendance and Success Patterns: An Interview with Clifford Adelman. *Journal of Developmental Education*, *31*(2), 14-16.

Aluko, F. R. (2014). From evaluation to reflection-on-action: Lessons learnt from the impact of a distance education program. *South African Journal of Higher Education, 28*(5), 1497-1512.

Aluko, F. R. (2011). Inclusion and exclusion in higher education: Paradoxes in distance education. *Progressio*, *33*(2), 122-136.

Aluko. F. R. (2009). The impact of an Advanced Certificate in Education (ACE) program on the professional practice of graduates. *International Review of Research in Open and Distance Learning*, *10*(4), 1-24. Available from: http://www.irrodl.org/index.php/irrodl/article/view/617/1315

Aluko, F. R. (2007). A comparative study of distance education programs assessed in terms of access, delivery and output at the University of Pretoria, unpublished doctoral thesis, University of Pretoria, Pretoria.

Aluko, F. R. & Hendrikz, J. (2012). Supporting distance education students: The pilot study of a tutorial model and its impact on students' performance. *Progressio*, *34*(2), 68-83.

Antony, S. & Gnanam, A. (2004). Quality assurance in distance education: The challenges to be addressed. *Higher Education*, *47*, 143-160.

Berg, C. A. R. (2005). Factors related to observed attitude change toward learning Chemistry among university students. *Chemistry Education Research & Practice*, *6*(1), 1-18.

Breier, M. (2008). *The RPL Conundrum: Recognition of prior learning in a teacher upgrading program*. Pretoria: HSRC Press.

Capaldi, E. D., Lombardi, J. V. & Yellen, V. (2006). Graduation Rates: A Simple Method That Works. *Change: The Magazine of Higher Learning*, *38*(4), 44-50.

Cosser, M, & Letseka, M, (2010) Introduction. In Letseka, M, Cosser, M, Breier, M and Visser, M, *Student Retention and Graduate Destination: Higher Education and Labor Market Access and Success*, (1-9). Cape Town: HSRC Press.

Council on Higher Education. (2010). *Higher Education Monitor 9: Access and Throughput in South African Higher Education: Three case studies*. Pretoria: Department of Education.

Council on Higher Education. (2004). *Enhancing the contribution of distance higher education in South Africa*, Pretoria: Council on Higher Education.

Department of Education (DoE). (2001). *National plan for higher education*, Pretoria: Department of Education.

Department of Education (DoE). (1997). *White Paper 3: Programs for higher education transformation*, Pretoria: Department of Education.

Department of Higher Education and Training (DHET). (2014). *Policy for the Provision of Distance Education in South African Universities*, Pretoria: Department of Higher Education and Training.

Department of Higher Education and Training (DHET). (2013). *Statistics on Post-School Education and Training in South Africa: 2011*. Pretoria: Department of Higher Education and Training.

Department of Higher Education and Training (DHET). (2012). *Green Paper for Post-school Education and Training*. Pretoria: Department of Higher Education and Training.

Dhanarajan, G. (1997). *Convergence of distance and conventional education: international perspectives*. Available from: http://www.col.org/speeches/cambridge97.html

Dreyer, J. M. (2010). Dropout in distance higher education in South Africa: A case study. *Progressio*, 32(2), 199-221.

Duval, E. (2005). *LearnRank: the real quality measure for learning materials.*: http://insight.eun.org/ww/en/pub/insight/thematic_dossiers/articles/quality_criteria/equali

Evans, T. (1997) *Understanding Learners in Open and Distance Education*, London: Kogan Page.

Fahy, P. J., Spencer, B. & Halinski, T. (2007). The self-reported impact of graduate program completion on the careers and plans of graduates. *Quarterly Review of Distance Education*, *9*(1), 51-71.

Fresen, J. W. & J. Hendrikz. (2009) Designing to promote access, quality and student support in an advanced certificate program for rural teachers in South Africa. *International Review of Research in Open and Distance Learning,* 10(4). http://www.irrodl.org/ index.php/irrodl/issue/view/37

Grobler, G. (2013) UNISA on the challenges facing higher education. 2013. The Association of Commonwealth Universities. 12 December. https://beyond2015.acu.ac.uk/submissions/view?id=50

Jones, B., Coetzee, G., Bailey, T. & Wickham, S. (2008). *Factors that Facilitate Success for Disadvantaged Higher Education Students: An Investigation into Approaches Used by REAP, NSFAS and Selected Higher Education Institutions*. Cape Town: Rural Education Access Program.

Knowles, M. (1975). *Self-directed Learning,* New York: Association Press.

Letseka, M. & Maile, S. (2008). *High University Drop-out rates: A Threat to South Africa's Future*, HSRC Policy Brief, Pretoria: HSRC.

Lewin, T. & Mawoyo, M. (2014). *Student access and success: Issues and interventions in South African Universities*. Cape Town: Inyathelo – The South African Institute for Advancement.

Lomas, L. (2004). Embedding quality: the challenges for higher education. *Quality Assurance in Education*, *12*(4), 57-165.

Louw, W. (2005). Taking the distance out of distance education through the means of mLearning. Paper presented at the 4th World Conference on mLearning, Cape Town, South Africa.

Lowe, S. D. (2005) Responding to learner needs in distance education: Providing academic and relational support (PARS). In *Making distance education work: Understanding learning and learners at a distance*, ed. S. J. Levin, 73-87. Okemos, MI: Learners Association.net.

MacGregor, K. (2012). Plan for 1.5 million students by 2030. University World News, 15 January 2012, Issue 88. http://www.universityworldnews.com/article.php?story=20120115093819516

Magagula, C. (2002). *Evaluation report of the course for distance education policy-makers in Southern Africa*. Vancouver: Commonwealth of Learning. http://dspace.col.org/handle/123456789/120

Mizikaci, F.(2006). A systems approach to program evaluation model in quality in higher education. *Quality in Education*, *14*(1), 37-53.

National Planning Commission (NPC). (2011). *National Development Plan 2030: Our Future - Make It Work*, Pretoria: National Population Commission.

Norway Statistics. (2014). Throughput of students in tertiary education (2012/2013. http://www.ssb.no/en/utdanning/statistikker/hugjen/aar/2014-06-26

Paterson, N. & Gordon, G. (2010). How one university examined graduation rates of its undergraduate student population. Available from: http://www.mona.uwi.edu/opair/managementreports/campusindicators/paperongradrates.pdf

Pulsipher, S. (2009). *Preparing quality teachers: Tracking a cohort of students from pre-admission to graduation*. http://education.byu.edu/cites/documents/Student%20ProfileSusan%20Pulsipher.pdf

Ramsden, P. & Dodds, A. (1989). *Improving Teaching and Courses: A Guide to Evaluation*, 2nd Edition, Parkville: Centre for the Study of Higher Education.

Ravhudzulo, A. (2014). Enhancing teaching and learning in Open Distance Learning: A mechanism to facilitate student success. *International Journal of Education Science*, *6*(1), 27-32.

Ravhudzulo, N. A. (2012). Keeping and getting students engaged in creating a successful learning environment at UNISA. *Journal of Emerging Trends in Educational Research and Policy Studies* (JETERAPS), *3*(5), 753-761.

Reindl, T. & Russell, A. (2004). Graduation Rates as a Measure of Institutional Performance: Why Now? Why Not? What Needs to be Done? *Policy Matters*, *1* (6), 1-4.

Richards, H. (2005). Education Guardian.co.uk@ Guardian Newspapers Limited.

Rockwell, K., Furgason, J. & Marx, D. (2000). *Research and evaluation needs for distance education: a Delphi study*. Available from: http://www.westga.edu/~distance/ojdla/ fall33/rockwell33.html

Saba, F. (2000). Research in distance education: A status report. *The International Review of Research in Open and Distance Learning*, *12*(6), 1-9.

Scott, I., Yeld, N. & Hendry, J. (2007). *Higher Education Monitor 6: A Case for Improving Teaching and Learning in South African Higher Education*, Pretoria: Council on Higher Education.

Simpson, O. (2000). *Supporting Students in Open and Distance Learning*, London: Kogan Page.

South African Institute for Distance Education (1999). *Initial overview of distance and open learning in Zambia*. http://www.saide.org.za/worldbank/countries/zambia/zamoverview. htm

Steyn, G. & de Villiers, P. (2006). *The impact of changing funding sources on higher education institutions in South Africa*. Pretoria: Council on Higher Education.

Steyn, M. & Van Zyl, M. (2001). *Like that statue at the Jammie stairs - some of the students perceptions and experiences of institutional culture at the University of Cape Town in 1999*. . Cape Town: The Institute of Multicultural and Diversity Studies in Southern Africa, Department of Sociology, University of Cape Town.

Telford, R. & Masson, R. (2005). The congruence of quality values in higher education. *Quality Assurance in Education*, *13*(2), 107-19.

Thune, C. (2005). *Standards and Guidelines for Quality Assurance in the European Higher Education Area*, Helsinki: European Association for Quality Assurance in Higher Education.

University of Cape Town. (2012). ADP position paper: Factors that affect throughput, Cape Town: University of Cape Town.

University of South Africa (UNISA). (2012). *An Institutional Profile of UNISA: UNISA Facts and Figures*, Pretoria: UNISA.

University of the Witwatersrand. (2003). *Success at the University of the Witwatersrand. Report of the working group on retention and throughput, November 2003. Document C2003/412*. Johannesburg: University of the Witwatersrand.

Watson, P. (2008). Measuring postgraduate cohort throughput: A case study. *South African Journal of Higher Education*, *22*(3), 725-739.

Welch, T. & Y. Reed (Eds). (2005). *Designing and delivering distance education: Quality criteria and case studies from South Africa*, Johannesburg: Nadeosa.

Yorke, M. (1999). *Leaving Early: Undergraduate Non-completion in Higher Education*. London: Falmer Press.

In: Open Distance Learning (ODL) in South Africa
Editor: Moeketsi Letseka
ISBN: 978-1-63463-890-6

Chapter 8

CONCEPTIONS OF SUCCESS IN OPEN DISTANCE LEARNING

Victor Pitsoe*[*1] and Gezani Baloyi[2†]
[1]Department of Leadership and Management
College of Education, University of South Africa, South Africa
[2]Adult Basic Education Training and Youth Development
College of Education, University of South Africa, South Africa

ABSTRACT

Despite the fact Open Distance Learning (ODL) continues to be an alternative or complementary mode of learning, in this chapter, we conjure that student support is a fundamental part of the delivery of quality distance education experiences and enhances students' success in a sustainable way. However, this chapter contributes to the debate on student success and academic success in higher education in South Africa, but with a focus on the University of South Africa's (UNISA) ODL. It makes a case for the potential of effective and efficient student success programs/systems to broaden access with success to higher education. For us, supporting students for success in a culturally diverse educational setting remains a complex challenge and calls for a rethinking. While success and the completion of studies are imposed by numerous tenacious factors, we argue that lack of appropriate support for ODL students can result in decreased student success and increased withdrawals. Although we acknowledge that the notion of Student Support Services in ODL has always been broadly perceived and a contested terrain, our take is that effective and efficient student support services should draw from theories that are consistent with the culturally diverse needs of the students. Among others, we contend that challenges of epistemological access, poor bandwidth and under preparedness (of both students and the institution) have great potential of failing the perceived initiatives of student success. We consider UNISA's *paradigm shift* from correspondence to cyberspace a policy imperative; and that it has far reaching implications for the student success. Central to this chapter is the assumption that with the increase of the barrage of cultural situations facing today's ODL practitioners, there is

* E-mail address: Pitsovj@unisa.ac.za.
† E-mail address: baloygp@unisa.ac.za.

a need to develop cultural intelligence, as a soft skill, to promote student success systems. Our thesis is that cultural intelligence has the potential and prospects to offer practitioners promising realistic, practical skills to meet the demands of a diverse student body, and can be considered to be a tool to improve student success. This chapter begins with conceptualization of "student success" and "student support services." Second, we critically reflect on the student success and retention. Third, we look into the designing of student support for success in ODL. Fourthly, we present cultural intelligence as a strategy to promote student success systems in ODL. Lastly, we offer the concluding remarks.

INTRODUCTION AND BACKGROUND

Student success in higher education remains a national priority and is an imperative at several South African universities. However, this chapter contributes to the debate on student success and academic success in higher education in South Africa, but with a focus on the University of South Africa's (UNISA) Open Distance Learning (ODL). It makes a case for the potential of effective and efficient student success programs/systems to broaden access with success to higher education. Globally, ODL continues to be an alternative or complementary mode of learning. Among others, it is believed that ODL can transform higher education, saving money and improving learning outcomes. While there has been a huge growth in ODL, as policy option for a growing number of African states, the question '*Why do we need success in ODL?*' becomes critical. For us, supporting students for success remains a complex challenge to some students.

Notwithstanding the provision for better access, flexibility, and convenience in ODL, student support is critical in the promotion of student success and retention in ODL. Success and the completion of studies are necessitated by numerous tenacious factors. Our central argument is that lack of appropriate support for ODL students can result in decreased student success and increases withdrawals. It is noteworthy to indicate that the notion of Student Support Services, as a closed and an open system, in Open Distance Learning (ODL) has always been a contested terrain – it is an elusive concept and is broadly perceived. As Potter (1998:60) observes, the term 'student support services' is used in a variety of ways. For some authors, particularly in the distance education world, it has been limited to describing the learning resources needed by students to complete course requirements. While we acknowledge that many factors contribute to student success, we argue that effective and efficient student support services should draw from theories that are consistent with the culturally diverse needs of the students.

Notwithstanding the grey area that defines UNISA's ODL, student support is an integral part of the delivery of quality distance education experiences and enhances students' success in a sustainable way. LaPadula (2010:127) notes that a successful online program allows its students to have the same opportunities and services as students in traditional classes. Additionally, distance students need to access services in the same way they access instruction: from a distance and at times that fit their schedules. Despite the fact that UNISA's ODL is attracting and serving a large numbers of students from a wide range of backgrounds, experiences and expectations, challenges of epistemological access, poor bandwidth and under preparedness (of both students and the institution) have great potential of failing the perceived initiatives of student success.

While we fully acknowledge the politics and hegemony of globalization with reference to ODL, for us, UNISA's *paradigm shift* from correspondence to cyberspace is a policy imperative and it has far reaching implications in terms of access, cost, quality of teaching and learning, and more specifically, student success. With this in mind, the purpose of this chapter is to gain a better understanding of the pedagogical issues concerning student success and student support services through a critical review of the relevant literature. With the increase of the barrage of cultural situations facing today's ODL practitioners; there is a need to develop cultural intelligence, as a soft skill, to promote student success systems.

Conceptualising Student Success and Student Support Services

The importance of learner support in ODL is crucial and many scholars reviewed above argue that it has a role to play in increasing the success rate of the students. The relative low pass rate and dropout is a cause for concern for distance students. Although there are best practices globally at UNISA learner support strategies and multiple challenges face the students and lecturers regarding learner support. UNISA uses technology to reach out to its students who are in urban and rural areas. However, problems face students and lecturers in using technology for teaching and learning. The learner support structures at UNISA depend on Information Communication Technology (ICT), group discussion classes using video conferencing (satellite broadcasting), mobile libraries in some selected provinces that being piloted now, etc.

It has been noted that one of the critical components in ODL is learner support. Learner support has frequently been identified as particularly important for student success in ODL. According to Simpson (2002), Tait (2000) and Thorpe (2002), learner support is a broad term referring to the services provided to distance learners so that they can overcome barriers to learning and complete their studies successfully. Learner support is defined in different ways in the distance and online learning literature (Brindley, Walti & Zawacki-Richter 2004). It might cover learning materials, teaching and tutoring and non-academic elements, administrative aspects, guidance and counselling.

In this chapter, learner support refers to all kinds of services including face to face teaching during group discussions or e-tutoring, etc. Most UNISA modules are tutor linked, and currently e-tutoring has come in to picture. These support systems and structures are increasing student success at UNISA. Dzakiria (2005:95) and Kelly and Mills (2007:149) add that "learner support has frequently been identified by open learning institutions as being of particular importance for student success in ODL". All these scholars are of the view that learner support is learner-centred and crucial for learner success in ODL.

The ODL model entails a student-centred approach that is based on integrated systems and engaged learning. The technologies, such as telephone, multimedia CDs and DVDs, video and audio conferencing, SMSs, cell phones, e-mail and discussion forums via myUNISA, mobile library etc., have been proposed to offer new possibilities for supporting learning at UNISA. UNISA has regional centres throughout the provinces to support students. However, most students are still in rural areas and they have to travel to cities and towns in order to access learner support services.

According to Rumble (2000), "distance education institutions have been instrumental in developing support services that will assist their students to perform." For Rumble, "the focus on providing student support services was driven by the need to address the high drop-out rates that were associated with correspondence education". With this in mind, the distance between the students and the institution is still a worrying factor. The effects of such isolation on distance learners can inhibit any possibility for engagement with teachers, study material and peers (Simpson 2002).

Moore (2012:167) ideally believed all students should receive some sort of orientation when they enter a program. This too will reduce the need for individual counselling later. It is particularly important to inform people of the time demands that accompany distance learning and to encourage them to think about how they will fit this in with their interests and obligations. According to Anderson (2008), "understanding of students is a prerequisite for knowledge, their learning environment, and their cultural attributes are starting points in the development of the student-centred support services." Therefore for students to succeed, it is important to understand their profile.

Reflections on Student Success and Retention

Student success and retention has a rich account in South Africa which has been well documented elsewhere (See for example Akoojee & Nkomo 2007; Scott et al. 2007; CHE, 2010; Letseka & Maile, 2008; Moleke, 2005). These scholars provide a more detailed account of student success via cohort studies, which track the number of students in a cohort who graduate. However, it is pertinent to declare that knowledge on economic divide in higher education students, lower socioeconomic status (SES) and lower-social-class environments is imperative to understanding student success problems today. Student success in ODL is both a very complex phenomenon and global challenge. Perhaps, it noteworthy to mention that there are voluminous contributing factors to explicate why some ODL programs fail. Nevertheless, there is symbiotic and multiplicative relationship between student success and retention. Even though widening access is increasingly associated with retention and success in higher education, some scholars (Rovai & Downey 2010; Grodsky & Jones 2007; Bound & Turner 2007; Howell, Kurlaender, Grodsky 2009; Young-Jones et al. 2013; Tinto 1975, 2007) argue that "when an increase in enrollment creates a crowding of students competing for scarce college resources, rates of degree completion tend to decline". Taking it further, Rovai and Downey (2010: 144) observe that "when enrollment growth declines, retention of current students becomes more critical and demands greater effort and investment."

Notwithstanding the challenges of 'under preparedness' and 'epistemological access' in ODL, student success and retention remain a policy imperative, particularly in developing and underdeveloped countries, Rovai and Downey (2010) write that "although the growth of online learning in higher education is well documented, a number of studies provide evidence that course-completion and program-retention rates are generally lower in distance education courses than in face-to-face courses". They further mention that "a major reason is that distance education programs attract a higher percentage of nontraditional students". On the one hand, a growing body of research suggests that "students who feel alienated by the institution, its faculty and staff, and other students are likely to leave the institution"

(Fontaine, 2014:111). On the other hand, Karp (2011) notes that "while it is likely that academic interventions need to be reformed to increase their efficacy, another possible explanation for these low success rates is that students have other needs that are not being met.

Experts (Baard et al. 2010; Steenkamp et al. 2009) in the field of students' success agree unanimously and capture the following as factors influencing students' success: (1) part-time work by students; (2) gender and motivation, whether it is a residential or distance learning institution, whether students are repeating the module, compared to first-time enrolments, prior exposure to the subject; and (3) language proficiency, study habits and reading ability. They further argue that "some of the factors could contribute to students' success in the modules while influencing other factors in predicting success" (Steenkamp et al. 2009). For instance, Baard et al.'s (2010) research showed that "a student who was not successful in the module included students who did not pass the exam, or who did not obtain entry into the exam, and students who discontinued the module during the year."

While there have been several replications, these experts left out some aspects of intelligence that people in other cultures would be likely to include. Much of the literature on student success deals with higher education institutions serving disadvantaged populations. Plenty of accounts or explanations given on student success studies revolve around social class, lower and higher SES. As Nisbett (2009:78) puts it, "social class is a consequence of intelligence". For him, "the poor are poor because they are not intelligent, and neither money, nor class, nor parenting practices play much of a role in making some people more intelligent than others – class is mostly a matter of genes." While lower socioeconomic status (SES) and lower-social-class environments are considered to be a major pivot in students' success, our take is that cultural intelligence (CQ) counts in the discourses of student success. Hence, there is a symbiotic relationship between cultural intelligence and student success.

Nevertheless, it is significant to indicate that ODL has received a lot of attention for many years. Notwithstanding the pockets of excellence and success stories, like other ODL institutions, UNISA is not immune to student success and retention challenges. Despite the hundreds of millions of Rands spent on innovative educational programs, ICT infrastructure and human resource development, student success and retention remain a policy imperative. Among others, it is facing a multiplicity of factors which influence culturally diverse students' success and retention. While culture can also confer advantages for the development of intelligence and academic achievement, among others, we conjure that social class, societal and cultural differences could be an account for a big impact on students' success, intelligence and academic achievement. Nisbett (2009:3) observes that "people of lower socioeconomic status have lower average IQs and achievement for reasons that are partly environmental—and some of the environmental factors are cultural in nature". For him, "most of the environmental factors relate to historical disadvantages but some have to do with social practices that can be changed."

An important aspect of ODL best practices, as way of promoting student success, is to develop students' ability to direct their own learning, encourage practices that keep students on track and develop the ability to identify study groups among students. However, information technology has created new opportunities for ODL; and reducing classroom and facilities cost, training cost, travel cost, printed materials cost, labour cost, and information overload, and more specifically, students' success remains a challenge and policy imperative.

As Tinto (1975) aptly puts it "student success is shaped by a complex, multi-layered, and dynamic set of events".

Akojee and Nkomo (2012) accept that "while there was considerable disagreement in the summit regarding the exact reasons for the student success, notably a combination of 'student preparedness' and 'educational resources', they emphasise the prevalence of a "de-contextualized curriculum that appeared socially removed from the realities facing the students to which it is directed." They further argue that "the need for a comprehensive institutional strategy designed to respond effectively to these considerations can no longer be avoided".

In the case of UNISA, Subotzky and Prinsloo (2011:177) contend that "the challenges and imperatives to enhance student success in higher education in South Africa are particularly formidable". They further lament that "despite substantial government funding incentives, numerous policy initiatives and well-intentioned institutional efforts, retention and success rates are notoriously poor".

The conclusion to be drawn is that ODL has fundamentally changed since the last two decades. To that end, the ever changing and increasing diversified student populations in UNISA's ODL intensifies the need for practitioners to take note of factors that may influence student success. Be that as it may, Tinto (1975, 2007) points out that "students are more likely to thrive, persist, and complete degrees in environments that provide clear and consistent information about institutional expectations and requirements". In line with this, we conclude that in order for students to be successful online learners, they must be self-directed, identify with their groups, and possess the skills that facilitate team goals, processes and tasks. Hence, For UNISA to improve student success and retention, among others, it should develop students' ability to direct their own learning, facilitate practices that keep students on track, increase students' ability to identify with their groups, enable student groups to achieve goals, and create opportunities for faculty to share best practices (Hubbard, 2013).

Designing of Student Support for Success in ODL

UNISA is an ODL institution that functions within an environment in which students are living at various geographical areas. The students enrolled at the university come from varied socio-economic backgrounds and also rural and urban areas. They come from the culturally diverse backgrounds and they are mainly scattered in the remote rural areas of the provinces of South Africa and other developing and underdeveloped countries. The institution assumes that when students enter higher education, they must have completed their general education. As McInnis 2001) puts it, "there is also an assumption that students come from backgrounds that equip them with the skills they need to adjust comfortably to the university environment". Qakisa-Makoe (2005:45) reveals that most of UNISA's African students come from homes where they are first-generation learners in higher education. Furthermore, they come from schools that are poorly resourced and are not adequately prepared for higher education. Yet when these students enter higher education, they are expected to learn complex new material independently and to adjust to new ways of learning in a distance learning environment. Therefore, designing of the support material that speak directly to the students is crucial in ODL.

It is important to have a learner profile in ODL. Therefore one will be able to design learner support systems for them. The designing of study material should be in line with the ODL policy (Robinson 2008:10). The students who register with UNISA have understanding of what ICT and other computer facilities can do to support them. In the words of Ringstaff and Kelly (2002) the students are aware of the impact technology has as a tool for achieving instructional goals (Ringstaff & Kelley 2002). South African distance education students are likely to own cellphone with internet features so they are in a better position to be supported using computer facilitites. In the UNISA environment, email is probably the most popular communication application of the internet. It is fast and conveys messages and files within a very short time. While there is an increased interest in the integration of technology in learning and teaching, very little remains known about how the use of ICTs is changing students' approaches to learning (Rumble 2000).

This is an issue which needs to be explored especially as most institutions are going online. Perraton (2000:11) notes that "technology has spurred the development of ODL in the global communities". Students can learn from computers, where technology is used essentially as a tutor and this serves to increase students' basic skills and knowledge. They can also learn by means of computers, where technology is used as a tool that can be applied to a variety of goals in the learning process and can serve as a resource to help develop higher-order thinking, creativity and research skills (Ringstaff & Kelley 2002). UNISA as an ODL institution use email, telephone, face to face sessions, radio, television, audio and videocassettes, compact discs, emails and other computer conventions and tele-conferencing systems.

Gulati (2008:1) believes learning using technologies has become a global phenomenon. The feedback that we are currently getting from students in incorporating technology to teaching and learning is quite positive. Learner support is developed for students to communicate with the university. The learner support in ODL is designed to enhance communication between the students and the university. The function of student support entails providing the students with as much assistance as possible in order to enable them to overcome difficulties that are often encountered by distance education students. Student support in ODL takes on different forms including the following, group discussion, contact session, learning management systems, mobile library etc. It should be noted that there is difference between group discussion and tutorial classes, and distance students tend to confuse group discussion and tutorial classes. The group discussion classes are defined as classes where lecturers meet students in the regional offices and teach them. Tutorial classes are classes where tutors who are appointed by the university or department guide and support students with their assignments etc.

The students also tend to combine direct teaching, facilitation and group discussion together. These also show that group discussions are effective because a large number of students actually attending it. Most students use the libraries in the regional centers to get resources and also as a place to study. Generally the distance students regard the library as quite places to study. In their home communities they do not have places to study. There are many different types of technologies that an institution can utilise in order to facilitate the delivery of teaching and learning. UNISA has an excellent Learning Management System (LMS) in place called myUNISA. It is an online tool that is available to all registered students who have an access to the internet.

When using technology, facilities like *myUNISA*, it makes it possible for the students to learn anytime, anywhere, and make learners have access to learning resources. The lecturers are able to interact with students at all times. There are also interactive responses between the students and the lecturers. It is asynchronous learning management system for students. Asynchronous delivery offer advantages and disadvantages. The white board sometimes is also used to support students who are scattered in the rural communities. In white board, which is synchronous the institution is able to connect most regions and reach out the students.

It is significant to mention that student support has positive implications on student success. In the context of South Africa, the majority of students do not have an access to the internet and they still rely on the print based materials. Although UNISA wants to go online and use the eLearning route, the majority of the students in rural areas will be left out in teaching and learning programme. However, UNISA is applauded for coming up with initiatives like mobile library to the rural provinces. Currently, pilot is being done to two provinces, namely, Limpopo and Eastern Cape. South African government is also encouraging the integration of ICT to the curriculum in the schooling system. These initiatives are putting the institution of higher learning in a better position to implement the ODL policies in their institutions.

In summary, *myUNISA,* as a learner support system bridges the distance between the institution and the students. It offers online courses and the students are able to participate in these learning meaningfully. The *myUNISA* enables the students to share their learning activities through this blogs and discussion forums. Hence, *myUNISA* makes students to feel less isolated. In spite to the challenges of access, *myUNISA* has a great potential of offering excellent learner support system easily.

Cultural Intelligence (CQ) as a Strategy to Promote Student Success Systems in ODL

In every industry, from manufacturing to higher education, working professionals are increasingly interacting with people from culturally diverse groups. However, culture as both an outcome and a product of our social interaction, continues to shape how people behave and learn, more specifically in ODL context. As Peterson (2008) writes, "we are culturally groomed to think and behave in certain ways from the time we are babies". Be it in the manufacturing or higher education sectors, cultural differences will always matter. Our take is that modern culture's demands on people require a more complex consciousness than ever before. We attest that ODL practitioners with high CQ are able to adapt to new global environments as well as effectively interact with students of diverse cultures.

Just like computers, students are culturally programmed and need *cultural operating systems* that fit their context. According to Peterson (2008:84), "in an increasingly accessible world, cultures play a bigger, not a smaller role in business". For him, cultural intelligence becomes more important, not less important. Hence, cultural intelligence, as a soft skill, fits to be used as a conceptual tool to promote student success systems in ODL. At the pedagogical level, cultural intelligence is consistent with Paulo Freire's emancipatory model which seeks to empower people to question their lives and position in society, leading to a struggle that is at the heart of praxis.

It is beyond the scope of this chapter to provide a detailed description of cultural intelligence (CQ). However, interested readers are referred to Livermore (2006, 2008, 2009, 2011), Li and Mobley (2010), Peterson (2008), MacNab (2012) and Ng et al. (2009). The concept cultural intelligence has a very rich history and was first formally introduced by Earley and Ang in 2003 in their book *Cultural Intelligence: Individual Interactions Across Cultures. Later,* in 2008, Ang and Van Dyne published the *Handbook of Cultural Intelligence: Theory, Measurement, and Applications,* which encompasses 24 conceptual and empirical contributions from intellectuals from different cultural and disciplinary backgrounds. Of late, in 2009 and 2011 respectively, Livermore wrote *Leading With Cultural Intelligence: The New Secret to Success,* and *The Cultural Intelligence Difference: Master the One Skill You Can't Do Without in Today's Global Economy*. These polemics focus on practical ways to increase CQ capabilities. Nonetheless, Gelfand, Imai, and Fehr (2008:376) see it as a "new kid on the scientific block".

Given the inclusiveness of the term cultural intelligence, it becomes apparent that differences and similarities among definitions could refer to any number of things. However, there is agreement among advocates of cultural intelligence that it is the ability to engage in a set of behaviors that uses skills (i.e., language or interpersonal skills) and qualities (e.g., tolerance for ambiguity, flexibility) that are tuned appropriately to the culture-based values and attitudes of the people with whom one interacts (Livermore 2006, 2008, 2009, 2011; Li & Mobley 2010; Peterson 2008; MacNab, 2012; Ng et al 2009; Prado 2006; Rockstuhl et al. 2009, 2010; Rockstuhl & NG 2008; Shokef & Erez 2008). Cultural intelligence, among others, involves aspects of knowledge (facts about places, economies, history, etc.), it involves awareness (knowing about yourself and others), and it involves skills (knowing how to do something (Livermore 2006, 2008, 2009, 2011; Peterson 2008).

The challenges of working with students from different cultures are well documented in ODL research. Although these challenges were largely constrained within the problems and constraints to enhance student success in higher education, few, if any, explored cultural intelligence as an alternative tool to encourage student success. At a deeper level cultural intelligence pose profound challenges with respect to ways of assessing and assuring the quality of ODL teaching and learning, more specifically student success. Like intellectual intelligence (IQ) and emotional intelligence (EM), cultural intelligence (CQ) is critical in developing efficient and effective student success systems in culturally diverse settings. Perhaps, it is noteworthy to indicate that CQ picks up where EM leaves off. For us, CQ guides the ODL practitioners how to work effectively with students who come from culturally diverse orientations. In this section we argue that student success system, as a multilayered construct, in culturally diverse ODL be guided and informed by cultural intelligence (CQ) framework.

As observed by Livermore (2009:36), "becoming culturally intelligent doesn't imply turning our backs on our own cultural backgrounds and preferences. He sees cultural intelligence as "a transformative model of cross-cultural behaviour and leadership rather than a model built primarily on behaviour modification strategies". Hence, CQ is uniquely suited for the barrage of cultural situations facing today's the ODL practitioners. It is pertinent to mention that cultural intelligence is a four-dimensional framework rooted in many years of research on intelligence and cross-cultural interaction. All four dimensions are essential in order to gain the benefits of CQ. The four dimensions are CQ drive, CQ knowledge, CQ strategy, and CQ action, usually referenced in the research as motivational CQ, cognitive CQ, metacognitive CQ, and behavioral CQ (see Figure 8.1).

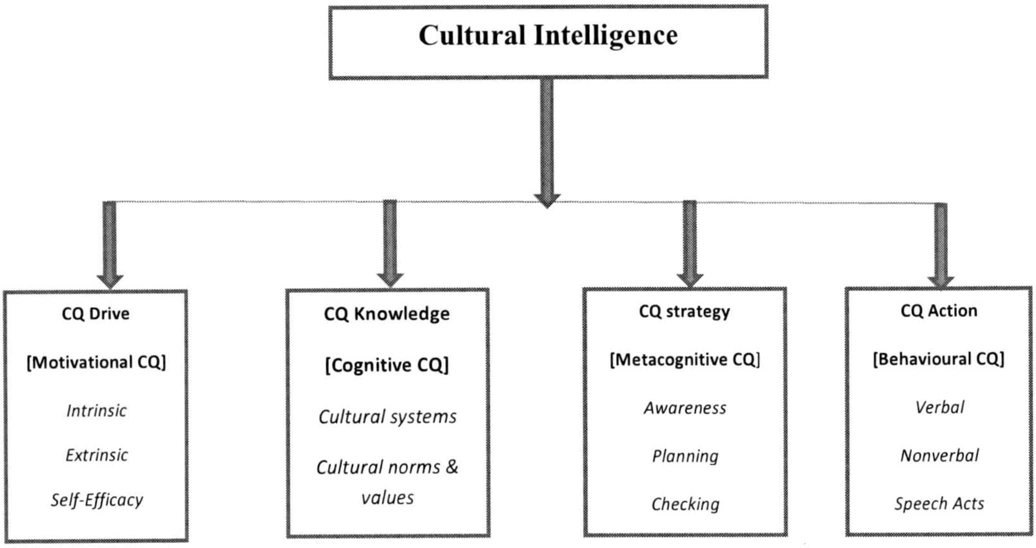

Figure 8.1 The Four Dimensional Model of Cultural Intelligence.
Adapted from Livermore (2009: 25)

Livermore (2009:37) contends that "just as leaders can grow in their social, emotional, and technical competence, they can grow in their ability to effectively lead across various ethnic and organizational cultures. For him, "as leaders move through the four-step cycle of cultural intelligence — CQ drive, CQ knowledge, CQ strategy, and CQ action — they gain a repertoire of perspectives, skills, and behaviors for use as they move in and out of the fast-paced world of globalization (p. 37)". With this in mind, there is a multiplicity of ways to apply the four dimensions of cultural intelligence to student success systems in culturally diverse ODL. As Livermore (2009.29) writes, "the four dimensions of cultural intelligence can be used as four areas to assess individuals you're considering for a cross-cultural assignment.

CQ Drive

Motivation in student success systems is essential. Livermore (2009: 41) observes that "leaders with high CQ drive are motivated to learn and adapt to new and diverse cultural settings. He maintains that "their confidence in their adaptive abilities is likely to influence the way they perform in multicultural situations".

CQ Knowledge

The capacity to understand and work with culturally diverse ODL setting does not just come intuitively. It requires a well-organized effort to develop the competency of cultural understanding, or CQ knowledge (cultural systems, norms, and values). While culture shapes the way we live and make sense of the world, ODL practitioners' knowledge on the understanding cross-cultural issues and differences plays a key role in student success. As Livermore (2009: 63) aptly puts it, "leaders high in CQ knowledge have a rich, well-organized understanding of culture and how it affects the way people think and behave. They possess a repertoire of knowledge in knowing how cultures are alike and different. They understand how culture shapes behavior". Hence, CQ knowledge provides a kind of understanding and perspective for the cultures with which ODL practitioners interact as instructional leaders.

CQ Strategy

Strategizing and making sense of culturally diverse experiences is central to student success systems. CQ strategy practitioners go beyond the surface and dive into the subtle but powerful issues that often make or break their leadership. For Livermore (2009: 113), "leaders with high CQ strategy develop ways to use cultural understanding to develop a plan for new cross-cultural situations". He further argues that "these leaders are better able to monitor, analyze, and adjust their behaviors in different cultural settings; and that are conscious of what they need to know about an unfamiliar culture". He suggests that, "CQ strategy is the key link between our cultural understanding and behaving in ways that result in effective leadership (p. 115).

While there are three important sub-dimensions to CQ strategy (namely, *awareness, planning,* and *checking*), CQ strategy guides the practitioners to plan their learning activities across-cultural interactions; and enables them to check if their assumptions and plans were appropriate. For this reason, culturally intelligent ODL practitioners understand that the themes they talk about, particularly in ODL space, are embedded in cultural values and conventions that can simply be understood with CQ strategy that looks beneath the superficial.

CQ Action

There is a causal relationship between CQ action and effective student success systems. While practitioners communicate with individuals across different cultural contexts, the ability to communicate effectively in a cultural diverse ODL context is a prime example of how CQ action becomes into being. CQ action, primarily the outcome of our drive, knowledge, and strategy, enhances efficient and effective student success systems. Livermore (2009: 133) claims that "leaders with high CQ action can draw on the other three dimensions of CQ to translate their enhanced motivation, understanding, and planning into action. They possess a broad repertoire of behaviors, which they can use depending on the context. It is noteworthy to indicate that CQ action enables the ODL practitioners to adapt their communication, negotiate differently, and know when to flex and when not to flex.

To end this section, today's ODL practitioners need cultural intelligence – it allows the possibilities for learning, personal growth, and relationships. CQ offers practitioners a promising realistic, practical skill set to meet the demands of leadership in today's fast-paced ODL world. More specifically, CQ is the most important theory relevant to measure of cross-cultural competence and encourages student success. Among others, CQ focuses on developing an overall repertoire of understanding, skills, and behaviors for making sense of the barrage of cultures we encounter daily; CQ emphasizes learned capabilities more than personality traits, and CQ is more than just knowledge (Livermore 2011). For this reason, CQ has become a critical component of everybody's résumé.

CONCLUSION

Higher education system still reflects the legacy of apartheid when it comes to student success. While there is an undeniable need to rethink UNISA's ODL student success systems, the recent concern of shocking statistics of attrition and high dropout rates, particularly of African students as compared to other sectors of the population remains both a policy challenge and political necessity. It is contended that a more comprehensive response is required to ensure that dropout rates are addressed effectively. This chapter makes the claim that today's ODL practitioners need to acquire cultural intelligence, as a soft skill, to allow the possibilities for learning, personal growth, and relationships. Cultural intelligence has the potential and prospects to offer practitioners promising realistic, practical skills to meet the demands of a diverse student body, and can be considered to be a tool to improve student success.

REFERENCES

Akoojee, S. & Nkomo, M. (2007) Access and quality in South African higher education: the twin challenges of transformation. *South African Journal of Higher Education,* 21 (3), 385-399

Baard, S., Steenkamp, L.P, Frick, B. L. & Kidd, M. (2010) Factors influencing success in first-year accounting at a South African university: The profile of a successful first-year Accounting student. *South African Journal of Accounting Research* 24(1), 129-147.

Bound, J., & Turner, S. E. (2007) Cohort crowding: How resources affect college attainment. *Journal of Public Economics*, 91, 877–899.

CHE (Council on Higher Education) (2010) Access and throughput in South African Higher Education - Three case studies. *Higher Education Monitor* No. 9, Pretoria: Council on Higher Education.

Fontaine, M. (2014) Student Relationship Management (SRM) in Higher Education: Addressing the Expectations of an Ever Evolving Demographic and Its Impact on Retention. *Journal of Education and Human Development*, 3(2), 105-119.

Gelfand, M. J., Imai, L. & Fehr, R. (2008) Thinking intelligently about cultural intelligence: The road ahead. In S. Ang & L. Van Dyne (Eds.), *Handbook of Cultural Intelligence: Theory, Measurement, and Applications*, New York: M. E. Sharpe, pp. 375-387.

Grodsky, E. S. & Jones, M. T. (2007) Real and imagined barriers to college entry: Perceptions of cost. *Social Science Research*, 36, 745–766.

Gulati S. (2008) Technology – Enhanced Learning in Developing Nations: A review. International Review of Research in Open and Distance Learning, 9 (1), 1-16.

Howell, J., Kurlaender, M. & Grodsky, E. (2009) *Postsecondary Preparation and Remediation: Examining the Effect of the Early Assessment Program at California State University*. Working paper, Sacramento: California State University.

Hubbard, R.S. (2013) How to Improve Student Success and Retention in Online Education Programs, *E-Learn*, 784-793.

Karp, M.M. (2011) Toward a New Understanding of Non-Academic Student Support: Four Mechanisms Encouraging Positive Student Outcomes in the Community College. CCRC Working Paper No. 28, Community Research College Center: New York.

Letseka, M. & Maile, S. (2008) *High University Drop-out Rates: A Threat to South Africa's Future*, Policy Brief, Pretoria: HSRC Press.

Li, M. & Mobley, W.H. (2010) The role of experiential learning in the development of cultural intelligence, paper presented at the annual meeting of the Academy of Management, Montreal, Canada.

Livermore, D. (2006) *Serving with Eyes Wide Open: Doing Short-term Missions with Cultural Intelligence,* Grand Rapids, MI: Baker Books.

Livermore, D. (2008) Cultural intelligence and short-term missions: The phenomenon of the fifteen-year-old missionary. In S. Ang & L. Van Dyne (Eds.), *Handbook of Cultural Intelligence: Theory, Measurement, and Applications*, New York, NY: M. E. Sharpe, pp. 271-285.

Livermore, D. (2009) *Leading with Cultural Intelligence: The New Secret to Success*. New York: Amacom.

Livermore, D. (2009) *Leading with Cultural Intelligence: The New Secret* to *Success*, New York: Amacom.

Livermore, D. (2011) *The Cultural Intelligence Difference: Master the One Skill you can't do Without in Today's Global Economy*. New York: Amacom.

MacNab, B. R. (2012) An experiential approach to cultural intelligence education. *Journal of Management Education*, 36 (1), 66-95.

McInnis, C. (2001). Researching the first year experience: Where to from here? Higher Education Research & Development 20 (2): 105-114.

Moleke, P. (2005) Inequalities in Higher Education and the Structure of the Labour Market. Cape Town: HSRC Press.

Ng, K.Y., Van Dyne, L. & Ang, S. (2009) From experience to experiential learning: Cultural intelligence as a learning capability for global leader development. *Academy of Management Learning and Education,* 8 (4), 511-526.

Nisbett, R.E. (2009) Intelligence and how to get it: Why Schools and Cultures Count. New York: W. W. Norton & Company.

Perraton, H. (2000) Open and Distance Learning in the Developing World. New York: Routledge.

Peterson, B. (2008) *Cultural Intelligence: A Guide to Working People from Other Cultures.* London: Intercultural Press, Inc.

Prado, W.H. (2006) The relationship between cultural intelligence and perceived environmental uncertainty, unpublished doctoral dissertation, University of Phoenix, Arizona.

Qakisa-Makoe, M. (2005) Reaching out: Supporting black learners in distance education. Progressio, 27 (1 & 2), 44-61.

Ringstaff, C. & Kelley, L. (2002) The Learning Return On Our Educational Technology Investment: A Review of Findings from Research. San Francisco: WestEd RTEC

Rockstuhl, T. & Ng, K.Y. (2008) The effects of cultural intelligence on interpersonal trust in multicultural teams. In S. Ang & L. Van Dyne (Eds.), *Handbook of Cultural Intelligence: Theory, Measurement, and Applications*, New York: M. E. Sharpe, pp. 206-220.

Rockstuhl, T., Hong, Y.Y., Ng, K.Y., Ang, S., & Chiu, C.Y. (2010) The culturally intelligent brain: From detecting to bridging cultural differences. *Neuro-Leadership Institute,* 3, 22-36.

Rovai, P.R. & Downey, J.R. (2010) Why some distance education programs fail while others succeed in a global environment. *Internet and Higher Education*, 13: 141–147.

Rumble, G. (2000) Student Support in Distance Education in the 21st Century: Learning from Service Management. Distance Education, 21(2), 216-235.

Scott, I., Yeld, N.& Hendry, J. (2007) Higher Education Monitor No. 6: A case for improving teaching and learning in South African higher education. The Council on Higher Education, Pretoria.

Shokef, E. & Erez, M. (2008) Cultural intelligence and global identity in multicultural teams. In S. Ang & L. Van Dyne (Eds.), *Handbook of Cultural Intelligence: Theory, Measurement, and Applications*, New York, NY: M. E. Sharpe, pp. 177-191.

Steenkamp, L. P., Baard, R. S. & Frick, B. L. (2009) Factors influencing success in first-year accounting at a South African university: A comparison between lecturers' assumptions and students' perceptions. *South African Journal of Accounting Research*, 23(1), 113-140.

Subotzky, G. & Prinsloo, P. (2011) Turning the tide: a socio-critical model and framework for improving student success in open distance learning at the University of South Africa. *Distance Education*, 32(2), 177-193.

Tinto, V. (1975) "Dropout from higher education: a theoretical synthesis of recent research", *Review of Educational Research*, 45: 89-125.

Tinto, V. (2007), "Research and practice of student retention: what next?". *Journal of College Student Retention: Research, Theory, and Practice*, 8: 1-19.

Young-Jones, AD., Burt, T.D., Dixon, S & Hawthorne, M.J. (2013) Academic advising: does it really impact student success? *Quality Assurance in Education*, 21(1), 7 – 19.

In: Open Distance Learning (ODL) in South Africa
Editor: Moeketsi Letseka
ISBN: 978-1-63463-890-6

Chapter 9

STUDENT SUPPORT FOR OPEN DISTANCE LEARNING (ODL)[*]

Shakila Dhunpath[†1] ***and Rubby Dhunpath***[‡2]
[1] Tuition and Facilitation of Learning
University of South Africa (UNISA), South Africa
[2]University Teaching and Learning Office (UTLO)
University of KwaZulu-Natal (UKZN), South Africa

ABSTRACT

UNISA's Academic Literacies provisioning over the past 9 years has served a disembodied interventionist role in student support, despite the dire need for substantive support, given the Institution's poor track record of student success. The absence of a clear vision to embed student support in the mainstream curriculum is likely to relegate academic development practitioners to sub-contractors, further marginalizing a vital support function which can be characterized as erratic and incoherent since the existing staff providing this function are on short-term contracts. The chapter argues that not only is this practice pedagogically unsound, but it contradicts UNISA's declared aspiration to be among this country's top universities, focusing more intently on the quality of teaching and learning (Senate Report, 2010:2). It argues that the need for academic development (AD), particularly for Open and Distance Learning (ODL) institutions is now direr than ever before and is central to the university's intention to improve its unsustainable throughput rates. By revisiting some of the theories supporting the need for explicit academic literacies support, the chapter contends that rather than devalue its status, the academic development provisioning at UNISA should be significantly up-scaled and institutionalized for optimal impact.

Keywords: Academic literacies, academic development. Epistemological access, pedagogic distance

---

[*] This chapter is an adapted version of an article which appears in the International Journal of Research in Social Sciences, Nov 2013, Vol. 13 No.3

[†] dhunpsb@unisa.ac.za.
[‡] Dhunpath@ukzn.ac.za.

INTRODUCTION

In his address to Senate on 26 August 2006, the Principal of UNISA said, [We face] "even more dire challenges to our aspiration to become 'the African university in the service of humanity.' Our throughput rates are simply disgraceful" (P1). He cited the following drop-out statistics: BSc 80%-90%; BA (Social Science) 85% - 96%; BCom 77%- 87%, noting that "this, by any measure, is a shocking indictment on this university" (p.5). He lamented that UNISA was "in danger of ruining whatever academic reputation this university has ever had" (p5). UNISA is therefore complicit in perpetuating the untenable situation where well under 5% of black youth are succeeding in any form of higher education. Seven years since this executive assessment, UNISA's throughput rate remains intractably low and unsustainable. This chapter argues that any prospect of improving this dismal record of student success is likely to be substantially diminished if students continue to be left to their own devices in ameliorating their own under-preparedness, especially in the context of structural inequities that characterize higher education in South Africa. We begin by situating the problem in its historical context; attempt to highlight our understanding of the underlying reasons for the crisis and examine some of the literature in the field wherein potential solutions may be located.

ODL FOR EQUITY AND ACCESS

Given the glaring inequalities in South African society, the high price tag of higher education in campus- based universities, coupled with exclusive admission criteria of most mainstream universities, UNISA has a critical role to play in providing access through its ODL programs, to those students who would otherwise be excluded from accessing higher education opportunities by conditions beyond their control. However, as articulated by Vincent Tinto (2008), access without support is not opportunity. In the absence of substantive student support, the country will continue to perpetuate access without success.

One of the key contributors to poor retention and graduation rates at UNISA is that the systems and resources supporting ODL teaching and learning are premised on the assumption that the university serves the needs of mature adult working students who have the capacity to take responsibility for their own learning; are capable of learning alone or in small groups; can learn at their own pace and in their own time; can learn from a variety of learning materials, are active rather than passive learners; need less frequent help from their teachers and learn from people other than their teachers, (see Letseka & Pitsoe, 2012).

The reality is that the university has long outgrown this idealized caricature, and the demographics of its student population in 2013 are quite different from what they were barely a decade ago. Today, UNISA is attracting young school leavers who cannot secure admission into full-time, campus-based, contact tertiary institutions. The new generation of UNISA students who are typically not in full-time employment spend most of their time in university learning centers studying for their respective courses and modules or participating in class discussions. Given these changing realities, Letseka & Pitsoe, (2012) question whether UNISA understands this new clientele of students correctly and whether it is theoretically defensible to continue to regard this new generation as ODL students, in the purist sense.

They note that part of meeting the demands of this new clientele of students, UNISA runs a series of Tutorials, Academic Literacies workshops and Peer Collaborative Learning sessions that can be described as quasi contact interactions (ibid). This means that the taken-for-granted ODL nature of the university poses a major conceptual challenge. While the initial focus of ODL was on distance constraints and approaches that bridge geographical barriers through organizational strategies such as mass production and delivery of learning packages, the changing landscape requires fundamental re-theorization of the ODL model currently on offer.

ODL and Pedagogic Distance

The South African Council on Higher Education (CHE) commissioned study on "Access and Throughput in South African Higher Education: Three Case Studies (2010) advances 3 explanatory factors for unsatisfactory access and throughput. The case studies "examined everyday academic practices and relationships, institutional rules and languages and taken-for-granted assumptions about hegemonic cultural constructs (e.g. 'race') as fluid and tentative descriptors of an institutional culture"(p.169). The findings generated from the cases may be summarized as follows:

Student-related factors: which include the notion of "underpreparedness' or students not being academically 'strong enough'; issues of students' prior learning and language skills; students' approach to learning, and their attitude and expectations; a diminished learning culture or students taking less responsibility for their learning; and issues of the students' life and other pressures such as personal, social, financial or family matters" (p30).

Staff-related factors: which include "outdated or simply different approaches to pedagogy; the attitudes of academic staff; the skills of academic staff in teaching and assessment practices (also referred to as staff 'underpreparedness'); pressures on the time and energy of academic staff, and staff being demotivated by changes in the university" (p30).

Systemic factors: which include the "inherent difficulty of some course content; increasing student numbers; resource constraints; too little support for students making the transition from school; a lack of coordination and systematic assessment of various 'solutions' that have been attempted, and a lack of recognition for teaching and academic development work that discourages academic staff from putting energy into their teaching duties" (p.31). The CHE case study engages with the theory of "pedagogic distance" which explains the "gap between teaching expectations and learning achievements as a function of separateness or disconnectedness" (p.98). It is argued that the distance is not confined to geographic or physical space, but evinces at least five dimensions: "emotional, political, pedagogical, linguistic and physical", each of which is further explicated in the CHE paper. If pedagogic distance is a crucial feature of higher education in general, then it should be self-evident that the problem facing ODL institutions is, to say the least, profoundly complex requiring creative institutional responses.

It is true that UNISA has seen an unprecedented increase in enrolments, exceeding its targets by more than 13% to 308, 768 headcounts in 2010, and to 387, 656 in 2013 (DISA website) raising a crucial question that the university leadership must answer: In its attempt to provide physical (administrative) access to higher education, which the university should be commended for, is the university providing concomitant epistemological access? (Lotz-Sisitka, 2009; Boughey, 2005; Morrow, 1992). The graduation and throughput statistics indicates that the university is in fact failing to provide epistemological access, especially to black learners who continue to bear the bruises of dysfunctional schooling. Therefore, logically, more rather than less, needs to be done to mitigate the deficits of its burgeoning student population. In this context, it is difficult to comprehend why student support, and in particular support for Academic Literacies development, is being considered a fiscal burden and relegated to an optional, marginal support function rather than a core function of the curriculum

Academic Development Mitigates the Effects of Dysfunctional Schooling

Academic development has a long history in this country and virtually all institutions invest heavily in mediating the effects of the articulation gap between secondary and higher education, particularly deficits in academic skills and literacies which accelerate dropout. The National Plan for Higher Education makes the point that the, "…role of academic development in improving the efficiency of the higher education system in terms of graduate output is critical" (DoE, 2001: 31). Universities now recognize Academic Development as a resource for institutional efficiency in relation to teaching and learning (See Boughey, 2012). Acknowledging the centrality of this function in improving retention and throughput rates, academic literacies practitioners, who previously held marginal positions, have been absorbed into the mainstream because of their demonstrated role in facilitating epistemological access. An examination of the attendance statistics at academic literacies workshops reveals that these services should be up-scaled rather than downgraded.

The challenges facing UNISA's capacity to deliver adequate support to its increasing young student population is compounded by the allegations of grade inflation and score-fixing by critics skeptical of the unprecedented increase in overall performance of the Grade 12 national examinations. If these allegations are credible, it suggests that cohorts of matriculants will be further disadvantaged as their nominal scores belie their de-facto capabilities, compounding the continuing lack of equity of outcomes. The skewing in who is benefiting from higher education – along racial and social class lines - is contrary to social justice for individuals and communities, and may well lead to social protest and declining public support for higher education (see Scott, 2012). In the absence of substantive systemic support, the current situation will not serve the interests of students who are gaining administrative access to higher education but are being set up for failure. Invariably, those most likely to fail are black learners who already bear the burden of inadequate schooling.

Academic Literacies and Epistemological Access

Without exception, the literature on access to higher education is replete with research findings which point to the inescapable role of academic literacies in providing access to academic discourses which in turn promote or inhibit access. Using the frame of epistemological access, Mgqwashu (2012:208) identifies the multiple skill levels students require in reading academic texts, which include accessing textual details, making inferences and drawing conclusions from texts they read. Mgqwashu adds that in the context of higher education, "the expectation goes beyond just these abilities, but includes students' ability to take a different position derived from values and attitudes related to what counts as knowledge, and how it can be known within various disciplinary discourses". The problem is considerably more acute for quantitative literacy as is evidenced in the dismal student performance in Mathematics, Science and Technology. Entrusting the development of these crucial skills to sub- contractors is another form of Band-Aid which will fail to heal the much deeper systemic maladies. For instance, Jacobs (2009) has consistently argued that the debates around the synergies between language and content in higher education need to be raised beyond understandings of language as a generic set of skills to be integrated across disciplines in higher education, or language as an instrument of communication; to understandings of language as Discourse and how language embodies and structures the conventions and philosophies of disciplines to provide epistemological access to students.

A critical function of academic literacies practitioners involves inducting students into the social practices, and the values and attitudes which underpin them, which characterize the university. For this to happen, those working within academic development environments must themselves master those social practices. This means that AD workers must be fully-fledged members of the academy who understand the ways knowledge is constructed through reading, writing and speaking (McKenna, 2012). Mainstream academics at ODL institutions have neither the means nor the opportunities to fulfil this lofty expectation, but AD practitioners do; and should be valued for their mastery of both generic and trans-disciplinary and discipline specific skills. The inextricable link between access, equity, redress and quality has long been a key imperative of Higher Education transformation in South Africa, requiring a synergy of creative strategies to ensure that the reconciliation of access (or equity) and quality is a matter of purposive policy, and is something that has been achieved when countries take policy courses where debate and experimentation result in improvements in both access and quality. (Crouch and Vinjevold, 2006; Akojee and Nkomo, 2012). That the imbalance between access and quality still exists, despite the obvious reasons for their interdependence is a function policy inertia, demonstrated clearly in the South African context, where unsatisfactory throughput and often considerable attrition and dropout rates has been addressed by the add-another-program syndrome, with little substantive impact. There is little pedagogic merit in conceiving academic development as another add-on luxury that the university funds at its discretion. Universities have a moral responsibility to provide the conditions for student retention and success. If students fail, it should not be because the university has failed to support them to succeed.

There can be little doubt that the call for a pragmatic, responsive approach to academic literacies is an appropriate and prudent response to what is now widely regarded as a literacy crisis facing the country. The need for a differentiated approach to literacies resonates with the work of Cummins' (1992) theoretical model in which he distinguishes between BICS (Basic Interpersonal Skills) and CALP (Cognitive Academic Language Proficiency) which we will explore briefly below. Whether or not we should focus "sequentially on reading and then writing" as discreet activities, are open to debate. However, we will explore some of the literature that might serve to support this claim or contradict it. The call for pragmatism also underscores the need to reassess the raison d'être of academic literacies at tertiary institutions which, traditionally, have a been grounded in an autonomous view of literacy, resulting in a curriculum that is often generic, sometimes disembodied from disciplinary knowledge and usually de-contextualized from students' actual needs. We now provide a brief philosophical and theoretical justification for the approach we propose in re-conceptualizing academic literacies at UNISA. Needless to say, the problems we have inherited are multiple and complex and there are no silver-bullet solutions.

To add to this historical cauldron, we need to consider the impact of language teaching methods, in particular, the complete swing in the language teaching pendulum from the teaching of grammatical structures often with little or no link to communicative competence (characteristic of the period up to the nineteen eighties), to the constructivist period where the teaching of grammatical structure was frowned upon as archaic. The new buzzwords of the eighties were: fluency rather than accuracy. This unfortunate dichotomy which was essentially an oversimplification (obfuscation?) of the tenets of Communicative Language Teaching (CLT) provided refuge for teachers who were themselves untrained and unprepared to teach effectively in a second language. This was followed by the era of Outcomes Based Education (OBE) which further entrenched the laissez faire approach to language teaching and learning. We now turn our attention briefly to explore the link between home language proficiency, cognitive development and additional language acquisition.

HOME LANGUAGE PROFICIENCY, COGNITIVE DEVELOPMENT AND SECOND LANGUAGE ACQUISITION

Over the years, research has provided a substantial body of empirical evidence which suggests a causal link between language acquisition and cognitive development. Lemmer, (2001) synthesizes Cummins as follows: Learners who have instruction from the beginning in a language they can understand are able to develop concepts and learn to read and write and calculate. When they enter an English-medium school, they are then able to transfer those abilities to the new situation. Second-language learners with no schooling in the first language may have difficulty with English instruction as they have missed out on important background knowledge, which the other group has received. Furthermore, learners who do not have a developed proficiency in first-language and whose first-language maintenance is not supported tend to lose proficiency in the former as they acquire an additional language. Moreover, their culture may be undermined. This is known as subtractive bilingualism. Conversely learners who are fluent in the first language and whose first language is respected and its maintenance supported acquire a second language while retaining home language and culture. This view is endorsed (by inference) by proponents of "Language Transfer"; the Nativists conception of "Universal Grammar"; and Noam Chomsky's theory of the Language Acquisition Device (LAD). Similarly, Eric Lenneberg (1964) advanced the Critical Period Hypothesis in which he suggests (somewhat controversially) that the critical period for language development and cognition ends at the onset of puberty. The theory has often been extended to a critical period for additional language acquisition, although this is much less widely accepted. What we do know is that older learners of a second language rarely achieve the native-like fluency that younger learners display, despite often progressing faster than children in the initial stages. If one hazards to extend the theory to adult learners, what we are witnessing in students is the accumulated deficits of inadequate exposure to and lack of proficiency in the home language as well as their second language. These are the deficits which language facilitators are required to remedy in a few contact sessions.

However, to paint the student body as monolithic and therefore requiring equal treatment (remedy) is the issue that invites more critical exploration. Lemmer (2001) reminds us that when language minority learners enter an English classroom, they bring with them a wealth of cognitive, social and linguistic skills which have been developed in their first language. However, lecturers are often under the impression that, if this prior knowledge is not stored in English, it does not exist at all. Frequently they perceive these learners as having no language and of suffering from impoverished thinking skills. This is simply not true. It is in fact the exclusive and exclusionary language policies of HE institutions (de-facto and de-jure) that cultivate deficits by promoting monolingual environments and not creating conditions for multilingual engagement. A nuanced understanding of this sociolinguistic complexity cannot be acquired from disembodied on-line textual interactions.

THE CHALLENGE FOR ACADEMIC LITERACIES

Let us turn our attention back to the challenge for academic literacies and the call for a differentiated approach. We draw attention to Jim Cummins' 4 quadrants of proficiency[1] represented in the graphic below:

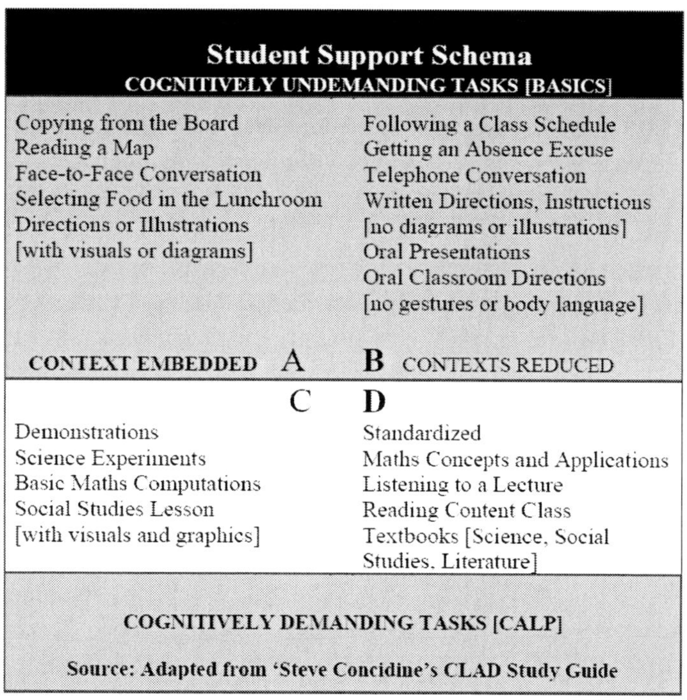

Figure 1. Cummins' Four quadrants.

[1] See also: Dhunpath, R & Joseph, M (2014) Multilingualism: Can Policy Learn From Practice? Nordic Journal of African Studies, 23(1): 1–15 (2014)

The 4 quadrants are based on two axes: the horizontal axis represents the C line: context embedded language and context-free language. This cline reflects linguistic complexity, the context-embedded being easiest for learners as it is linguistically less complex (use of everyday language, supported by gestures, interactions, visuals, syntactically elliptical language, lexis drawn from the colloquial). On the other end – context-free language is the opposite as it represents language that is academic, with specialist terminology, full blown syntax, discourse that is coherent and cohesive, messages that are explicit and appropriate to the genre, monological.

The vertical cline represents cognition, that is to say: the cognitive effort learners are required to make and their cognitive competence in doing so. The top end of the vertical axis, namely the context undemanding end, as it suggests, makes low level thinking demands on learners. An example is phatic conversation or small talk, ritualistic forms of talk like greetings, and a lot of everyday conversation. The lower end, i.e. cognitively demanding, is the effort to process knowledge through reasoning. It is not about language as such, but cognition.

Cummins' separation of linguistic and cognitive complexity, we believe, represents an advance over his earlier BICS (Basic Interpersonal Skills) and CALP (Cognitive Academic Language Proficiency) emphasizing that intervention should ultimately aim at achieving higher order thinking skills but that these facilitative pedagogies or 'scaffolding' in quadrant B, are central in providing the means for learners to achieve quadrant D – which requires demonstration of academic literacy and advanced reasoning to be manifest in writing of essays, and exams etc.

The 4 quadrants model allows us to assess students proficiency levels, quadrant D being the highest and the goal of education, quadrant A being the language proficiency of their first language that they acquire naturally in their homes and bring to schools as a resource. The 4 quadrants can also be used to examine classroom discourse: the language varieties used in interactions, the tasks / materials used and what linguistic and cognitive demands they make on the students, in other words: what kinds and levels of language proficiency are being developed in learners.

The 4 quadrants enable us to see language varieties in terms of use or function. They enable us to see the difference between the use of a non- standard variety used for lower order thinking – like conversation, and the same non-standard variety used for thinking/reasoning processes. They allow us to see whether for instance the African language is being used for reasoning processes but in context-embedded situations associated with oracy, and whether English is being used for cognitive and academic literacy purposes that fall into quadrant D. This has profound implications for facilitators' attitudes to code switching and the value of code switching as a cognitive crutch for Additionally English L2 learners whose proficiency is limited to Quadrant B.

Reading and Writing: Sequential or Generative?

What then are the implications for the two streams of intervention: the Critical (foundational) and the more advanced writing conventions (cognitively demanding); and what are the implications for teaching and writing? There is a multitude of reading strategies most of which focus on ways of optimizing comprehension. These include prediction, inferential reading, annotation of the text, use of mind maps, the noting of key concepts, the use of sociograms and a host of others. We will not delve into them here, except to say that it is mandatory for reading to be taught as an active skill - even to competent additional Language users. The reason for our dogmatic position here is based on the premise that in many South African classrooms, reading was, and continues to be a passive process. The teacher reads a given text from cover to end (including the publishers' details and endnote citations). The student is required to listen while the teacher attempts to excavate the gospel from the Holy Grail with no prospect of alternative or contending meanings. The assumption behind this approach is that meaning resides in the text and the text alone.

This disembodied approach to reading has dire implications for multicultural societies where indigenous knowledges and socio-cultural influences mediate learning and learning outcomes. For instance, not admitting the role of the "spiritual" in mediating learners' understandings of scientific concepts or the role of "Ubuntu" in mediating their understanding of economic concepts is to negate the prospect that these essentially western constructions of knowledge are sometimes in conflict with learners' intuitive knowledges. What does this mean for the selection of reading strategies and our approach to materials design? Central to any selection is the acknowledgement that all human beings possess categorical rules or scripts that they use to interpret the world. New information is processed according to how it fits into these rules, called schema. Schema Theory popularized by Carrell, Eisterhold, Driscoll and others remind us that information that does not fit into our schema may not be comprehended correctly, or may not be comprehended at all. The most important implication of schema theory is the role of prior knowledge in processing new content. Facilitators therefore need to be judicious in their choice of materials, texts, artefacts and other technologies of learning. They need to be acutely mindful of selecting materials that do not alienate students and undermine the schemata that form the building blocks of new knowledges.

We now briefly ponder the question of whether reading and writing should be conceived as two parallel sequential streams. In the early 1990s British sociologist Basil Bernstein saw reading as basic to the progression through the sequence. He suggested that "It is crucial to read early in order to acquire the written code, for beyond the book is the text book, which is the crucial pedagogic medium and social relation" (Bernstein, 1990:53). This links to Bernstein's notions of access to the Elaborated Code which enable learners to move beyond their Restricted Code essential for academic success. This implies that in the early stages, students must be exposed to a variety of exemplary models to enrich their schema. This resonates with Stephen Krashen's Monitor Hypothesis (Krashen, 1981) in which he proposes the provision of "Maximum Comprehensible Input" to remove affective filters that impede language acquisition. Bernstein's early work which revolved around issues of deficit and difference earned him the label of a structuralist.

However, there is now consensus that reading and writing are dialectical processes which are deeply contextual and interdependent. We subscribe to Bernstein's view that students need exposure to exemplary models of writing on which they can model their own writing. However, these cannot be discreet or mutually exclusive activities. Writing is an iterative process that must be complemented and enriched by reading. We are therefore inclined towards the Genre Approach (GA) in which explicit teaching of the structural and linguistic conventions of different genres give a clear sense of audience, purpose and the way in which they are staged as well as the language patterns used to achieve that purpose effectively. GA uses methodology where the facilitator begins with several exemplar texts to demonstrate how the writer has organized the text and used language to achieve the purpose of the text. This is followed by active engagement with the text through a range of authentic activities in an attempt to activate students' schemas and arouse the awareness that writers are not gifted or infallible.

The next stage involves the facilitator jointly constructing a text with the learners in the genre they are dealing with. This is accompanied by explicit guidelines on structure and negotiated criteria on what makes for effective writing. The facilitator supports students through their drafting stages by providing feedback based on the criteria. The iterative dialogical processes identified above require substantive contact time with students in combinations of whole-class interactive sessions with small-class personalized support to embed these cognitively demanding skills.

CONCLUSION

The facilitation skills required to mediate the challenges above cannot be achieved by periodic ad-hoc on-line consultations. Neither can they be achieved by staff without deep socio and psycholinguistic teaching and learning skills. Relegating academic development practitioners to the level of casualized labor provided by independent contractors undermines the value of academic development work and is counter- intuitive to virtually all contemporary research which affirms the centrality of such work to successful access and success in higher education. While UNISA, the largest university on the continent does indeed facilitate administrative access not least by affordable fees, and its recognition of prior learning (RPL) policy, it continues to face challenges of articulation, the challenges of student support, and the challenge of throughput rate. Collectively these cast a shadow over its accomplishment and unless the challenge of throughput is fixed, "talk of access with success will only be like a fleeting illusion that is pursued, but never attained" (Letseka & Pitsoe, 2012). The issue of poor schooling remains our biggest hurdle, but increasingly, academics are becoming aware of the futility of focusing on this (Scott et al, 2007, Scott 2009). The ethics of calling exclusively on the problem of poor schooling to justify low student throughput and retention in higher education is being brought into question, and Scott cautions us against "a deterministic throwing up of our hands and pointing of fingers at the school system. It seems unlikely that there will be substantial change in the school sector in the short term" (Scott et al 2007). We are therefore morally obliged to refrain from using the on-going problems in that sector as an excuse for retaining the flawed *status quo* in higher education. Instead, we need to take responsibility for the factors within the control of the higher education sector which can contribute to improved students success. Academic literacy is part of that solution, not the problem. Scott urges us to acknowledge "that valuable knowledge and experience have been gained through the development of alternative approaches to access, curriculum design and teaching, but, to serve the majority of students and the wider interests of the country, what has been alternative now needs to become mainstream" (Scott:2012).

REFERENCES

Alexander, N (2004) Language Planning and Policy in South Africa, Occasional Paper, PRAESA, UCT.

Akojee, S., & Nkomo, M (2012) Access, Equity and Quality in Higher Education: Academic Versus Institutional Development in Dhunpath, R., & Vithal, R, *Access to Higher Education: Underprepared Students or Underprepared Institutions*, Pearson Publishers, Cape Town.

Bernstein, B. (1971) Education cannot compensate for society. In B. R. Cosin, I.R. Dale, G. M. Esland & D. F. (Eds.) *School and Society: A Sociological Reader*, Open University Press: London.

Boughey, C. (2012) The Significance of Structure, Culture And Agency In Supporting And Developing Student Learning At South African Universities in Dhunpath, R & Vithal, R, *Access to Higher Education: Underprepared Students or Underprepared Institutions*, Pearson Publishers, Cape Town.

Boughey, C. (2005) Epistemological access to the university: an alternative perspective, *South African Journal of Higher Education,* 19 (3), 638-650

Council on Higher Education (2010) *Who Participates in Higher Education*, CHE: Pretoria.

Council on Higher Education (2009) *The State of Higher Education in South Africa*, Higher Education Monitor No.8. CHE: Pretoria.

Cummins, J.,(1985) Language Planning in multilingual settings, in Ed. Bickley, V. Language in Education in a Bilingual or Multilingual setting.

Dhunpath, R & Joseph, M (2014) Multilingualism: Can Policy Learn from Practice? Nordic Journal of African Studies, 23(1): 1–15 (2014)Dhunpath, R & Dhunpath, S (2013) The Centrality of Learner Support for Enhanced Student Progression in Open & Distance Learning, International Journal of Research In Social Sciences, Vol. 3, No.3

Gee, J, P. (1990) *Social Linguistics and Literacies: Ideology in Discourses*, Falmer Press: Hampshire.

Jacobs, C (2009) Plenary paper presented at the 3rd Annual Teaching & Learning Conference, University of KwaZulu-Natal, South Africa, 21-23 September, 2009.

Krashen, S. D. (1981) *Principles and Practice in Second Language Acquisition*. Prentice-Hall International: London.

Lenneberg, E. H.(1967).*Biological Foundations of Language.* Wiley: New York.

Lemmer, E. M. (2002) Fostering language development in multicultural schools in South Africa, *Educare: Journal of the Faculty of Education*, 31(1-2), 38-60.

Letseka, M., & Pitsoe, V, (2012) Access to Higher Education Through Open Distance Learning (ODL): Reflections On The University Of South Africa (UNISA) in Dhunpath, R & Vithal, R, *Access to Higher Education: Underprepared Students or Underprepared Institutions*, Pearson: Cape Town.

Lotz-Sisitka, H. (2009) Epistemological access as an open question in education, *Journal of Education,* 46:57-79.

McKenna, S (2012) The Context Of Access And Foundation Provisioning In South Africa in Dhunpath, R & Vithal, R (2011) *Access to Higher Education: Underprepared Students or Underprepared Institutions*, Pearson Publishers, Cape Town.

Mgqwashu, E (2012) On Teaching Reading for Epistemological Access in Dhunpath, R & Vithal, R (2012) *Access to Higher Education: Underprepared Students or Underprepared Institutions*, Pearson Publishers, Cape Town.

Mirramontes, O B., Nadeau, A., & Commins, N L. (1997) Restructuring schools for linguistic diversity: Linking decision making to effective programs. New York: Teachers Colleges.

Morrow, W. (1992) Epistemological access in university. *AD Issues*, 1: 3-5.

Pityana, B. (2006) Principal's Statement to Senate, UNISA, Pretoria.

Pityana, B. (2010) Principal's Statement to Senate, UNISA, Pretoria.

Scott, I. (2012) Access, Success and Curriculum: Aspects of their Organic Relationship in Dhunpath, R & Vithal, R (2012) *Access to Higher Education: Underprepared Students or Underprepared Institutions*, Pearson Publishers, Cape Town.

Street, B., V. (1993) *Literacy and Theory and Practice*, Cambridge University press, UK.

Tinto, V. (2008) Keynote address given at the annual conference of the National Institute for Staff and Organizational Development, University of Texas at Austin, May 26, 2008.

Webb, V. (2004) The non-use of African languages in Education in Africa Paper presented in a panel discussion on *Language Policy in Education: Local Experiences in a Global Context* at the conference of the African Studies Association on *The Power of Expression: Identity, Language, and Memory in Africa and the Diaspora* New Orleans, November 11-14.

In: Open Distance Learning (ODL) in South Africa
Editor: Moeketsi Letseka
ISBN: 978-1-63463-890-6

Chapter 10

THE NEXUS BETWEEN OPEN DISTANCE LEARNING AND THE LABOR MARKET

Maximus Monaheng Sefotho*
Department of Educational Psychology
Faculty of Education, University of Pretoria, South Africa

ABSTRACT

This chapter is about the nexus between Open Distance Learning (ODL) and the labor market. The chapter starts with the review of the philosophy of ODL and links it with andragogy as a philosophical approach and the art and science of adult learning. Central to the discussion is the issue of how ODL provides the much needed qualified human resources to the labor market, found to be complex within the South African context. This is due to many factors paramount to which is labor immigration. Historically, continued labor market discrimination against previously disadvantaged groups, blacks, women and persons with disabilities in senior and executive management positions is a thorn in the South African employment sector. Given the status of South Africa as an emerging market, its labor market is becoming a kaleidoscope with various aspects to be considered. For instance, recruitment and appointments tend to be biased against graduate from historically black universities, many experience extended waiting periods before absorption into the labor market. Their counterparts from historically white universities on the contrary wait less. Sometimes the whites are guaranteed jobs while still studying. The chapter reviews work-based learning as a contributory factor to the development of ODL graduates. The last part links ODL and the labor market with career adaptation of the ODL graduates and how this answers to the needs of the ever changing labor market.

* Maximus.Sefotho@up.ac.za.

Introduction

Open and Distance Learning (ODL) has been instrumental in shaping many lives and opening avenues into the labor market. Education is the bedrock of human and socio-economic development. ODL is the nexus between underdevelopment and prosperity. In its early developments, ODL was perceived as catering for learners who could not access traditional educational institutions. Indeed many learners who missed that traditional route for learning resorted to the ODL mode to empower themselves. Letseka and Pitsoe (2013) highlight access to higher education as paramount to self-empowerment of previously disadvantaged persons, especially those already participating in the labor market. In South Africa, ODL played a pivotal role as most formerly marginalized learners were able to shape their future despite the odds. The University of South Africa (UNISA) has been very instrumental in this regard.

The advent of globalization and the ever evolving technological advancements have made it possible for ODL to advance and improve its modes of delivery. The philosophy of ODL also changed over time in order to meet the needs of its clientele. Labor market demands required of ODL a specific kind of supply that would answer to the plight of the labor market. Globalization brought with it complexities of the labor market in a variety of ways. Mostly, the labor market has been open for global access, be it in terms of employment, goods and services as well as human capital development. ODL has been instrumental in providing opportunities for labor force development, especially for the least developed and emerging economies. Many workers were able to study as they continued with their work. This has been transformational, liberating and empowering. It is through ODL that most people who may have lost hope as they were marginalized and denied access by traditional education institutions fulfilled their dreams. The open mode of learning allows effective use of time and resources for the attainment of self-development via lifelong learning (Louw, 2014).

This chapter establishes a link between ODL and the labor market by reviewing ODL and the labor market, interrogating the philosophy of ODL and examining the labor market. The composition of the labor market in South Africa is considered and work-based learning support examined. The review takes into account ODL and the rapidly changing labor market, and it links that with career adaptability of the ODL graduate. The chapter closes by examining the employability skills of the ODL graduates and prospects of retention in the labor market.

The Philosophy of Open Distance Learning and the Labor Market

Open and Distance Learning (ODL) emerged to redress the imbalances (Bhorat, 2007) endemic to the South African society that left the majority of the formally excluded groups outside the sphere of education and the labor market. The philosophy of ODL is anchored onto filling the lacuna left by political, socio-economic and education systems of South Africa. ODL is premised on the philosophy of transformation, social change and equal access to education and the labor market. The philosophy of ODL is andragogical (Muongmee,

2007) and heutagogical (Msila, 2014). Andragogy is generally juxtaposed with pedagogy and is considered the art and science of helping adults learn (Knowles, 1990). It is designed in response to the needs of adult learners (Wang & Sarbo, 2004). The assumption is that learners in ODL are adults with responsibilities for their own career management, family, place of employment and the country. Andragogy then forms a firm foundation in setting a tone for learning that can mainly be self-directed and tailored towards meeting the needs of the adult learner. The following are the assumptions of andragogy as conceived by Knowles:

- **The need to know** - adult learners need to know why they need to learn something before undertaking to learn it.
- **Learner self-concept** - adults need to be responsible for their own decisions and to be treated as capable of self-direction
- **Role of learners' experience** - adult learners have a variety of experiences of life which represent the richest resource for learning. These experiences are however imbued with bias and presupposition.
- **Readiness to learn** - adults are ready to learn those things they need to know in order to cope effectively with life situations.
- **Orientations to learning -** adults are motivated to learn to the extent that they perceive that it will help them perform tasks they confront in their life situations.

Atherton (2013) based on Knowles (1990:57)

Heutagogy is another fundamental philosophy of ODL that supports andragogy. The Greek etymology of heutagogy indicates that *Heuto* means 'self' while *agogy* means 'again'. The idea is based on the expectation that a learner 'self' interacts 'again' with the subject once the teacher-learner process has taken place. This is done with the aim of the learner re-designing the learning experience in a manner tailor-made to their learning needs as well as learning style. The learner takes charge of their own learning in line with the expectations of ODL. Self-determination in learning underpins heutagogy (Blaschke, 2012). The learner drives the process of learning to accommodate a variety of contexts such as time, space, resources and context. Learning is the responsibility of the learner heutagogically speaking.

The philosophy of ODL considers its learners to be mature people who can make informed choices about what they want to learn, the medium of instruction, the place of study, the pace of study and support mechanisms. Letseka and Pitsoe (2013) suggest that the UNISA ODL programs are a viable option for access to higher education. Nonetheless, most learners participating in ODL require well thought out and properly resourced support. Letseka and Pitsoe encourage an ODL framework characterized by flexibility, open admission, equitable access and affordability. These characteristics are reflective of the kind of learner who in many ways may be the product of the apartheid regime, whether directly or indirectly. ODL then becomes the largest program to redress the educational and economic ills resulting from the legacy of the past dispensation in South Africa. The philosophy of ODL follows the principles of the philosophy of adult education underpinned by lifelong learning (Smidt & Sursock, 2011) and self-directed learning (Silén & Uhlin, 2008).

The main driver for the emergence of ODL was to address educational and labor market needs of the majority of adults who for various reasons could not go through normal schooling or who were obliged to obtain a qualification later in life. Thus, establishing a nexus between ODL and the labor market. In such circumstances, most adults may not have accessed the labor market due to lack of necessary qualifications. The relationship between education and the labor market clearly defines possibilities of sustainable employment. In South Africa, attempts have been made to address disparities in the education and labor market, mainly through the affirmative action (Moleke, 2005). Nonetheless, unemployment still prevails and new trends of graduates who do not access employment are becoming significant (Levinsohn, 2007). The youth rank high among those who are unemployed in South Africa although most may be graduates (Yu, 2013). Pauw, Oosthuizen, and Van der Westhuizen (2008) note a paradox embedded in unemployment in South Africa. First, it is the acknowledgement that unemployment is structural concerning a general mismatch between supply and demand. Secondly, a realization that university graduates are not in high demand within the South African labor market. Samuel and Thakhathi (2012) extend the debate on the paradox of skills shortage and growing unemployment. Similar experiences of graduate unemployment are also found in the Nigerian economy, regarded as being on par or even more stable than the South African economy (Bassey & Atan, 2012).

Education and the labor market are inextricably intertwined and lack of education generally mirrors lack of access to the labor market, particularly employment. South Africa's unemployment levels are very high (Magruder, 2012) at about 26 percent (Banerjee, et al. 2008). According to Statistics South Africa's Quarterly Labor Force Survey (2013), "the number of unemployed persons for the periods of Q1: 2008 to Q1: 2013 average 4.3 million…and the trend seems to be increasing" (p. xiii). Unemployment by education level is rated at 6.4 %. Although this may seem lower, it is still significant given the skills shortage within the South African labor market. There have been clarion calls about the quality of education in South Africa. Part of what I argue could be the ever raw sore on the skin of the South African education is absence of comprehensive school guidance and counseling, especially well-developed and technologically friendly career guidance courses and programs. Education that is not supported by auxiliary career guidance courses and programs deprives its citizens of the opportunities to construct careers from a lifelong perspective. Many of the graduates who are unemployed might not have made informed decisions about their careers, therefore followed any course through which it was a possible or easy way to graduation. Thus, the mismatch between education and the world of work also becomes a reality for many, not addressing the labor market needs of South Africa.

South Africa's labor market is characterized by significant wage gaps and the labor market supply and demand are incongruent. While higher levels of education are strongly rewarded in the labor market (Branson, & Leibbrandt, 2013); formerly marginalized adults do not enjoy wages enabling them to sustain healthy livelihoods. O'Gorman (2010) recognizes the earnings gap between Africans and whites in the post-Apartheid period. This is an area where ODL plays a crucial role of skilling and re-skilling the formerly undereducated sections of the population to redress the employment and wage disparity gaps. ODL is attempting to fill the wage gap experienced by many disadvantaged persons by giving access to higher education and training. Samuel and Thakhathi (2012) refer to a skills misalignment prevalent within the South African economy and warn that if no change is implemented, South Africa may find it difficult to experience sustainable economic growth. In recent years, wage disparities have manifested in recurring salary disputes part of which has been the prolonged Marikana strike which resulted in several deaths and has shaken the South African economy (Odeku, 2014).

The labor market landscape is marked by yearly strikes which sometime shake the foundations of the South African economy (O'Gorman, 2010). Recent prolonged strikes by miners are a living example of this trend, dating back as far as 1973 (Bhorat, Van der Westhuizen, & Goga, 2007). While there may be gains in terms of salary increases and other benefits, there could be high costs such as retrenchments resulting from the prolonged strikes. This will exacerbate the problem of unemployment; testimony to South Africa's Gini coefficient regarded as the highest in the world (Bosch, Rossouw, Claassens, & du Plessis, 2010). The strike phenomenon in South Africa (Odeku, 2014) reflects deep seated dissatisfaction of the workers as well as echoes the cries of wage differentiation review. These strikes also may point out to the composition of the labor market in South Africa.

Composition of the Labor Market in South Africa

According to Leibbrandt, Woolard, McEwen & Koep (2010:7) 'South African labor force participation rates are particularly low for men'. Historically, the rates were also low on the bases of race, but that changed since 1994. 'Exclusion from the formal economy begins in the labor market' notably with highest levels of unemployment among females aged between 15 and 24 years and the Black population (Gordhan, et al, 2011:11). Nonetheless with more females participating in education, since 1995 the proportion of women entering the labor market has been greater than that of men (Sibanda, 2008). This advancement regarding the inclusion of women in the labor market is a welcome move given global trends in giving space for the recognition of women. Women can now perform any job as well as men. Around our cities, women drive buses, trains and fly airplanes. These were formerly domains for men.

Another section of the population usually forgotten is persons with disabilities. Participation in the labor market for persons with disabilities displays very uneven landscape. Statssa's Census 2011 indicates that "...2.9 million South Africans or 7.6% of the total population are classified as disabled. Persons with disabilities are often excluded from employment due to a number of factors such as discriminatory attitudes and practices, past ineffective labor legislations, inaccessible and unsupportive work environments, and inadequate access to information, inaccessible public transport, and lack of skills" (p.116). Most are considered Not in Education, Employment or Training (NEET), they are relegated to manual work and end up with low salaries.

The labor market composition in South Africa is complex. This is compounded by labor migration endemic to the economy that has attracted workers from across the SADC region (Sibanda, 2008). This phenomenon is also known as the South–South migration which could lead to a decline in natives' (formal) employment rates (Facchini, Mayda, & Mendola, 2013: 4). Migrants might arrive in South Africa highly qualified. If this is not matched by the natives, it leaves many unanswered questions as to why this should still be the case after 1994. It may also be a call to the natives to rise above mediocrity and transcend towards meritocracy. The era for blaming the past has now become obsolete. The labor market requires well prepared and competent labor force, but alas, most may still be inadequately prepared. ODL then becomes an alternative for those who need to remain working while they continue studying.

OPEN DISTANCE LEARNING AND WORK-BASED LEARNING SUPPORT

ODL re-aligns higher education with the world of work and opens avenues for the 21st century student to undertake work-based study while on the job (Helyer, 2012). Work-based learning dovetails with lifelong learning. Work-based learning can be experiential in nature and it depends mainly on employer-determined competencies. It is learning acquired daily on the job, but once it is supported, it then becomes semi-formalized. Work-based learning forms part of the motivation to propel workers to aspire for ODL while they continue working. This is for purposes of acquiring suitable qualifications. There ought to be a direct link between employer-determined competencies and the decision to participate in ODL. 'A competency is the capability of applying or using knowledge, skills, abilities, behaviors, and personal characteristics to successfully perform critical work tasks, specific functions, or operate in a given role or position' (Ennis, 2008, p. 4). Adult learners undertake learning to meet the job requirements. They need skills and competencies which allow them to perform their duties.

Although adult learners may have greater needs to engage in ODL to acquire the necessary skills and competencies, most might not have had sound foundations in the lower levels of their education. Therefore, there may be need to rectify this situation. It is also possible that many possible ODL candidates might not have required entry qualifications into higher education.

Some might use recognition of prior learning (RPL) to enter tertiary institutions or mature age. Even though work-based experience could have been accumulated, those skills and competencies acquired through education may be lacking. Thus the ODL candidates require high-quality learning support to be able to undertake their studies. ODL is a very solitary learning experience with less contact with the facilitator in most cases. If students do not understand learning material, the processes to support them may be time consuming yet necessary.

Learning support for ODL students provides mechanisms to overcome frustration and confusion (Floyd & Casey-Powell, 2004). Successful online support services should be the norm in ODL in providing further links with the labor market for continuous alignment with employer requirements. 'Successful online support services aid both students and faculty' (Floyd & Casey-Powell, 2004:55). The challenges could be around students' own technological proficiency, access to most current and advanced technology, balanced with those whose proficiency and technology pose access problems. Technological advancement should facilitate bringing the classroom atmosphere to technology most accessible to the student! For instance, are there ways in which e-learning could be accessible on students' mobile technologies along the same lines as the 'Learning Anytime Any place Partnership?' (Floyd & Casey-Powell, 2004:57).

ODL students should feel a sense of connection at different levels, top of which should be with the instructor. Equally important could be connection with other students in the same course. This promotes continued connections beyond studies into the labor market.

OPEN DISTANCE LEARNING AND THE RAPIDLY-CHANGING LABOR MARKET

Change is inevitable. The globalization agenda set in motion a plethora of changes leading towards establishing a global labor market. ODL is equally compelled to align itself to the globalized labor market. The changing patterns in the world of work are assuming a pattern of a kaleidoscope (ILO, 2006). There are changes all around; policies change, careers change, curricula change, migration patterns change on the bases of availability of employment and worker demands are changing under democracy. Parallel immigration patterns are also developing around the world, bringing along both desirable and undesirable economic immigrants (Somerville, 2009). Employment patterns are also changing as a consequence. Savickas (2000) re-focuses the change from life-time employment to life-time employability. More women are now free to participate in the labor market (Perrons, 2009). There may also be a need to re-define work, career or profession following changes in the labor market.

Career Adaptability of Open Distance Learning Graduates

Career adaptability has become an important ingredient of the 21st century worker (Härtung, Porfeli & Vondracek, 2008). Along with the labor market changes, ODL graduates may have to make careful career adaptation to align with their jobs and the qualifications they have acquired. The career adaptability of ODL graduates is an imperative that could drive labor market demands of the 21st century. Generally career adaptability is perceived as 'the capability of an individual to make a series of successful transitions where the labor market, organization of work and underlying occupational and organizational knowledge bases may all be subject to considerable change' (Bimrose, Brown, Barnes, & Hughes, 2011: ii).

Career adaptability provides ODL graduates with opportunities for career mobility either within the same places of employment or across working environments. Most likely, upwards mobility is possible after acquisition of new qualifications or even some kind of recognition within the same job. Within career psychology, contemporary careers (Baruch, 2006) that relate to career adaptability are the protean careers (Hall, 2004) and boundaryless careers (Briscoe & Hall, 2006; Segers, et al, 2008). Protean careers are named after a Greek God Proteus, '... notable for being the origin of the adjective ''protean''-the ability to take on many different self-representations' (Yee & Bailenson, 2007: 271). The adaptable nature of a protean career could allow ODL graduates the flexibility required to make the necessary changes in the careers in tandem with the demands of the changing labor market. Boundaryless careers are another metaphorical representation of contemporary careers required within the global labor market. Boundaryless careers are not confined by boundaries. They transcend the boundary of a single path within the boundaries of a single employer (Baruch, 2006). The boundaryless careers also fit within the paradigm shift of the ever changing global labor market. If ODL graduates embrace these career changes, they may be able to adapt their careers in line with contemporary changes in the labor market. 'The interplay of boundaryless and protean careers [can lead to] self-awareness and motivation to change' (Briscoe & Hall, 2006:16).

'Survival in this turbulent career environment requires workers to continually manage change-in themselves and their contexts' (Fugate, Kinicki, & Ashforth, 2004:15). ODL graduates face the task of continuously managing not only their careers but their studies during the duration of preparing for career adaptability. If the studies are not effectively managed and suffer at the expense of the job, failure is imminent. The majority of ODL students study while they are employed. This is encouraging lifelong learning and continuous acquisition of skills and competencies required by the globalized labor market. It is important to establish through research whether graduates of ODL programs are competitive to meet the demands of the global labor market.

Employability Skills of Open Distance Learning Graduates and Retention in the Labor Market

Moleke (2010) identifies a paradox of a mismatch regarding general graduate output and labor market requirements. Key to employability is the match between the graduate qualifications, competences and the labor market skills requirements. ODL has been noted to provide its graduates with satisfactory levels of proficiency in various fields (Das & Bordoloi, 2012). Thus employability skills and retention of the ODL graduates appears possible. Jackson (2013) notes that 'graduate employability is multifaceted and encompasses academic performance, career management skills, and labor market awareness' (p. 271). Many employability skills repertoires can be displayed, but it is the generic skills that form the basis of many other skills which are normally decided upon by the employer. One of the most important skill clusters relate to critical thinking and problem solving skills.

Conclusion

Open Distance Learning has been instrumental in shaping graduate careers to answer to the needs of the ever changing labor market. Today ODL is perceived as a vehicle towards career adaptation in view of enhancing work-based learning. Although the composition of the South African labor is complex due to labor immigration, the challenges this poses could serve as launch pad for South Africans to engage vigorously in ODL as they continue with their daily jobs. The rapidly changing labor market urges ODL students to fine tune their careers to remain employable. Open Distance Learning contributes to the South African labor market, and indeed to the global market as many of its participants are located globally.

References

Atherton, J. S. (2013) Learning and Teaching; Knowles' andragogy: an angle on adult learning [On-line: UK] retrieved 7 July 2014 from http://www.learningandteaching.info /learning/knowlesa.htm

Banerjee, A., Galiani, S., Levinsohn, J., McLaren, Z., & Woolard, I. (2008) Why has unemployment risen in the new South Africa? 1. *Economics of Transition*, 16(4), 715-740.

Baruch, Y. (2006) Career development in organizations and beyond: Balancing traditional and contemporary viewpoints. *Human Resource Management Review*, 16:125-138.

Bassey, G.E., & Atan, J. A. (2012) Labor Market Distortions and University Graduate Unemployment in Nigeria: Issues and Remedies. *Current Research Journal of Economic Theory*, 4(3): 67-76.

Beneria, L. (2001) *Changing Employment Patterns and the Informalization of Jobs: General Trends and Gender Dimensions*, Geneva: International Labor Office.

Bhorat, H. (2007) Unemployment in South Africa: Descriptors and Determinants, unpublished consultant report for OECD, Paris: OECD Publishing.

Bhorat, H., Van der Westhuizen, C., & Goga, S. (2007) *Analyzing Wage Formation in the South African Labor Market: The Role of Bargaining Councils*, Cape Town: Development Policy Research Unit (DPRU).

Bimrose, J., Brown, A., Barnes, S. A., & Hughes, D. (2011) *The Role of Career Adaptability in Skills Supply*, Technical Report for the UK Commission for Employment and Skills, South Yorkshire: UKCES.

Blaschke, L. M. (2012) Heutagogy and lifelong learning: A review of heutagogical practice and self-determined learning. *The International Review of Research in Open and Distance Learning*, 13(1), 56-71.

Bosch, A., Rossouw, J., Claassens, T., & du Plessis, B. (2010) *A Second Look at Measuring Inequality in South Africa: A Modified Gini Coefficient*, Working Paper No 58, prepared for the South African Reserve Bank, Pretoria.

Branson, N., & M. Leibbrandt (2013) Educational Attainment and Labor Market Outcomes in South Africa, 1994-2010, OECD Economics Department Working Papers, No. 1022, Paris: OECD Publishing.

Briscoe, J. P., & Hall D. T. (2006) The interplay of boundaryless and protean careers: combinations and implications. *Journal of Vocational Behavior*, 69: 4-18.

Dare, L. A., Zapata, L. P., & Thomas, A. G. (2005) Assessing the needs of distance learners: A student affairs perspective. *New Directions for Student Services*, 112: 39-54.

Das, P and Bordoloi, R (2012) Effectiveness of Open and Distance Education and the Relevance of ICT: A North-East Indian Perspective. *Information and Knowledge Management*, 2 (1), 38-45.

Ennis, M. R. (2008) *Competency Models: A Review of the Literature and the Role of the Employment and Training Administration (ETA)*, Washington, D. C: US Department of Labor.

Facchini, G., Mayda, A. M., & Mendola, M. (2013) South-South migration and the labor market: Evidence from South Africa. IZA Discussion Paper No 7262, Bonn: Institute for the Study of Labor.

Floro, M., & Meurs, M. (2009) *Global Trends in Women's Access to" Decent Work*. Geneva: Friedrich-Ebert-Stiftung/International Labor Organization.

Floyd, D. L., & Casey-Powell, D. (2004) New roles for student support services in distance learning. *New Directions for Community Colleges*, 128: 55-64.

Fugate, M., Kinicki, A. J., & Ashforth, B. E. (2004) Employability: A psycho-social construct, its dimensions, and applications. *Journal of Vocational Behavior*, 65(1), 14-38.

Gordhan, S., Manxeba, R., Hughes, C., Foley, P., Maroc, C., Lolwana, P., & Nell, M. (2011) *Towards a Youth Employment Strategy for South Africa*. Midrand, Johannesburg: Development Bank of Southern Africa.

Hall, D. T. (2004) The protean career: A quarter-century journey. *Journal of Vocational Behavior*, 65: 1-13.

Helyer, Ruth (2011) Aligning higher education with the world of work. *Higher Education, Skills and Work-based Learning*, 1 (2), 95-105.

Hirschi, A. (2009) Career adaptability development in adolescence: Multiple predictors and effect on sense of power and life satisfaction. *Journal of Vocational Behavior,* 74(2), 145-155.

Hughes, K. L., Moore, D. T., & Bailey, T. R. (1999) *Work-Based Learning and Academic Skills*. IEE Working Paper No. 15, New York: Columbia University.

ILO (2004) *Changing patterns in the world of work, Report of the Director-General*, International Labor Conference, 95th Session, Geneva: ILO.

Jackson, D. (2013) Student Perceptions of the Importance of Employability Skill Provision in Business Undergraduate Programs, *Journal of Education for Business*, 88 (50, 271-279.

Knowles, M. S. (1990) *The Adult Learner: a neglected species* (4th edition) Houston: Gulf Publishing.

Leibbrandt, M., Woolard, I., McEwen, H., & Koep, C. (2010) Employment and inequality outcomes in South Africa. *University of Cape Town: Southern Africa Labor and Development Research Unit.*

Lester, S., & Costley, C. (2010) Work-based learning at higher education level: value, practice and critique. *Studies in Higher Education*, 35(5), 561-575.

Letseka, M., & Pitsoe, V. (2013) The challenges and prospects of access to higher education at UNISA, *Studies in Higher Education*, doi: 10.1080/03075079.2013.823933.

Levinsohn, J. (2008) Two policies to alleviate unemployment in South Africa, CID Working Paper No. 166, Harvard University: Center for International Development (CID).

Louw, W. (2014) Designing Learning Experiences to Prepare Lifelong Learners for the Complexities of the Workplace, in Melinde Coetzee (ed) *In Psycho-social Career Meta-capacities*, Dordrecht: Springer International Publishing, pp. 307-319.

Lowden, K., Hall, S., Elliot, D., & Lewin, J. (2011) Employers' perceptions of the employability skills of new graduates. Glasgow: Edge Foundation, University of Glasgow, SCRE Center.

Magruder, Jeremy R. (2012) High Unemployment Yet Few Small Firms: The Role of Centralized Bargaining in South Africa. *American Economic Journal: Applied Economics*, 4(3), 138-66.

McCord, A., & Bhorat, H. (2003) Employment and labor market trends. *Human Resources Development Review 2003*, Cape Town: HSRC Press, pp.112-41.

Moleke, P. (2005) *Finding Work: Employment Experiences of South African Graduates.* Cape Town: HSRC Press.

Moleke. P. (2010) The graduate labor market. In Moeketsi Letseka, Michael Cosser, Mignonne Breier and Mariette Visser (eds) *Student Retention and Graduate Destinations: Higher Education and Labor Market Access and Success*, HSRC Monograph, Cape Town: HSRC Press, pp.87-94.

Moseki, M. F. (2011) *Migrating to South Africa: experiences of 'skilled' and 'unskilled' Lesotho workers*, unpublished Master of Social Sciences dissertation, University of Pretoria, Pretoria.

Msila, V. (2014) Heutagogy, Africanization and Learning: Experiences from an Open and Distance Learning (ODL) Program at the University of South Africa. *Mediterranean Journal of Social Sciences*,5 (14), 214 -220.

Muongmee, S. (2007) The role of lifelong learning and self-directed learning in educational reform in Thailand. *Educational Journal of Thailand*, 1(1), 33-42.

O'Gorman, M. (2010) Racial earnings inequality in South Africa: An assessment of policy options. *Journal of Policy Modeling*, (32), 703–718.

Odeku, K.O. (2014). An Overview of the Right to Strike Phenomenon in South Africa. *Mediterranean Journal of Social Sciences*, 5(3), 695-702,

Oosthuizen, M., & Bhorat, H. (2004) The Post-apartheid South African Labour Market, Working Paper 05/93, Cape Town: Development Policy Research Unit (DPRU).

Pauw K, Oosthuizen M, van der Westhuizen. C. (2006) Graduate unemployment in the face of skills shortages: A labor market paradox. *South African Journal of Economics*, 6: 45-57.

Perrons, D. (2009) Women and gender equity in employment: patterns, progress and challenges. London: Institute for Employment Studies, London School of Economics and Political Science (LSE).

Price, D. W. (2000) Philosophy and the adult educator. *Adult Learning*, 11(2), 3-5.

Savickas, M. L. (2000). Renovating the psychology of careers for the twenty-first century, in A. Collin & R. A. Young (eds.) *The Future of Career*, Cambridge: Cambridge University Press, pp. 53-68.

Sibanda, N. (2008) The impact of immigration and the labor market: evidence from South Africa, unpublished Doctoral dissertation, Alice: University of Fort Hare.

Silén, C., & Uhlin, L. (2008) Self-directed learning–a learning issue for students and faculty! *Teaching in Higher Education*, 13(4), 461-475.

Smidt, H., & Sursock, A. (2011) *Engaging in Lifelong Learning: Shaping Inclusive and Responsive University Strategies*, Brussels: European University Association.

Somerville, W. (2009) Future immigration patterns and policies in the United Kingdom. Washington, D.C: Migration Policy Institute.

Statistics South Africa (Statssa) (2011) *Mid-year Population Estimates*, Pretoria: Statssa.

Wang, V. C., & Sarbo, L. (2004) Philosophy, role of adult educators, and learning How contextually adapted philosophies and the situational role of adult educators affect learners' transformation and emancipation. *Journal of transformative education*, *2*(3), 204-214.

Yee, N., & Bailenson, J. (2007) The Proteus effect: The effect of transformed self-representation on behavior. *Human Communication Research*, 33(3), 271-290.

Yu, D. (2013). Youth unemployment in South Africa since 2000 revisited. Stellenbosch Economic Working Papers:04/13, University of Stellenbosch.

Zoellick, E. M. (2009) Philosophical orientation to adult learning: A descriptive study of Minnesota environmental education practitioners, unpublished Doctoral dissertation, University of Minnesota Duluth.

In: Open Distance Learning (ODL) in South Africa
Editor: Moeketsi Letseka
ISBN: 978-1-63463-890-6

Chapter 11

SHIFT FROM OPEN DISTANCE LEARNING TO OPEN DISTANCE E-LEARNING

***Sindile Ngubane-Mokiwa**[*1] **and Moeketsi Letseka**[†2]*
[1]Institute for Open Distance Learning
College of Graduate Studies, University of South Africa (UNISA), South Africa
[2] Department of Educational Foundations
College of Education, University of South Africa (UNISA), South Africa

ABSTRACT

This chapter explores the University of South Africa (UNISA)'s immanent shift from open distance learning (ODL) to open distance e-learning (ODeL). It considers UNISA's initial mandate as an ODL institution that provides higher education opportunities to previously disadvantaged, predominantly African students who would otherwise not be able to obtain a higher education qualification were they to be left at the mercy of full-time, campus-based and contact higher education institutions. The move from ODL to ODeL presumes existence of an established culture, use of, and reliance on modern electronic technologies. But while South Africa has pockets of urban cosmopolitan enclaves in the form of major modern cities and sub-urban areas, the larger spatial spread of the country remains rural, communal, invariably poor and excluded from the broader benefits of modern electronic technologies in what is known as the 'digital divide'. UNISA needs to reconcile its commitment to the mandate to provide higher education learning opportunities for the majority poor and previously marginalized Africans with the envisaged shift to ODeL. It needs to vigorously deal with the probable perception that the shift to ODeL might have the unintended consequence of perpetuating inherited socio-economic inequalities; that it might potentially exclude the poor from access to open distance learning opportunities as a result of a policy shift that equates access to higher education opportunities with possession of, and access to modern electronic technologies, which the mass of the poor might not afford. The chapter grapples with the perceived social benefits of the shift to ODeL. It argues that the promise of the global e-learning system can only be realized at UNISA if the university were to strive for a better

[*]To whom all correspondence should be directed; mokiwsa@unisa.ac.za.
[†]letsem@unisa.ac.za.

understanding of the views on teaching and learning that pertain to the specific socio-economic and cultural context of South Africa.

INTRODUCTION

Open Distance Learning (ODL), also known as Distance Education (DE) continues to play a critical role in the educational development of the black peoples in South Africa, most of whom were previously denied opportunities to higher education by the apartheid policies and legislation. Different ODL institutions in South Africa and on the African continent use a wide variety of modern and/or affordable technologies to facilitate the sharing of learning content with, and among their geographically distant students. ODL is characterized by use of new Web 2.0 tools (Mbatha, 2014), which allow for more interaction between the lecturer and the students, the students and the learning environment, the student and fellow students, and the students and the institutions at which they are affiliated. This is different from the previous First, Second and Third Correspondence models where the lecturer was the only constant link between the student and the learning environment (Anderson and Dron, 2011; Taylor, 1995, 2001; Fozdar and Kumar, 2007).

In this chapter we consider the University of South Africa (UNISA)'s immanent transition from ODL to open distance e-learning (ODeL). We ask, and attempt to answer pertinent questions with respect to the envisaged transition. For instance, and in the context of South Africa in particular, how plausible is it for an institution that has marketed itself as open, flexible, and affordable to the poor masses of previously disadvantaged African people to suddenly embrace e-learning? Isn't this a shift that is likely to exclude the previously marginalized groups that the university purports to include? Is e-learning even feasible in the context of a country such as South Africa, that is reeling under the burden of a high gini coefficient, high unemployment rates, and growing numbers of young people who are not in employment, not in education, and not in training (NEETs)?

The chapter is divided into six sections. We start with a brief exploration of the ODL framework, within which UNISA is currently operating. The exploration shall be brief given that a more detailed ODL framework has been done elsewhere by one of the authors (Letseka and Pitsoe, 2013, 2012). Thus here we shall only make cursory remarks and observations. In the second section we consider the ODeL framework. The notion of ODeL is a contested terrain. For while UNISA strives to move toward the ODeL mode, others have expressed concern that a clear and unambiguous distinction between, on the one hand, 'distance education', and on the other hand, 'e-learning', is necessary given that the two are "not the same thing" (Guri-Rosenblit, 2005). E-learning presumes the ubiquity of, and an establish culture of the use of various modern electronic technologies to facilitate communication and to share information between the lecturers and the students. We question the viability of such a presumption. In the third section we sketch some of the initiatives that are being rolled out at UNISA to prepare the University for ODeL compliance. In the fourth section we reflect on the perceived gains of shifting to ODeL. In the fifth section we mull over the plausibility of the envisaged shift to ODeL. In the last section we offer some concluding remarks. We now turn to the ODL framework.

ODL FRAMEWORK

By their very nature ODL institutions provide educational opportunities to mature non-traditional, working students who are often unable to access higher education in full-time, contact, and campus-based institutions. Former Vice Chancellor and Principal of UNISA Barney Pityana (2009) postulates that ODL is a form of education delivery model that promises to solve the ongoing challenge of limited access to higher education. It is his contention that ODL has the potential to widen access and facilitate increased participation in higher education. It is Pityana's view that ODL is cost-effective in comparison to face-to-face contact mode of delivery. He warns though of the imperative to guarantee quality of delivery of teaching and learning in ODL. UNISA (2008) defines ODL as a learning model that endeavors to bridge the time, geographical, economic, social, educational and communication distance between the institutions and the students, the academics and the students, the learning materials and the students and amongst the students themselves. There is consensus among ODL practitioners that the common ODL feature is that it is not defined by the distance between the academic (the teacher) and the student (Commonwealth of Learning 2004; Perraton, Robinson and Creed 2001; Perraton 2000; UNESCO 2002; Peters 1998; Rowntree 1996; Moore and Kearsley 1996; Holmberg 1995).

It can therefore be reasonably argued that the success of ODL depends on functional and optimal student support systems, a point that is well argued by Dunpath and Dunpath in this volume. Before the advent of modern electronic technologies student support was provided through detailed and sometimes laborious written feedback on hardcopy assignments; lengthy landline telephone conversations, or scheduled face-to-face contact either individually or in groups (Perraton, Robinson and Creed, 2001; Perraton, 2000; UNESCO, 2002; Peters, 1998; Rowntree, 1996). Moore and Kearsley (1996) postulate that ODL is an organized learning activity that is deliberately designed to afford learning opportunity to everyone, everywhere they are located. The students would be required to study and complete their degrees without physically attending classes. According to Letseka and Pitsoe (2013) ODL has been marketed through the use of fancy descriptors such as open, accessible, flexible, supportive and affordable. They argue that these descriptors are premised on the assumption that distance learners are responsible adults who can self-regulate their own learning; and that the mere provision of learning materials like tutorial letters, audio-visual media and ongoing self-assessment would result in the acquisition of knowledge and requisite skills. Given that ODL students are expected to learn on their own, they tend to form their own peer support groups where they support one another to reach their goals. ODL has two distinct characteristics that make it totally different from full-time campus-based contact learning. First, it is never synchronous in nature. This is attributable to the distance element that requires learning to be correspondence based (Keegan, 1996). Second, it is guided by educational theories that put emphasis on the teacher being the Centre of knowledge, termed "teaching by telling" (Dede, 1996:1).

But how should distance learning be managed in the era of increasingly proliferating modern electronic technologies such as the internet; internet-linked computers; Wi-Fi; DVDs; videos and video links; Tablets; smartphones, and associate satellite technologies. These technologies have lifted the lid off the generation and dissemination of 'knowledge'; on conception, dissemination and control of 'knowledge' or 'what's knowable'? As a result the position of the teacher as the 'Center of Knowledge' has either taken a new form or gradually 'withered away'. Conceptions of 'knowledge' have become negotiated, porous and decentered terrains. In the next section we briefly explore the ODeL framework. Our aim is to reflect on its implications for conceptions of knowledge and the place of a conventional teacher in the era of modern electronic technologies.

ODeL Framework

The ODeL framework is premised on the assumption that every student learning can be optimally supported by modern electronic technologies and other digital facilities. The operating term here is 'assumption'. ODeL students are assumed to have access to, and to be able to make optimal use of modern electronic technologies to access their study material and to interact with their lecturers without necessarily being required to make physical contact. Carswell, Thomas, Petre and Price (2000) argue that increased interaction in ODeL leads to reduction in transactional distance between the lecturers and the students. Thus modern electronic technologies result in e-learning, online learning or digital learning through the use of remote electronic communication.

A further assumption of ODeL is that it shall be guided by learner-centered educational theories. Benson and Samarawickrema (2009) contend that learning designers in ODeL should consider the impact of context on the student's learning journey. In the same vein Laurillard (2002) posits that technology-based learning would be more effective if its design is based on the conversational framework. There are specific technologies that can be used to facilitate the conversational framework of teaching and learning. For instance, videoconferencing can be used to facilitate dialogue and discussions between the lecturers and the students, and amongst students at different locations. Such dialogue and discussions provide spaces for students to analyze each other's views (peer-to-peer assessment) and to develop critical thinking skills. In some instance lecturers might make use of electronic discussion forums to promote collaboration, synthesis and reflection. The three activities bridge the spatial distance that might exist between the lecturers and the students; the students and the learning content, and amongst the students themselves. Some lecturers use blogs to facilitate learning in an online environment. Blogs get the students, the lecturers and/or e-tutors to reflect on the processes of teaching and learning. They provide a form of support that enables students to have an asynchronous communication while also enabling support during learning. Podcast is another tool that is used quite often to facilitate ODeL. Anderson (2010) argues that the benefits of podcast are that it augments the clarification of specific details in the learning content and enhances understanding. Generally though, podcasts facilitate the consolidation of knowledge acquired during learning. They could also be instrumental in providing students with illustrations or demonstrations of the element of the learning content.

In the next section we touch on some of the initiatives that UNISA is putting in place in order to facilitate teaching and learning and roll out of student support in the ODeL mode of delivery. These initiatives include, but are not limited to e-tutoring; learning design approaches, and digital literacy.

UNISA ODeL Initiatives

This section presents the different initiatives that the Department of Tuition and Facilitation of Learning at UNISA has introduced as part of facilitating support for Online Learning or e-Learning. A number of these initiatives aim at making use of Web 2.0 tools to facilitate an interactive student support system (Mbatha, 2014).

E-Tutoring

E-tutoring is part of the Integrated Tutor System (ITS). The aim of ITS is to enable the Information and Communication Technology (ICT) system to facilitate positive learning experiences for UNISA students. Matoane and Mashile (2012) define e-tutoring as a tool that can be used to facilitate learning, steer students towards successful completion of their course and effectively manage the conducive learning environment. E-tutoring offers four main roles; pedagogical, managerial, technical and social.

- The pedagogical role enhances collaboration, knowledge construction and critical thinking.
- The managerial role augments the practical and administrative element of learning.
- The technical role ensures that the ICT system and the software provided adequately support students' digital and pedagogical competence.
- The social role provides an environment for the students to freely collaborate and learn from each other in a relaxed manner.

As part of UNISA's intended shift to ODeL mode; three tutoring programs were introduced. These are the Science Foundation Program (SFP), the Face-to-Face (F2F) program, and the E-tutoring program. Besides the F2F which is based on the student and the tutor interacting face-to-face, both the SFP and the e-tutoring system are run electronically.

Challenges

We now briefly touch on the challenges faced by the UNISA academic community as a result the institution's intention to introduce the ODeL framework. These can be summarized as learning design approaches, digital illiteracy, and lack of consensus on ODeL approaches. We briefly tease out each of these challenges.

Inappropriate Learning Design Approaches

As alluded to earlier, there are challenges with respect to the ODeL approach. One of these is the common mistake of using the learning approaches that were initially meant for the correspondence model. For instance, there is a tendency among some lecturers to simply upload the pdf versions of old learning materials onto the *MyUNISA* online portal. Oliver and

Herrington (2001) propose a conceptual framework that is an important element of e-learning design. This framework, which is constructivist, emphasizes the design of learning tasks that are parallel to specific outcomes and assessment. The tasks should inform the kind of support that is to be given to the students.

Learning Design for Accessibility

Shifting to ODeL poses learning and instructional design concerns (Mashile and Matoane, 2012; Muirhead, 2007). These revolve around ensuring that all learning material is accessible to UNISA's diverse groups of learners. Twigg (2003) presents five different approaches to redesigning courses which can be incorporated into the shift to ODeL. The first is the Supplemental model, which keeps the course structure unchanged but adds online activities to supplement learning delivery. The second is the Replacement model, which reduces the paper-based tutorial activities with technology-enhanced activities. The third is the Emporium model, which allows the students to make their own choices on what learning materials would best enable them to learn. The students decide on the pace at which they want to learn. The Emporium model is characterized by individual learner support. The fourth is the Fully Online model. This is resource laden, student-focused and interactive. The fifth is the Buffet model, which provides a variety of learning activities through different media with courses that use different instructional strategies to facilitate learning. The success of this approach depends on ongoing learner support and use of different collaboration styles. Ngubane-Mokiwa (2013) proposes the Inclusive Universal use of Technology Framework (IUuT) which emphasizes the importance of designing learning programs that can facilitate learning across different abilities and disabilities. This framework promotes critical and inclusive use of ICTs for learning as well as ICT tools that conform to accessibility and usability principles. It encourages dialogue between and among students and lecturer, leading to autonomy and learning as emancipation. Ngubane-Mokiwa (2013) emphasizes the pertinence of continuously seeking students' learning experiences and using them to inform authentic educational practices.

Digital Illiteracy

Partly due to the enduring historical inequalities that are widespread in South Africa (Letseka and Pitsoe, 2012), most people are technologically illiterate. Technological habits show that some people might not improve their digital skills, which are critical to improving their educational engagement (Khalil, 2013; Goyal, Purohit and Bhagat, 2010). This phenomenon prevails at UNISA. Ncube, Dube and Ngulube (2014) report that most lecturers have no idea of how they can implement e-learning to enhance teaching. Since there are few e-learning champions at UNISA there is an urgent need to conduct further research into the learning design and learning facilitation strategies for e-learning. Equally, more studies are needed on student e-learning readiness in order to determine the kind of interventions that need to be implemented by the student support structures especially at UNISA's regional offices.

Lack of Consensus on the ODeL Approach

The principle of Change Management requires that research is conducted to determine the attitudes of different stakeholders towards any planned changes. In this regard, two commissioned studies led by Roger Mills of Cambridge University in the United Kingdom, and the South African Institute for Distance Education (SAIDE) are worthy of mention. On the one hand Mills (2011) cautions that UNISA might not be ready for e-learning or ODeL. He is doubtful that UNISAis not yet in a position to function like ODeL universities such as Athabasca in Canada or Phoenix in Arizona, United States of America (USA). On the other hand, the SAIDE (2012) study expresses a hopeful view for UNISA to facilitate interactions with students through digital approaches. While the two studies convey different messages it stands to reason that UNISA needs to pay careful attention to the development of robust ICT infrastructure and other emerging digital technologies if hopes to hit the ground running in its roll out of the ODeL mode of teaching and learning. It is crucial at this stage to mention that there is a tendency at UNISA to think that the use of modern electronic technologies implies a form of panacea to our modern day challenges to teaching and learning. This tendency is predicated on the belief that traditional distance education methods like correspondence through hardcopy material, telephonic discussions with distance students, and traditional library holdings in the form of hardcopy textbooks and scholarly journals are outdated and should therefore be done away with. Our view is to the contrary. And that is, the two approaches to teaching and learning can be optimized by viewing, and using them as complementary to one another. Print media still has many miles to go, and a lot to live for.

Implications of the Shift to ODeL

The introduction of new teaching approaches and tools will no doubt be met with resistance by less technologically competent lectures. This is because modern electronic technologies force traditionally-inclined lecturers out of the comfort zone of their customary and familiar techniques and pedagogies. Ncube, Dube and Ngulube (2014) argue that lecturers become apprehensive when they are expected to change the way they have always been designing and facilitating teaching and learning. Ncube et al. (2014) are acutely aware that adoption of ODeL will mean lecturers will not only have to change the way they teach, but they will also need to change the way they design their learning programs and respond to their respective learning environments. They will be required to design learning material that are easily accessible to the diverse student populations online; are intended for collaboration learning; for student-centered engagement; for authentic and transformative learning, and for critical engagement. Teaching and learning would need to radically shift from assessing students through once-off summative assessments to more bite size formative assessment activities that encourage creativity and originality.

While advocates of e-learning see it as a necessary and long overdue educational paradigm shift that should make obsolete all forms of distance/correspondence education that preceded it, Bates (2005:14-25) cautions that this is fundamentally mistaken given that "distance learning can exist without online learning, and online learning is not necessarily distance learning". In the same vein Guri-Rosenblit (2005:468) argues that on the one hand 'distance education' and 'e-learning' do overlap in some cases, but are by no means identical. Distance learning reaches out to students wherever they live or wish to study. On the other hand e-learning relates to the use of electronic media for a variety of learning purposes that range from add-on functions in conventional classrooms to full substitution for the face-to-face meetings by online encounters (Guri-Rosenblit, 2005:469).

What these views highlight? Our view is that they provide a window of opportunities for UNISA to approach ODeL with caution, cognizant that while modern electronic technologies do indeed optimize the work than was previously done, it would indeed be imprudent to treat them as panacea to our teaching and learning challenges.

PERCEIVED GAINS OF ODEL

In a country such as South Africa, which is characterized by routine service delivery and trade union protests, there is a pressing need for the realization of the promise of learning 'anywhere, anytime' factor that is offered by e-learning (Marimo, Mashingaidze and Nyoni, 2013; Cooper, 2009; Aydin and Tasci, 2005). For instance, the fact that the student can access their study environment and material wherever they are, and that it would no longer be necessary for them to wait for study guides to be delivered by postal services when they can be downloaded from the internet to expedite e-teaching and e-learning. E-learning is said to providethe lecturers with opportunities to offer 'just-in-time training' (So & Swatman, 2006). We would like to see this as 'just-in-time learning facilitation'. The lecturers are able to provide feedback to students' assignments through a click of a button from any location in the world through 'on-screen-marking'. The student benefits by receiving their feedback on time, having a chance to engage with their lecturers and peers, which potentially improves understanding of the learning concepts. With well-functioning e-learning programs in place the students need not complain about late feedback on assignment, which compromises preparation for examinations. It has been argued that e-learning opens opportunities for e-student support where the student can have access to cognitive, affective and systemic support at a click of a button (Tait, 2000).

Student-centered learning (Abu-Hassan-Assari, 2005) and student-centered support (Sewart, 1993) are two crucial elements for nurturing students' critical thinking skills and positive learning experiences. Student-centered learning is premised on the assumption that the students should be the core element in the design of learning material, learning environment, assessment and support services (Beheler, 2009). Student-centered support implies that the students' needs are the determining factor of how support is structured and provided (Sewart, 1993). Tait (2000) postulates that learner support services should comprise of a functional technological platform, authentic student characteristics, course demands, effective management system and scalability. Regarding scalability, Hüllsman (2004) suggests that learner support models should be based on economies of scale. He argues that the increased cost of learner support should be justified by positive learning experience and progressive retention rates. To assist in understanding the cost involved in learner support; Simpson (2008) designed a cost versus benefit of learner support formula. This formula can be used with different learner support interventions, for instance, interaction between lecturers and students, students and the learning material, students and students and students and learner support specialists (De Villiers, 2005; Yun, 2008; Ryan, 2004). In the case of one ODL university in Africa practitioners like Hüllsman (2004) question the use of the tutor-student ratio of one e-tutor to two hundred students (1:200 ratio). Although this argument is based on the idea that e-tutor/student interaction is more effective when the e-tutor has less number of students to support, Hüllsman argues that there should be evidence of the impact of learner support on the learner performance. According to Lentell and O'Rourke (2004) the desired norm for European ODL institutions is one tutor to twenty to thirty students (1:20-30 ratio). To counteract the high costs involved in learner support, Brindley (2014) suggests effective use of peer-to-peer support in order to cater for large numbers. Peer-to-peer support would also lead to students forming collaborative learning networks which Kretovics (2003) calls the Communities of Students (CoP).

Collaborative learning goes beyond geographical locations (Aydin and Tasci, 2005; Cooper, 2009; Marimo, Mashingaidze and Nyoni, 2013). It can occur in two forms: on a face-to-face or virtual mode. Face-to-face collaboration would be in form of study groups formed amongst peers with the aim of supporting each other. In undergraduate studies the peers are united by common causes like the same module content, same level of study and the need for peer support. Similarly in postgraduate level, students' collaboration could be based on academic and motivation needs. Virtual collaboration can be facilitated through Web 2.0 tools like social networks, vodcasts, podcasts, blogs, wikis, shared docs, YouTube, bookmarks, multimedia sharing and tagging (Mbatha, 2014). The benefits of virtual collaborative learning include among others; being able to collaborate online, having access to evolving content, limitless and safe data sharing and storage through cloud computing, increased user participation and rich user experience. These are indeed laudable prospects for institutions intending to adopt the ODeL mode of learning to consider. The presumption driving such considerations would necessarily be advancement in, and ubiquity of modern electronic technologies. In the next section we mull over the plausibility of ODeL at UNISA given South Africa's level of modern electronic technologies' penetration, especially in the vast rural areas where the majority of UNISA's student clientele resides.

How Plausible Is ODeL at UNISA?

When a proportion of UNISA lecturers is reported to resist ODeL because they are not fond of modern electronic technologies (Ncube, Dube and Ngulube, 2014) the greatest concern is that UNISA will lose out on the Web 2.0 tools which support constructivist student-centered approaches to teaching and learning. Not being supportive of the use of modern electronic technologies can only deprive UNISA students of an opportunity to engage in the digital world. Makoe (2012) highlights the importance of the need for academics to embrace the digital learning habits of their students. She uses the term 'digital natives' to describe modern technology users who have 'hypertext minds…leap around…function best when they are networked…thrive on instant gratification and frequent rewards' (Prensky, 2001:2). Makoe (2012) argues that at UNISA, as in other higher education institutions the lecturers tend to be digital immigrants who are not socialized into learning through different tools but only through engagement with structured courseware. Research shows that most of UNISA students are comfortable with the use of social media tools like Facebook, Instagram,

Twitter, Mxit, and other synchronous platforms. Not embracing these tools would deny UNISA lecturers and students the opportunity for interaction and instant feedback through easily accessible mobile technologies like cellphones, smartphones, MP3 players, Tablets, iPads and others (Rao, 2011; Prensky, 2004). Global learning trends are such that lecturers have to change from being knowledge banks to being a learning process design experts (Makoe, 2012). This approach to teaching and learning is not only becoming universal, but it also encourages authentic learning (Reeves, Herrington & Oliver, 2004; Ralabate, 2011), promotes higher order thinking skills and active learning (Laurillard, 2004) and cultivates a sense of responsibility to learn and self-development (Seymour & Fourie, 2004:5). Another consequence of not embracing the ODeL model through the use of modern electronic technologies is that UNISA might not benefit from the uses of emerging technologies such as Cloud computing, mobile technologies, gaming and simulation software, open content, learning analytics, personal learning environments (Johnson, Adams Becker, Cummins, Estrada, Freeman & Ludgate, 2013). The use of different electronic technologies provides lecturers and students with a variety of means for interaction. It positions the students to access different learning approaches, mediation and engagement.

CONCLUSION

The literature on teaching and learning at UNISA shows that the students are pretty much at home with modern electronic technologies and social media tools. It would therefore be a terrible disservice should the university not embrace the ODeL model (Mbatha, 2014; Makoe, 2012). It is our submission in this chapter that the ODeL model holds the key to huge benefits for UNISA lecturers and students to be key role players in accessible, open, inclusive and interactive learning practices. But in order for this to happen, UNISA needs to sufficiently prepare its lecturers for the transition from ODL to ODeL. It needs to ensure that academics and support staff, as well as the students receive appropriate and sufficient training, retraining and continuous support to deal with the envisaged shift to ODeL. There is also the imperative to strengthen the provision of the ICT infrastructure in order to avoid costly glitches such as the slow uptake when logging into the system because of poor bandwidth. Given that UNISA's estimated student headcount is currently in excess of 400 000 the number of technical and learning technologies support staff would have to be increased and availed on a 24/7 basis in order to meet the demand created by this astronomical growth in student headcount. There is no doubt therefore that one of UNISA's glaring priorities is to provide adequate bandwidth infrastructure to ensure fast and reliable internet connectivity. The greatest challenge though is going to be how well UNISA reaches out to the vast majority of students that reside in rural, communal, invariably poor parts of the country and who might be excluded from the broader benefits of modern electronic technologies through the 'digital divide'. Designing ODeL program that are able to transcend the 'digital divide' would be a measure of UNISA's successful provision of the ODel mode of teaching and learning.

REFERENCES

Abu-Hassan-Assari, M.H. (2005) Adult learners and e-learning readiness: a case study. A paper presented at the European College Teaching & Learning Conference, 13-17 June.

Anderson, T. & Dron, J. (2011) Three Generations of Distance Education Pedagogy. *The International Review of Research in Open and Distance Learning* 12 (3), 80-97.

Anderson, T. (2010) Three Generations of Distance Education Pedagogy. DEANZ Conference. Available online at cloudworks.ac.uk/cloud/view/3381.

Aydin, C.H. & Tasci, D. (2005) Measuring readiness for e-learning: reflections from an emerging country. *Educational Technology & Society 8*(4), 244-257.

Bates, A. W. (2005) *Technology, E-learning and Distance Education* (2nd ed.) London: Routledge Falmer.

Beheler, B. (2009) Student Centered Learning Environments and Technology Applied to Special Education, Learning Theory and Educational Technology. EdTech, Boise State University https://sites.google.com/a/boisestate.edu.edtech504/behelerb. Accessed on 23 September 2014.

Benson, R. & Samarawickrema, G. (2009) Addressing the context of e-learning: using transactional distance theory to inform design. *Distance Education,* 30(1), 5-21.

Brindley, J.E. (2014) Learner Support in Online Distance Education: Essential and Evolving, in O. Zawacki-Richter & T. Anderson (Eds.), *Online Distance Education: Towards a Research Agenda* (pp. 287-310). Oldenburg, Germany: Bibliotheks- und Informationssytem der Universität Oldenburg.

Carswell, L., Thomas, P., Petre, M. & Price, B. (2000) Distance education via the Internet: a report on students' experiences. *British Journal of Educational Technology*, 31 (1), 29-46.

Commonwealth of Learning. (2004) Planning and implementing open and distance learning systems: A handbook for decision makers. Vancouver: Commonwealth of Learning.

Cooper, H.M. (2009) *Research Synthesis and Meta-analysis: A Step by Step Approach*, 4th edition. Thousand Oaks, CA: Sage.

De Villiers, M.R. (2005) E-Learning artefacts: are they based on learning theory? *Alternation* 12(1b), 345-371.

Dede, C. (1996) The evolution of distance education: Emerging technologies and distributed learning. *The American Journal of Distance Education,* 10(2), 4-36.

Fozdar, B.I. & Kumar, L.S. (2007) Learning and Students retention, *The International Journal Review of Research in Open and Distance Learning,* 8(2), 1-19.

Goyal, E., Purohit, S. & Bhagat, M. (2010) Factors that affect Information and Communication Technology usage: A case study in management education, *Journal of Information Technology Management,* XXI (4), 38-57.

Guri-Rosenblit, S. (2005) "Distance education and 'e-learning': Not the same thing", *Higher Education*, 49: 467–493.

Holmberg, B. (1995) *Theory and Practice of Distance Education*, 2nd Ed. London: Routledge.

Hüllsman, T. (2004) The two-pronged attack on learner support: Costs and the centrifugal forces of convergence. In J.E. Brindley, C. Walti, & O. Zawacki-Richter (Eds.), *Learner Support in Open, Distance and Online Learning Environments*, Oldenburg, Germany: Bibliotheks- und Informationssytem der Universität Oldenburg, pp.241-50.

Johnson, L., Adams Becker, S., Cummins, M., Estrada, V., Freeman, A. & Ludgate, H. (2013) *NMC Horizon Report: 2013 Higher Education Edition*. Austin, Texas: The New Media Consortium.

Keegan, D. (1996) *Foundations of Distance Education*, 3rd Ed. London: Routledge.

Khalil, S.M. (2013) From resistance to acceptance and use of technology in academia. *Open Praxis,* 5 (2), 135-150.

Kretovics, M. (2003) The role of student affairs in distance education: Cyber-services or virtual communities, *Online Journal of Distance Learning Administration,* 6(3). Available online at http://www.westga.edu/~distance/ojdla/fall63/kretovics63.html. Accessed on 09 October 2014.

Laurillard, D. (2002) *Rethinking University Teaching: A Conversational Framework for the Effective use of Learning Technologies*. 2nd Ed. London: Routledge.

Laurillard, D. (2004) E-Learning in Higher Education. *Changing Higher Education*, Edited by Paul Ashwin. Routledge Falmer.

Lentell, H. & O'Rourke, J. (2004) Tutoring Large Numbers: An Unmet Challenge. *The International Review of Research in Open and Distance Learning,* 5(1).

Letseka, M. & Pitsoe, V. (2012) Access to higher education through open distance learning (ODL): Reflections on the University of South Africa (UNISA). In R. Dhunpath& R. Vithal (Eds.).*Access to Higher Education: Under-prepared Students or Under-prepared Institutions?* Cape Town: Pearson.

Letseka, M. & Pitsoe, V. (2013) The challenges and prospects of access to higher education at UNISA. *Studies in Higher Education.*

Makoe, M. (2012) Teaching digital natives: Identifying competencies for mobile learning facilitators in distance education. *South African Journal of Higher Education* 26(1), 91-104.

Marimo, S.T., Mashingaidze, S. & Nyoni, E. (2013) Faculty of Education Lecturers' and students' perceptions on the utilization of e-learning at Midlands State University of Zimbwabwe. *International Research Journal of Arts and Social Science,* 2(4), 91-98.

Mashile, E.O. & Matoane, M.C. 92012) E-Learning development-The case of UNISA.

Matoane, M.C. & Mashile, E.O. (2012) Key considerations for successful E-tutoring: Lessons learnt from an institution of Higher Learning in South Africa. *E-Learn 2013*.

Mbatha, B. (2014) Global Transition in Higher Education: From the Traditional Model of Learning to a New Socially Mediated Model. *The International Review of Research in Open and Distance Learning* 15(3), 258-274.

Mills, R. (2011) *Report of the Investigation into the Regional Networks of the University of South Africa*. Report commissioned by the management committee of UNISA.

Moore, M.G. & Kearsley, G. (1996) Distance Education: A systems view. Belmont: Wadsworth.

Muirhead, B. (20070 Interactivity challenges facing online educators, in *The Twelfth Cambridge Conference on Open and Distance Learning,* pages 2-9.

Ncube, S.; Dube, L. & Ngulube, P. (2014) E-Learning Readiness among Academic Staff in the Department of Information Science at the University of South Africa. *Mediterranean Journal of Social Sciences* 5(16), 357-366.

Ngubane-Mokiwa, S.A. (2013) Information and Communication Technology as a learning tool: experiences of students with blindness. Unpublished doctoral thesis, University of South Africa: Pretoria.

Oliver, R. & Herrington, J. (2001) *Teaching and Learning Online: A Beginner's Guide to e-learning and e-Teaching in Higher Education*, Mt Lawley, Western Australia: Edith Cowan University.

Perraton, H. (2000) *Open and Distance Learning in the Developing World*, London: Routledge.

Perraton, H., Robinson, B. & Creed, C. (2001) *Teacher Education through Distance Learning: Technology, Curriculum, Cost, Evaluation*, Paris: UNESCO Division of Higher Education.

Peters, O. (1998) *Learning and Teaching in Distance Education: Analyses and Interpretations from an International Perspective*. London: Kogan Page.

Pityana, B. (2009) Open distance learning in the developing world: trends, progress and challenges. Keynote speech delivered on the occasion of the M-2009 23rd ICDE World Conference on Open Learning and Distance Education, 'Flexible Education for All: Open-Global-Innovative', Maastricht, the Netherlands, June 7-10.

Prensky, M. (2001) *Digital Natives, Digital Immigrants*,On the Horizon, NCB: University Press.

Prensky, M. 2004. What can you learn from a cell phone? *Innovate Online Magazine*, Available online at http://www.innovateonline.info. Accessed on 21 September 2014.

Ralabate, P.K. (2011) Universal design for learning: meeting the needs of all students. Available online at http://www.asha.org/Publications/leader/2011/110830/Universal-Design-for-Learning-Meeting-the-Needs-of-All-Students/. Accessed on 23 September 2014.

Rao, M. (2011) Mobile Africa Report: Regional hubs of excellence and innovation. Available online at http://www.mobilemonday.net/reports/MobileAfrica_2011.pdf, accessed on 22 September 2014.

Reeves, T.C., Herrington, J. & Oliver, R. (2004) A development research agenda for online collaborative learning. *Educational Technology Research & Development,* 52(4), 53-65.

Rowntree, D. (1996) *Exploring Open and Distance Learning*, Milton Keynes: Open University.

Ryan, Y. (2004) Pushing the boundaries with online learner support. In J.E. Brindley, C. Walti, & O. Zawacki-Richter (eds.), *Learner Support in Open, Distance and online learning environments* (pp. 125-34). Oldenburg, Germany: Bibliotheks- und Informations system der Universität Oldenburg.

SAIDE. (2012) Report of SAIDE on the Organizational Architecture for the University of South Africa. Report commissioned by the management committee of UNISA, *South African Institute for Distance Education.*

Sewart, D. (1993) Student support systems in distance education. *Open Learning,* 8(3), 3-12.

Seymour, L. & Fourie, R. (2004) ICT literacy in Higher Education: Influences and Inequality. Available online at http://web.up.ac.za/ecis/SACLA2010PR/SACLA2010/Papers /SACLA002.pdf. Accessed on 24 September 2014.

Simpson, O. (2008) Cost benefits of student retention policies and practices. In W. Bramble and S. Panda (Eds.), *Economics of Distance and Online Learning*, London, UK: Routledge, pp. 162-78.

So, T. & Swatman, M.C. (2006) e-Learning readiness of Hong Kong teachers.

Tait, A. (2000) Planning student support for open and distance learning. *Open Learning*, 287-298.

Taylor, J. (2001) Automating e-Learning: The Higher Education Revolution. Available online at http://www.usq.edu.au/users/taylorj. Accessed on 18 September 2014.

Taylor, J.C. (1995) Distance education technologies: The fourth generation. *Australian Journal of Educational Technology* 11(2), 1-7.

Twigg, C. (2003) Improving learning and reducing costs: New models for Online Learning. Available online at http://net.educause.edu/ir/library/pdf/erm0352.pdf

UNESCO. (2002) *Open and Distance Learning: Trends, Policy and Strategy considerations*, Paris: UNESCO Division of Higher Education.

UNISA. (2008) *Open Distance Learning Policy*, Pretoria: UNISA Press.

Vygotsky, L.S. (1978) *Mind in Society: The Development of Higher Psychological Processes*, Cambridge, M.A: Harvard University Press.

Yun, C.C.L. (2008) Effects of personal characteristics on learner online learning readiness. Proceedings of the EDU-COM, International Conference, Perth, Western Australia 19-20 November. Available at http://ro.ecu.edu.au.ceducom/31, accessed on 20 September 2014.

In: Open Distance Learning (ODL) in South Africa
Editor: Moeketsi Letseka
ISBN: 978-1-63463-890-6

CONCLUSION: AFTER THOUGHT

Moeketsi Letseka*
Department of Educational Foundations,
College of Education, University of South Africa (UNISA), South Africa

With an estimated 400 000 in student headcount enrollments UNISA is no doubt a mega-university. The university's student intake cannot be confined to the borders of South Africa. Consistent with its mission, UNISA is an African university with a sizable number of students from Botswana, Ethiopia, Kenya, Lesotho, Malawi, Namibia, Swaziland, Tanzania, Uganda, Zambia, Zimbabwe, the Middle East, Europe and the Americas. Indeed UNISA has had its share of producing some of Africa's leaders in the form of heads of states, judges, media personalities, authors and scholars. To cap it all in 2013 UNISA celebrated 140 years of existence, making it one of the oldest universities on the African continent. But size (quantity), and longevity (in terms of many years of existence) should not be conflated with desired impact (quality) in terms of UNISA's ability to deliver on teaching and learning to its student clientele. This book is an assembly of thirteen (13) ODL practitioners who have gathered to celebrate the sterling work of UNISA as the only South African university that is dedicated to offering access to higher education opportunities, especially to the previously excluded majority black people who were marginalized by apartheid policies and legislation. UNISA continues with its mission of expanded access to affordable higher education especially given that the price tag of higher education at full-time contact universities is out of reach for the vast majority of mature working adults who yearn for a higher education qualification.

And yet, notwithstanding these accolades, the team of ODL practitioners and experts assembled in this book were each given an explicit mandate – to celebrate UNISA's achievements in their respective areas of specialty; to shed light on specific highlights. But also to be critical. To use the literature and research data to make authoritative statements, to offer informative and invaluable clarifications, to minister to potential students and to shake them from the comfort zones and slumber of uncritical allegiance to UNISA. In short, to educate them about UNISA. At a strategic level each author was give the free range to

* E-mail: letsem@unisa.ac.za.

exercise their knowledge and depth on ODL and to interrogate some of the salient issues about which others might be uncomfortable to write. It is my conviction that it is what robust scholarship should be about; to go where others fear to tread, and yet to write about such sensitive and contested issues professionally, scholarly, ethically, and with passion.

Eventually though, I hope that these chapters have, individually and collectively, generated debate on the ODL mission of UNISA. The challenges of UNISA's poor pass rates, poor completion rates, poor graduation rates, and poor throughput rates are the challenges that should inspire anyone associate with this illustrious institution to want to sit at the *pitso* (public assembly) and engage with likeminded UNISA loyalists about ways of forging long-term sustainable solutions. They are challenges that should drive concerned parties to come together to re-imagine strategic plans and institutional policies whose main aim should be to drive the implementation that ensures that UNISA 140-years legacy is retained. The burning issues that preoccupied the thirteen authors are the issue of access to UNISA as an ODL institution, which Makoe took up. In the aftermath of the transition from apartheid to democracy the topical issue at education conferences or strategic planning retreats was how to roll out access to higher education so that the previously marginalized majority of blacks were afforded the opportunity to equitably access the best higher education institutions from which the apartheid laws and policies excluded them. At the time of writing (2014) South Africa had just celebrated twenty years of democracy. A critical question all South African should ask is, should we, twenty years later still be quibbling about access issues. Maybe yes and may no. Yes because given the glaring socio-economic inequalities vast numbers of black African households continue to irk out a living under conditions of dire poverty. It is such household whose children we should be most concerned about when we debate issues of access. These are children who grow up and experience lack of 'epistemological Access' at the time when their ages permit them to enroll at higher education institutions. The corollary question here should be, how should we improve such children's chances of attending schools that have the capacity to adequately prepare them to exit the schooling system with requisite intellectual and emotional resources to enter university and succeed regardless of their poor socio-economic backgrounds? Such preparation should nip in the bud the challenge of participation in higher education that Prinsloo addressed in chapter three. Participation rates can be improved if the educational reach of poor family households and state support in the form of full coverage social grants are made available to economically strained family households.

Ruth Mampane, Victor Pitsoe and Matsephe Letseka have interrogated the twin issues of assessment and 'best practice'. How well should ODL practitioners assess their student? Are they clear about what assessment in real terms presupposes? So that their assessment practices can be said to add value to the learners in so far as the aim of assessment is to improve teaching and learning? Moeketsi Letseka, Kelelco Karel, and Ruth Aluko addressed the two related issues of pass rates and throughput rates at UNISA. Both chapters highlighted a major concern of enduring and shocking poor pass rates and throughput rates. When a university's graduation rates are in single digits and are worse than the national average then there should be cause for concern. And the two did exactly that. They raised alarm bells to say something is terribly wrong in the teaching, assessment or the management of the entire ODL learning and teaching project and drastic measures need to be taken.

Chapters eight (Victor Pitsoe and Gezani Baloyi), and nine (Shakila Dhunpath and Rubby Dhunpath) dealt with conceptions of success in ODL and student support as key indicators of ODL. Dhunpath and Dhunpath in particular were vocal on how best traditional student support practices that have been tried and tested appeared to have been neglected or otherwise treated with disdain at UNISA. It is their view that the majority of student-support related challenges UNISA struggles with can be easily resolved were these age-old tried and tested support programs to be resuscitated and supported.

The role ODL plays to support the labor market was dealt with by Monaheng Sefotho in chapter ten. Sefotho does a good job of highlighting the deep seated dangers of continued discrimination in the labor market which still entertains the fantasy that graduates from previously black and disadvantaged universities are not good enough compared to graduates from previously white privileged universities. . South Africa's labor market analysts and the Commission on Employment Equity continue to highlight the fact that senior management positions and top executive positions are dominated by white males while blacks and women continue to swell the the lower ranks of the value chain, in a country in which blacks constitute 80% of the population. In chapter eleven Sindile Ngubane-Mokiwa and Moeketsi Letseka mull over the potential shift from ODL to open distance e-learning (ODeL). While they embrace the seeming proliferation and ubiquity of modern electronic technologies in ODL they advocate a reasonable balance between the use of modern electronic technologies and traditional distance learning techniques given that vast swathes of South Africa remain rural, traditional and often excluded from knowledge-carrying modern electronic technologies such as computers, laptops, Tablets, internet connectivity, and WiFi..

INDEX

#

21st century, ix, 51, 52, 53, 122, 123

A

academic development programs, 33
academic learning, 54
academic performance, 124
academic success, x, 74, 85, 91, 92, 113
accessibility, 10, 17, 134
accommodation, 83
accountability, 41, 54, 63
accounting, 102, 104
accreditation, 13, 14, 60
acquisition of knowledge, 131
action research, 56
adaptability, 118, 123, 124, 126
adaptation, xii, 56, 117, 123, 124
administrators, 53
admission policy, x, 65
adult education, 34, 35, 119
adult learning, xi, 74, 117, 124, 127
adults, vii, x, 65, 66, 119, 120, 131, 143
advancement, 8, 121, 122, 137
advocacy, 16
affirmative action, 120
African Council for Distance Education (ACDE), viii, 7, 12, 13, 15
African languages, 116
African National Congress (ANC), 2
African-American, 63
age, 24, 31, 40, 61, 68, 70, 122, 145
agencies, 13, 43
alienation, 70
anatomy, 74
annotation, 113
apartheid, vii, viii, 1, 2, 24, 29, 30, 33, 35, 68, 72, 73, 80, 102, 119, 127, 130, 143, 144
appointments, xii, 5, 117
articulation, 24, 84, 108, 114
aspiration, xi, 105, 106
assessment, vii, ix, 3, 4, 13, 14, 24, 28, 29, 30, 31, 39, 40, 41, 42, 43, 44, 45, 46, 47, 48, 49, 50, 51, 52, 53, 54, 55, 56, 57, 58, 59, 60, 61, 62, 63, 79, 81, 83, 84, 85, 106, 107, 127, 134, 135, 136, 144
assessment tools, 44, 46
asynchronous communication, 132
atmosphere, 122
attitudes, ix, 4, 39, 45, 54, 57, 58, 63, 71, 80, 99, 107, 109, 112, 121, 135
attribution, 32
audio-visual media, 40, 131
audit, 14, 17
Austria, 19
authority, 55, 59
autonomy, 11, 16, 134
awareness, 46, 56, 99, 101, 114, 124

B

background information, 53
bandwidth, xi, 83, 91, 92, 138
banking, 55
banks, 138
barriers, 8, 19, 24, 32, 57, 93, 103, 107
base, ix, 51, 53
basic education, 2
behaviors, 58, 99, 100, 101, 102, 122
benchmarks, vii, 66, 68, 69, 72
benefits, xii, 6, 43, 55, 82, 100, 121, 129, 132, 136, 137, 138, 141
best practice, vii, ix, 3, 4, 51, 52, 54, 55, 59, 60, 61, 93, 95, 96, 144
bias, 119

bilingualism, 110
blame, 79, 80
blindness, 56, 140
blogs, 98, 132, 137
Botswana, 143
brain, 104
budding, viii, 1
building blocks, 113
bureaucracy, 55

C

candidates, 122
caricature, 106
case study(s), 75, 80, 83, 87, 89, 102, 107, 139
causal relationship, 101
cell phones, 94
certificate, 25, 81, 87
certification, 42
challenges, ix, x, xi, 3, 4, 5, 8, 35, 51, 52, 56, 60, 61, 64, 65, 67, 69, 70, 75, 78, 80, 87, 88, 91, 92, 93, 94, 95, 96, 98, 99, 102, 106, 108, 114, 122, 124, 126, 127, 133, 135, 136, 140, 141, 144, 145
changing environment, 34
character traits, 18
chunking, 11
circulation, 16
city(s), xii, 6, 94, 121, 129
citizens, 17, 120
citizenship, 6, 32, 75
civil society, 32
clarity, 26
classes, 68, 92, 93, 97, 131
classification, 43, 85
classroom, 8, 46, 58, 96, 111, 112, 122
cleavages, 30
Cloud computing, 138
clusters, 124
cognition, 58, 110, 112
cognitive abilities, 46
cognitive development, 110
cognitive effort, 112
collaboration, 2, 33, 85, 132, 133, 134, 135, 137
color, 58
Commonwealth of Learning, (CoL), viii, 7, 12, 13, 15, 17, 18, 131
communication, 29, 40, 42, 57, 75, 79, 85, 97, 102, 109, 130, 131, 132
communication technologies, 75
community(s), viii, 1, 2, 15, 16, 17, 35, 57, 59, 64, 79, 97, 98, 108, 133
comparative costs, 30
competitiveness, viii, 1
complexity, 27, 32, 111, 112
compliance, 130
composition, 27, 118, 121, 124
comprehension, 48, 113
computer, 49, 52, 97
computer technology, 49
computing, 137
conception, 3, 110, 131
conceptualization, xi, 41, 92
conference, 35, 116
conflict, 113
Congress, 2
congruence, 89
connectivity, 138, 145
consciousness, 98
consensus, 52, 53, 60, 61, 67, 79, 82, 113, 131, 133, 135
consolidation, 132
constituents, 10
construction, 24, 32, 42, 55, 133
constructivist learning, 46
contact time, 80, 114
controversies, 36
convergence, 25, 139
conviction, 2, 144
coordination, 35, 107
cost, 8, 11, 27, 29, 30, 32, 34, 67, 68, 85, 93, 96, 103, 131, 136
counseling, 60, 120
course content, 107
covering, 3
creativity, 15, 59, 97, 135
critical analysis, 48, 64
critical period, 110
critical thinking, 48, 124, 132, 133, 136
cultural differences, 95, 98, 104
cultural heritage, 58
cultural identities, 61
cultural influence, 113
cultural intelligence, xi, 92, 93, 95, 98, 99, 100, 102, 103, 104
cultural values, 101
culturally diverse educational setting, xi, 5, 91
culturally relevant pedagogy (CRP), ix, 4, 51, 52, 57, 58, 59, 60, 61, 63
culture, viii, xii, 7, 12, 19, 27, 43, 46, 53, 57, 58, 59, 62, 70, 71, 89, 95, 98, 99, 101, 107, 110, 129, 130
cure, 62
curricula, 84, 123
curriculum, xi, 2, 5, 6, 24, 30, 34, 41, 42, 46, 47, 53, 54, 56, 58, 60, 61, 62, 79, 85, 96, 98, 105, 108, 110, 114
curriculum development, 54, 56

cyberspace, xi, 91, 93

D

danger, 73, 106
data collection, 62
database, 16
deaths, 120
decision makers, 16, 139
deep learning, 45
democracy, vii, 1, 2, 3, 6, 123, 144
democratization, 33
demographic change, 83
demonstrations, 132
Department of Education, 1, 14, 19, 50, 66, 68, 72, 73, 78, 87, 117, 129, 143
Department of Labor, 125
depth, 31, 42, 46, 75, 143
designers, 132
developing countries, 8, 78
dichotomy, 110
digital divide, xii, 33, 35, 129, 138
digital technologies, 6, 8, 52, 135
disability, 61
disadvantaged students, 8
discrimination, xi, 5, 29, 117, 145
discs, 97
dissatisfaction, 54, 121
distance learning, vii, viii, ix, x, xii, 1, 3, 15, 16, 17, 21, 22, 23, 24, 25, 30, 35, 36, 39, 40, 41, 42, 49, 60, 62, 63, 65, 66, 67, 71, 75, 84, 94, 95, 97, 104, 125, 129, 131, 135, 139, 140, 141, 145
diversification, 22, 27, 30
diversity, 61, 64, 80, 116
DOI, 34, 35, 36, 37
drawing, 109

E

earnings, 120, 127
earnings gap, 120
ecology, 46
economic competitiveness, x, 65
economic development, 118
economic status, 24, 61
economies of scale, 136
educational background, 60, 84
educational institutions, 20, 118
educational opportunities, 29, 30, 33, 67, 131
educational practices, 134
educational process, 17, 41
educational programs, 57, 95
educational quality, 10
educators, 127, 140
effective use of time, 118
e-learning, xii, 3, 122, 129, 130, 132, 134, 135, 136, 139, 140, 141, 145
electronic portfolios, 62
e-mail, 94
emotional intelligence, 99
emotional processes, 59
empirical studies, 12
employability, 118, 123, 124, 126
employers, 53
employment, vii, xii, 5, 106, 117, 118, 119, 120, 121, 123, 127, 130
energy, 107
engineering, 29
enrollment, 28, 29, 30, 66, 67, 78, 81, 83, 85, 94
environment(s), 32, 40, 44, 55, 57, 66, 69, 70, 94, 95, 96, 97, 98, 104, 109, 111, 123, 124, 130, 132, 133, 136, 138, 141
environmental factors, 79, 95
epistemology, 57
equality, 29
equipment, 33
equity, x, 8, 11, 15, 17, 18, 30, 33, 65, 67, 70, 73, 78, 108, 109
ETA, 125
ethics, 114
ethnic groups, 57, 58, 59
ethnicity, 58
Europe, 143
evidence, ix, 13, 42, 44, 46, 48, 51, 52, 54, 81, 82, 83, 84, 94, 110, 127, 137
evolution, 139
examinations, 43, 79, 108, 136
exclusion, 67, 86
exercise, 143
expertise, 46
exposure, 84, 95, 111, 113

F

Facebook, 137
face-to-face education, viii, 3, 21, 22
facilitators, 111, 112, 140
fairness, 46
families, 69
fantasy, 145
fear, 144
filters, 113
financial, 42, 79, 80, 85, 107
financial support, 85
first generation, 69

fitness, 9, 10, 15, 18
flex, 102
flexibility, viii, 3, 7, 10, 16, 17, 24, 30, 40, 56, 92, 99, 119, 123
fluctuations, 81
fluid, 55, 107
force, 135
Fordism, 55
foreign direct investment, 3
formal education, 11, 23
formula, 136
foundation programs, 84
foundations, 121, 122
freedom, viii, 1
full-time contact institutions, vii, x, 65, 66, 68
full-time employment, vii, 106
funding, 27, 33, 67, 83, 89, 96
funds, 109

G

GDP, 3
gender equity, 127
general education, 96
genes, 95
genre, 112, 114
geography, 29, 30
Germany, 139, 141
gestures, 112
gifted, 114
global knowledge, ix, 39
globalization, 93, 100, 118, 123
God, 2, 123
goods and services, 118
google, 139
governance, 3
governments, 5
grades, 40, 43
grading, 42, 46, 50
graduate program, 87
graduate unemployment, 120
graduation rates, x, 4, 33, 65, 68, 69, 71, 72, 81, 88, 106, 144
grants, 144
growth, 11, 22, 27, 78, 92, 94, 102, 138
guidance, 67, 70, 93, 120
guidelines, 43, 47, 114
guiding principles, 46

H

hazards, 110
hegemony, 55, 93
high school, 79
higher-order thinking, 97
historical overview, 22
history, 10, 11, 55, 57, 99, 108
homes, 68, 96, 112
Hong Kong, 2, 141
host, 68, 113
human, xi, 2, 3, 56, 59, 72, 75, 95, 113, 117, 118
human activity, 56
human capital, 118
human dignity, 2
human resource development, 95
Human Resource Management, 125
human resources, xi, 72, 117
human right(s), 2, 3
hybrid, 22
hypertext, 137

I

ICT(s), ix, 19, 29, 34, 51, 52, 93, 95, 97, 98, 125, 133, 134, 135, 138, 141
ideals, vii, 1, 58
identification, 42, 85
identity, 17, 57, 104
illiteracy, x, 65, 68, 133
illusion, 114
imbalances, 118
immigrants, 123, 137
immigration, xi, 117, 123, 124, 127
improvements, 33, 109
income, 42, 79
incubator, 34
independence, 40
India, 60, 62
Indians, 24, 31
indigenous knowledge, 113
individuals, 12, 24, 32, 58, 59, 100, 101, 108
industry, 10, 98
inefficiency, 84
inequality, 29, 126, 127
inertia, 109
infancy, 2
inferences, 45, 109
inflation, 108
information technology, 96
infrastructure, 30, 33, 67, 95, 135, 138
instructional design, 11, 134
instructional practice, 58
integration, 13, 97, 98
integrity, 43

intelligence, xi, 92, 93, 95, 98, 99, 100, 102, 103, 104
interdependence, 109
internalization, 45, 55
international trends, viii, 3, 15, 21
interpersonal skills, 99
intervention, 112
investment, 29, 30, 85, 94
iron, 11, 29, 32, 34, 35
irony, viii, 1
isolation, 41, 59, 84, 94
issues, vii, ix, 9, 11, 12, 14, 21, 23, 29, 30, 32, 49, 69, 80, 84, 85, 93, 101, 107, 113, 143, 144

J

Japan, 2, 62
Jordan, 2, 6
justification, 41, 110

K

Kenya, 143
Korea, 2

L

labor force, 36, 118, 121
labor force participation, 121
labor market, vii, xi, 3, 5, 66, 71, 73, 117, 118, 119, 120, 121, 122, 123, 124, 125, 126, 127, 145
labour market, 75
landscape, viii, 21, 22, 30, 36, 107, 121
language acquisition, 110, 113
language barrier, 79
language development, 110, 115
language proficiency, 95, 110, 112
language skills, 80, 107
languages, 107
laws, 2, 144
lead, 46, 52, 60, 100, 108, 121, 123, 137
leadership, 3, 13, 19, 83, 99, 101, 102, 107
learner support, 17, 24, 93, 94, 97, 98, 134, 136, 139, 141
learners, 13, 24, 25, 40, 50, 60, 61, 67, 68, 70, 73, 85, 88, 93, 94, 96, 98, 104, 106, 108, 110, 111, 112, 113, 114, 118, 119, 122, 125, 127, 131, 134, 139, 144
learning activity, 131
learning culture, 50, 80, 107
learning environment, 40, 58, 59, 61, 89, 94, 130, 133, 135, 136
learning outcomes, ix, 39, 40, 41, 43, 44, 46, 47, 48, 54, 57, 92, 113
learning process, 41, 42, 48, 53, 59, 81, 82, 97, 138
learning skills, 71, 74, 114
learning styles, 58
learning task, 134
legislation, 25, 35, 68, 70, 130, 143
lens, ix, 23, 26, 51, 53, 55
liberalism, 6
liberation, 6
life satisfaction, 126
lifelong learning, 15, 23, 24, 60, 68, 118, 119, 122, 124, 125, 127
lifetime, 52
light, 4, 30, 56, 72, 84, 86, 143
Limpopo, 98
literacy, 63, 69, 109, 112, 114, 132, 141
locus, 32, 55
logging, 138
loneliness, 84
longevity, 143
longitudinal study, 82
long-term retention, 46

M

magnet, 64
magnitude, 44
majority, vii, x, xii, 28, 65, 67, 68, 72, 79, 98, 114, 118, 119, 124, 129, 137, 138, 143, 144, 145
management, xi, 5, 11, 13, 16, 75, 83, 84, 97, 98, 117, 119, 124, 136, 139, 140, 141, 144, 145
management committee, 140, 141
manufacturing, 98
marital status, 68
marketing, 61
Marx, 85, 89
Maryland, 62
mass, xii, 8, 26, 27, 33, 107, 129
materials, 11, 14, 16, 24, 30, 40, 44, 48, 58, 60, 84, 85, 87, 93, 96, 98, 106, 112, 113, 131, 133, 134
mathematics, 75
matter, 4, 11, 46, 52, 55, 85, 95, 98, 109
measurement, ix, 51, 53, 59
media, 11, 35, 36, 134, 135, 136, 137, 138, 143
mediation, 18, 138
medicine, 6
Mediterranean, 49, 127, 140
meritocracy, 121
messages, 97, 112, 135
metacognition, 80
metaphor, 19
methodology, 46, 82, 114

Middle East, 143
migration, 121, 123, 125
misconceptions, 81
mission(s), viii, 2, 3, 7, 9, 10, 11, 12, 13, 15, 16, 17, 18, 19, 20, 42, 53, 84, 103, 143, 144
mission statement, viii, 3, 7, 9, 10, 12, 15, 16, 17, 18, 19, 20
models, 20, 22, 31, 34, 84, 113, 130, 136, 142
modules, 28, 29, 66, 67, 71, 83, 84, 93, 95, 106
Moon, 56, 63
motivation, 41, 43, 61, 84, 85, 95, 101, 122, 123, 137
multidimensional, ix, 3, 21, 32
multimedia, 93, 137

N

Namibia, 19, 143
narratives, 56
National Association of Distance Education Organisation of South Africa (NADEOSA), viii, 7, 12, 14
national policy, 69, 72, 82, 83, 86
Nelson Mandela, 6, 28
Netherlands, 11, 75, 141
neutral, 9
New England, 20
New Zealand, 75
Nigeria, 3, 19, 35, 125
Norway, 79, 88
NPC, 78, 88
nursing, 63

O

OECD, 19, 125
online learning, 36, 64, 93, 94, 132, 135, 141, 142
open distance learning, vii, viii, x, xii, 1, 3, 15, 16, 17, 21, 22, 23, 24, 25, 30, 36, 42, 49, 60, 62, 63, 65, 66, 104, 129, 140
openness, 8, 10, 19, 22, 25, 40, 74
operating system, 98
opportunities, vii, x, xii, 3, 4, 8, 9, 10, 16, 24, 29, 42, 48, 58, 64, 65, 66, 68, 70, 72, 92, 96, 106, 109, 118, 120, 123, 129, 130, 136, 143
organizational culture, 11, 13, 100
organize, 44, 45
originality, 60, 135
overlap, 136

P

pacing, 24, 84, 85
Pakistan, 60
paradigm shift, xi, 91, 93, 123, 135
parallel, 13, 113, 134
parenting, 95
participants, 124
part-time employment, vii
pass rates, vii, x, 3, 4, 65, 66, 67, 68, 69, 70, 71, 72, 81, 144
pathways, 33
peace, 3
pedagogy, ix, 4, 28, 46, 51, 52, 55, 57, 58, 59, 60, 61, 63, 64, 107, 119
peer assessment, 132
peer review, 11
peer support, 131, 137
performance indicator, 13, 15
permit, 144
personal autonomy, 40
personal learning, 138
personality, 102
personality traits, 102
persons with disabilities, xi, 5, 117, 121
persuasion, 55
Perth, 142
pilot study, 87
pipeline, 70
PISA, 2
platform, 12, 41, 136
plausibility, 130, 137
playing, 86
policy initiative, 96
policy issues, 52
policy makers, 8
policy options, 127
political party, viii, 1
political system, 2
politics, 36, 62, 93
poor performance, 73, 84
population, 4, 8, 26, 27, 29, 88, 102, 106, 108, 120, 121, 145
postal service, 136
post-school system, ix, 21, 28, 35
potential benefits, 78
poverty, 74, 79, 83, 144
practical activity, 48
pragmatism, 109
praxis, 99
preparation, 12, 47, 48, 67, 136, 144
preparedness, xi, 67, 69, 70, 71, 79, 80, 91, 92, 94, 96, 106
prevention, 62
principles, viii, 3, 7, 10, 15, 16, 24, 25, 43, 44, 45, 46, 47, 49, 52, 55, 60, 119, 134

prior knowledge, 111, 113
private good, 27
probability, ix, 39, 42
problem solving, ix, 39, 48, 56, 124
procedural knowledge, 52
professional development, 23
professionals, vii, 57, 98
profit, 22, 27
project, 52, 144
proliferation, viii, 5, 21, 145
proposition, 27
prosperity, 118
psychology, 74, 123, 127
puberty, 110
public policy, 35, 52
public support, 108

Q

qualifications, vii, 16, 28, 29, 31, 60, 67, 68, 71, 72, 120, 122, 123, 124
quality assurance, 8, 11, 12, 13, 14, 24, 41, 52, 83
Quality Assurance Criteria, viii, 7, 10
quality control, 9
quality improvement, 5, 82, 83
quality standards, 8
questioning, 39, 55
quizzes, 48

R

race, 29, 30, 58, 61, 66, 107, 121
radio, 97
rationality, 55, 57
reading, 46, 48, 95, 109, 112, 113
real terms, 2, 144
real time, 56
reality, vii, 8, 12, 43, 68, 106, 120
reasoning, 112
recall, 45
recognition, 24, 46, 55, 80, 107, 114, 121, 122, 123
recommendations, 48, 72
reconciliation, 109
reflective practice, ix, 4, 51, 52, 54, 55, 56, 60, 61, 62, 64
reflectivity, 57
reform(s), 2, 34, 55, 63, 70, 73, 75, 127
regulatory agencies, 13
regulatory bodies, 12, 13
regulatory framework, 13, 32
relevance, 40, 45, 46, 57
reliability, 41
relief, 82, 86
religion, 61
reproduction, 62
reproductive mechanism, 32
reputation, 73, 106
requirements, 10, 13, 17, 23, 25, 28, 32, 70, 72, 92, 96, 122, 124
researchers, 78, 85
resistance, 55, 135, 140
resources, 5, 8, 13, 17, 29, 34, 35, 40, 44, 48, 67, 80, 83, 85, 92, 94, 96, 97, 98, 102, 106, 118, 119, 144
response, viii, 12, 13, 21, 64, 66, 102, 109, 119
responsiveness, 74, 75
restrictions, 17, 40, 68
retention rate, 41, 73, 95, 136
rewards, 40, 137
rhetoric, 19
rights, 83, 86
risk, x, 66, 85
romanticism, 33
rubrics, 47
rules, 107, 113
rural areas, 17, 70, 93, 94, 96, 98, 137

S

SAQA, vii
schema, 113
schemata, 113
scholarship, 15, 16, 17, 41, 46, 144
school, viii, ix, x, 1, 8, 19, 21, 28, 30, 35, 56, 58, 59, 62, 63, 64, 65, 70, 79, 84, 87, 96, 106, 107, 110, 112, 114, 115, 116, 120, 144
school success, 62
schooling, 66, 69, 70, 71, 98, 108, 110, 114, 119, 144
science, xi, 29, 75, 117, 119
scope, 22, 23, 24, 25, 27, 33, 47, 78, 84, 99
scripts, 113
second language, 110
security, 44
self-assessment, 13, 40, 42, 48, 131
self-awareness, 123
self-concept, 119
self-efficacy, 32
self-empowerment, 118
self-esteem, 42
self-monitoring, 46
self-regulation, 40
separateness, 107
sequencing, 24, 84
services, xi, 13, 60, 84, 92, 93, 94, 108, 122, 136, 140
SES, 24, 94, 95

silver, 110
simulation, 138
Singapore, 2
skin, 120
social benefits, xii, 129
social change, 35, 118
social class, 29, 79, 95, 108
social construct, 46, 125
social context, x, 77, 79
social contract, 31
social development, 17
social group, 8, 33
social influence, 55
social justice, 17, 34, 108
social life, 59
social network, 69, 137
social phenomena, 81
social status, 68
social structure, 29, 58
societal factors, ix, 3, 21, 32
society, 9, 15, 16, 55, 57, 58, 62, 71, 99, 106, 115, 118
socio-economic inequalities, x, xii, 65, 68, 129, 144
socio-economic opportunities, x, 65
socioeconomic status, 94, 95
software, 133, 138
solution, 45, 86, 114
South Africa's Qualifications Authority, vii
South Africans, vii, 2, 29, 30, 121, 124
specialists, 137
specialization, 36
species, 126
speech, 141
spending, 30
spreadsheets, 32
stakeholders, ix, 9, 10, 12, 16, 18, 51, 52, 53, 73, 82, 83, 85, 135
standardization, 46
state(s), 2, 11, 22, 25, 27, 28, 31, 33, 44, 56, 81, 92, 143, 144
statistics, x, 31, 32, 42, 43, 65, 71, 78, 102, 106, 108
storage, 137
storms, 34
strategic planning, 144
structure, 34, 40, 43, 45, 52, 67, 84, 85, 110, 114, 134
student achievement, 41, 43, 58
student enrollment, 69, 83
student motivation, 59
student populations, 22, 96, 135
student success, x, xi, 5, 30, 31, 36, 80, 82, 88, 91, 92, 93, 94, 95, 96, 98, 99, 100, 101, 102, 104, 105, 106
student support, x, xi, 4, 5, 11, 27, 61, 66, 67, 72, 83, 84, 85, 87, 91, 92, 93, 94, 97, 98, 105, 106, 108, 114, 125, 131, 132, 133, 134, 136, 141, 144
Student Support Services, xi, 91, 92, 93
style, 119
sub-Saharan Africa, 3
subsidy, 79
substitution, 136
success rate, 28, 30, 31, 68, 81, 93, 95, 96
supervision, 55
supervisor, 42
support services, xi, 16, 91, 92, 93, 94, 122, 125, 136
support staff, 138
sustainability, 15, 17
sustainable economic growth, 120
swelling, 66
syndrome, x, 17, 77, 78, 86, 109
synthesis, 48, 104, 132

T

talent, 84
Tanzania, 143
target, 69
taxonomy, 44, 45, 47
Taylorism, 55
teacher preparation, 2
teachers, 5, 6, 40, 42, 55, 56, 58, 59, 61, 63, 85, 87, 88, 94, 106, 110, 141
teaching experience, 55
teams, 104
technician, 56
techniques, 44, 135, 145
technological advancement, 118
technology(s), viii, xii, 5, 11, 17, 21, 22, 25, 27, 29, 32, 33, 34, 35, 36, 50, 60, 68, 84, 93, 97, 98, 113, 122, 129, 130, 131, 132, 134, 135, 136, 137, 138, 139, 140, 145
telephone, 93, 97, 131
telephone conversations, 131
tensions, 63
tertiary education, 79, 88
testing, 41, 52
textbooks, 83, 135
Thailand, 127
thoughts, ix, 6, 51, 53
throughput rates, vii, x, xi, 3, 4, 65, 66, 69, 71, 72, 78, 79, 80, 81, 82, 86, 105, 106, 108, 144
tooth, 5
trade, 136
trade union, 136
training, ix, x, 2, 8, 21, 24, 28, 30, 35, 42, 55, 65, 96, 120, 130, 136, 138

trajectory, 34
transformation, 11, 22, 29, 32, 87, 102, 109, 118, 127
transmission, 58
transparency, 46
transport, 83, 121
treatment, 2, 29, 111
Truth and Reconciliation Commission (TRC), 3
tuition, 15, 16, 17
tutoring, 93, 132, 133, 140

U

unemployable, vii
unemployed, vii, 120
unemployment rate, 130
UNESCO, 8, 19, 24, 33, 131, 141, 142
United Kingdom (UK), 2, 25, 36, 62, 70, 75, 116, 124, 125, 127, 135, 141
Universal Declaration of Human Rights, 8
universities, viii, xi, xii, 2, 4, 5, 13, 21, 26, 28, 30, 33, 34, 35, 60, 68, 69, 70, 71, 78, 79, 80, 83, 84, 85, 92, 105, 106, 117, 135, 143, 145
university education, 68, 78, 82
urban, xii, 93, 96, 129
urban areas, xii, 96, 129
USA, 19, 81, 135

V

videos, 131
virtual communities, 140
vision, xi, 5, 15, 16, 42, 46, 71, 80, 105
vocational training, 28
vulnerability, 70

W

wages, 120
Washington, 19, 64, 73, 125, 127
water, 2
wealth, 111
web, 36, 141
well-being, x, 65
Western Australia, 141, 142
White Paper, 24, 28, 29, 30, 78, 87
Wi-Fi, 131
wood, 2
work environment, 121
workers, 109, 118, 121, 122, 124, 127
workforce, 77
workload, 44
workplace, 32
worldwide, 79

Y

young people, 130

Z

Zimbabwe, 60, 143